•Lhasa

Canton•

0   800 km

A Siberian Encounter

ALSO BY GAIA SERVADIO
Melinda
Salome and Don Giovanni

A Siberian
Encounter

Gaia Servadio

FARRAR, STRAUS AND GIROUX
New York

To Owen and Allegra, my children

Contents

'Nowhere does time fly as quickly
as it does in Russia; in prison, they
say, it flies even faster.'

Turgenev, FATHERS AND SONS

'And then it seemed to me that
even in a prison, an immense life
could be found.'

Dostoievsky, THE IDIOT

Part One
Siberia

A Telephone Call

It was two o'clock in the morning here, so for Kostia it must have been nine a.m., just after breakfast.

'Is there much delay in getting through to Irkutsk?' I asked the operator.

'Irkutsk? And where is it?' He had a French accent.

I explained.

'Let's see, it is in Zone Two of the Soviet Union . . . up to half an hour's delay. I'll call you back.'

I began to think about what I would say to Kostia; I had nothing particular to talk to him about . . . but the telephone rang back after a few seconds.

'Now, we'll try your number.' The operator was dialling Moscow.

I heard a woman's voice repeating the number as she dialled directly.

Kostia answered the telephone himself. It had taken a few minutes to get through.

'Kostia, it's me.'

'You? . . . You? . . . How are you?'

I could hear him so well, though our voices echoed slightly. We were both embarrassed by the telephone.

'I'm so happy to hear from you,' Kostia said.

'What are you doing? How are you?' I asked.

'I am working, I'm well. What about you?'

'I'm all right, really – working too.'

We talked about nothing: I hate telephones as well. A sudden shyness comes over me when I use them.

'Is it morning there?' I asked. Oh God, why did I ask him that? I knew perfectly well what time of day it was in Irkutsk.

'Yes, I was just starting work.'

'I must say good-bye now, Kostia.'

'Tell me, tell me something . . . are you, are you still the same?'

Of course I was not.

'Yes, I'm the same,' I lied.

Irkutsk

Compared with other Siberian cities, Irkutsk looks like Paris or New York. It is a city with a past; its name has not been changed and I was able to look it up in my 1902 Baedeker guide-book. But Herr K. Baedeker devotes only a few, though well-chosen, words to Irkutsk: '. . . situated on the right bank of the *impétueuse* Angara'. '*Impétueuse*.' What a splendid word to describe that river. I am sure that Herr Baedeker never went there himself; if he had he would have known better. He might have described some of Irkutsk's churches in detail, instead of saying only: '*La cathédrale de le Ste Vierge de Kazan, a cinq dômes avec un clocher isolé.*' He says that Irkutsk was founded in 1652, and he mentions a Lutheran church and an interesting geographical museum, both of which still exist.

I was staying at the Grand Hotel Siberia: incongruously-named, since to a Western mind the very word 'Siberia' spells cold and discomfort. But I had a nice room, a study, the bath worked, the lavatory functioned, it was well heated and it looked out onto the main street.

There was a radio too, which I listened to in the mornings to practise my Russian. There were programmes on health and gymnastics: 'And now, children, breathe deeply, one-two-and-three,' accompanied by dull piano notes. Then there were incessant talks on Lenin's childhood and his writings. There was music, Komsomol songs and Moscow's ubiquitous voice. Preceded by a lovely and nostalgic tune, Moscow gives the news: the fraternal Czechoslovakian

4

peoples, the signing of pacts between the Soviet Union and the friendly Czechs.

Siberians listen to the Voice of America and to the BBC foreign service; the stations are not usually jammed and they come across clearly. The BBC, I was told, is fiercely anti-Soviet but the Voice of America is more relaxed. Sometimes the latter reported on aspects of Soviet life which amazed some of my friends. Once, for example, they broadcast particulars about an atomic centre in Siberia and gave biographical details about the plant's director. This centre is closed both to Soviet citizens and to foreigners so what was revealed was top secret.

But back to Irkutsk. One sunny day I went out for a walk. Children were coming out of their schools, the ice and snow were melting, water rushed into the streets eating away the asphalt. This is the Siberian spring and it is disliked by the inhabitants. It is still cold, nature is bare and violent, it is nothing like our soft image of spring.

Summer is equally violent: heavy heat and clouds of mosquitoes. During this time Siberians take refuge in the *taiga,* the Siberian fir forest, and in drink. Even when the temperature rises to thirty degrees centigrade, the Siberian's diet remains exactly the same as it is in winter: heavy food, onions, potatoes and vodka. This is well suited to cold weather but indigestible in the summer, unless washed down with great quantities of liquid in various forms: *Kvas,* the brewed Russian drink *par excellence,* mineral water and 'fruit juice'.

I was beginning to feel at ease in Siberia. During my first few days in Moscow and Khabarovsk I had been constantly on my guard: every time I travelled by bus or train I wondered whether my movements were being followed, and when on the telephone, I suspected that an extra ear might be listening; I also felt far, too far, from my family, and I especially missed my children.

People were looking at me as I walked along, staring at my clothes as if an inhabitant of Mars had descended among them. I stared straight back, wondering if they were hostile. But it suddenly occurred to me that nobody minded what I did – that people were only looking at me because I was a foreigner.

I turned into a side street, hoping to reach the Angara. I had also learnt to avoid main streets: in the Soviet Union they are all the same and their purpose is to make a town look modern. Lenin Avenue in Alma Ata is exactly the same as Marx Prospect in Kuybyshev. The Russians are childish in this respect: they like things to be new and shiny, and they prefer quantity to quality. This is a particularly Soviet leaning, but the Cecil B. de Mille taste for the colossal has always existed in Russia. Ivan's Kremlin, for example, is a Citizen Kane citadel of extravaganza, and Tsarina Elisabeth's concept of architecture is exaggeration.

'In every way there is something gigantic about this people: ordinary dimensions have no application to them. . . . Their boldness, their imaginativeness knows no bounds. With them, everything is colossal rather than well-proportioned, audacious rather than well-considered, and if they do not attain their goals, it is because they exceed them.' (Madame de Stael.)

The Siberians would like to live in cities composed of modern skyscrapers. The beauty of theatres, institutes, universities, is measured in size. 'This is the largest hall in . . .' and they take you to see it. Nor can you escape 'the biggest theatre or culture house in the world'.

The centre of the road had become a river: during the night it would freeze. Every time a truck passed by, I jumped onto the snow covered pavements, grateful for my high boots, the most treasured item of my wardrobe. In Siberia, one is literally sunk without them.

My Scottish woollen cap, another essential object was

of particular interest to the children. They would call out to me, sometimes asking the time which is a universal way of finding out whether one speaks Russian or how well. Telling the time in that language is as difficult as improvising a Bach cantata. I used to avoid their trap by shouting back: 'You know what time it is,' or, 'My watch doesn't work.'

The Two Girls

I asked a passer-by whether I was on the right road: unusually for me, I was. I decided to take some photographs. I had a small automatic camera with me which I didn't use very often, because people don't like foreigners taking pictures.

I prefer the wooden houses to the already decaying gigantic blocks of flats, but passers-by usually suspect that one is planning to discredit their country abroad by showing photographs of poor districts.

This is understandable since they do this themselves when they travel abroad and also because years of Stalinist propaganda have marked out foreigners as the ambassadors of Satan, at the very best as imperialist spies.

'Will you take a picture of us?' said a little girl who seemed to have appeared from nowhere. She and her friend must have been about eleven or twelve.

'I'd be delighted,' I said. 'Why don't you go over there and stand in the sun?'

'Where do you come from?' they asked.

It was always difficult explaining that I live in England but am Italian by birth.

'You are the first foreigner we have met. How old are you?'

After meeting a few people in the Soviet Union one gets quite used to being asked questions in the most direct way, and generally without malice or shyness.

From the other side of the street a woman began shouting. 'What are you doing, children? Come here. Why does she want to photograph you?'

'Don't pay any attention to her,' said one of the girls, 'she's just an old bore.'

The woman came closer and asked me why I wanted to take pictures of the girls. 'Why not?' I answered. 'Besides, they asked me to.'

'Leave our children alone,' she said and went off grumbling.

When she was out of the way, I took the famous picture and the girls asked me where I was going. 'For a walk,' I answered. 'I want to get to the river.'

'Can we come with you?' they asked. I was, of course, delighted.

The huge Angara was half-covered with ice. From the other side one could see the new city, factories and flats. One bridge linked the two cities and another carried the Trans-Siberian railway. As I looked at it, the girls asked proudly: 'Do you like our river? Do you like our city?'

People stopped and stared at what must have been an amazing sight: an obvious foreigner accompanied by two obviously Siberian children. 'Shall we go down to the river?' On the banks of the Angara we sank into deep snow. Under new instructions, I took another photo of Masha and Liena. Then we walked around the city. 'We've had lunch at school, so we have all the afternoon free,' they told me. This was an open invitation, but I couldn't accept it. I had to meet Nadia and Leonid within a quarter of an hour. 'But then, could you come to the theatre with us, tonight?' Liena insisted. 'It is a good comedy, a modern work by an Irkutskian, I'm sure you'd like it. Shall we meet this afternoon?' I had no plans for the immediate future. Nadia and Leonid had come to collect me at the airport and I hardly knew them.

Leonid was a solid, silent young man, with blue slit-eyes. He was an APN journalist and the first thing I asked him was to save me from Intourist: that is from Nadia. Not that

I had anything against her personally, but Intourist guides take their victims to as few of the places they want to see as possible, and they insist on arranging visits to institutes, universities, electric plants. They also keep a close watch on the tourists' activities and try to prevent them meeting other people. The trouble was also that I was determined not to be a tourist, while, on the other hand, I knew I was one.

The girls took me back to my hotel. 'Shall we meet this afternoon at four?' they asked. I agreed, half suspecting that I would have to let them down.

Nadia joined me. She was thin, pretty and red-haired. She had delicate features and looked more Irish than Siberian.

'Let's have a look at the city: churches and museums.'

Leonid came along and met us in the street. He was with a friend of his, Konstantin Borisovich Burkov, a blue-eyed young man who wore one of those pale grey woollen caps worn by Siberians in the spring when the proverbial fur hat is too hot.

'What are you doing tonight?' Konstantin Borisovich asked me. I told him that I had thought of going to the theatre. 'It's a terrible play, you'd be mad to go to it. I'll take you to the circus.'

The idea of the circus did not please me at all. To be a tourist in Russia equals guided tours during the day plus the circus in the evenings. But Konstantin, one son holding his hand, another gripping his legs, insisted, 'I'll pick you up at twenty to seven.'

The Flowers

I was consuming a large glass of *smietana*, a liquid sour-cream, when Konstantin arrived at the hotel to pick me up, surprisingly punctual for a Russian.

This time he was wearing a gold sable hat. Men's faces look marvellous under fur hats, as Titian and Rembrandt often demonstrated.

Konstantin, smiling happily, handed me a bunch of tulips. I had spent the afternoon at the Irkutsk open market which has a strong Asiatic flavour. There are seeds of all kinds, prettily hand-painted tags, dried fruit beautifully arranged, mounds of nuts from the *taiga* tasting of resin. I had noticed that there were very few flowers on sale, only red tulips, and that they cost half a rouble each. People still bought them, even though they were so expensive. The Siberians love flowers and plants which they grow indoors and care for lovingly.

Most fresh fruit, vegetables and flowers in Siberian markets come from Kazakhstan. The Kazakhs deliver them by plane – a very cheap form of transport in the Soviet Union – and sell them for a large profit. But the originators and real masters of this trade are the Georgians and Armenians, the source of capitalism in the Soviet Union.

Why the government is incapable of distributing these goods is a mystery. But since the State is not prepared to organize it itself, it has to tolerate this open market, on which a small duty has to be paid.

I wonder if Konstantin realized how grateful I was for the tulips? Or how welcome he and the town of Irkutsk had made me feel? A Western man would have been very unlikely to turn up with a bunch of flowers: awkwardness and embarrassment would probably inhibit him.

'Shall we have a drink in the restaurant?' Konstantin asked, looking round the gloomy cafeteria where I was sitting.

While Konstantin found a table and ordered the drinks I hurried upstairs to my room and filled two vases with the tulips. I wondered why Konstantin's wife wasn't with him: perhaps she was still working or putting the children to bed; perhaps she would join us later at the circus. In Siberia, unlike in Moscow, Soviet men are good husbands; they always go out with their wives in the evenings. Moscow operates more according to an Asiatic-Italian code: women stay at home while men drink together.

The table Konstantin had got was shared by an Australian couple, a tiny wife and a majestic husband whom I had often noticed in aeroplanes and museums.

We smiled faintly at each other.

'I could not find a single free table,' said Konstantin as if he had noticed my lack of enthusiasm at the sight of the Australians. 'What would you like to drink?'

'Have we really got time? The service is so slow here.'

'With me, it's different.'

In fact the waitress was beside our table in a flash. 'Hello, Kostia, what can we do for you?'

Obviously Konstantin was popular in town. I liked this lack of servility and absence of class-consciousness on the waitress's part.

'I'd like a vodka,' I said.

'Vodka?'

This is not a lady-like drink in the Soviet Union, especially in the provinces. Anyway it is generally, and wisely, drunk with food. Nor do girls smoke, or if they do, not in public places.

'Shall we have 200 grams? Yes, 200, but very quickly. We are going to the circus.'

'It's a new programme,' said the waitress. 'Tell me later if it's any good.'

The Circus

'I've brought a dictionary with me.' I showed it to Konstantin. 'If we get stuck on a word, we'll be able to continue our conversation.'

Seeing it, the Australian husband asked me whether I spoke English. He thought I was Russian. Although I had been hiding myself from them behind some unreadably dull

11

Pravda editorials, I wouldn't have thought that anybody could have taken me for Russian. Sometimes, in the Soviet Union, I was taken for a Pole and, due to my rather colourful clothes, for a Polish folklore singer or dancer.

Konstantin and I walked to the circus; the sun was going down and it had become very cold. When we arrived, an assistant took us to our box. I enjoyed the circus: the clowns had a dry, witty manner, they were very good acrobats and did not exaggerate the pathos of their parts. I laughed a lot and felt Konstantin's eyes on me at times, glad that I was enjoying myself.

We went to a huge, modern restaurant. There was no free table and we settled down in a vast empty room, next to the crowded restaurant. Although in most Soviet restaurants the food is almost always lamentable and the decor tends to remind one of a hospital, it is frequently impossible to find a free table. Since higher education is easily available to everyone, it is very difficult for any management to find staff prepared to work as waiters, waitresses or cooks. So restaurants are expensive. But Soviet people nowadays have money and not much else to spend it on. They love to eat and drink in company, and, as there is no form of night-club, a restaurant is the only place to go. The larger ones have private side-rooms for banquets, tourists and special occasions like the one Konstantin and I had settled in.

Outside the sky was dark blue and blazing with stars.

'Why didn't you bring your wife with you?' I asked.

'She's dead,' he answered.

Kostia

Konstantin Borisovich was not yet twenty-seven. Naturally sure of himself, he enjoyed analyzing ideas and events and thinking about people. When I got to know him, I found him extraordinarily intuitive about people's motives and thoughts. His friends described him as a serious, rather gloomy person who preferred to be alone. They said that in company he was silent most of the time. But I never knew this side of Kostia and the fact that he had recently become so gay amazed his friends. Almost naive at times, with flamboyant bursts of enthusiasm followed by periods of introspection, overcome at times by fits of sadness, he was unconscious of class divisions and indifferent to material wealth.

He worked as an engineer and liked his job. But he also longed for his holidays so that he could wander alone in the *taiga,* sailing on the rivers for weeks at a time, camping alone with only bears and wild animals for company.

Kostia believed in the system and was a member of the Communist party. This is by no means universal in the Soviet Union, because it requires dedication and extra time spent in organization and political work. Party members are also meant to set a good example at work. Kostia himself and both his parents, now dead, had been born in Siberia, and he would not have dreamt of living anywhere else; the only time he went to Moscow was on business.

Kostia didn't smoke, he drank very little and he didn't like pop music. Although he no longer played, he had once studied the piano and sometimes practised on the clarinet. He didn't have girl friends and he had always been diffident with foreigners.

If the Soviet Union had to choose its ideal product, they might have chosen Konstantin.

He was also very sensible, always coming up with good suggestions, and he combined this good sense with a typically Russian sense of humour.

Since his wife's death three years earlier, Kostia had been living with his children and an old aunt who looked after them. He spent plenty of time with them and said that his children were his best and closest friends.

'. . . He had just the type of intellect which women like: pliant and observant, utterly unpretentious and gaily

13

ironical. He was simple and unconstrained in his manner towards Marya Gavrilovna, but his eyes and his whole mind closely followed everything she said or did.' (A. Pushkin, *The Snowstorm*.)

He treated me as a friend and consulted me on different subjects and at different levels. He was also able to convince me of facts that I knew rationally to be fantasies or plain lies but which he believed himself to be true.

Kostia wanted to know about my friends, my travels, my impressions, the details and routine of my life, the food I liked to cook and good recipes for spaghetti sauces.

In spite of the many differences between us, we understood each other very well and often did not have to have recourse to words at all.

'How much do you *really* know about Czechoslovakia?' I asked him one day.

'What do you mean "how much do I know"? I know everything.'

Konstantin accepted the party line; he believed in the necessity and ethics of Soviet intervention: it had been the voice of the Socialist Czechs which called for Soviet help. In the summer of '68 there were a hundred thousand West German tourists there and all of them had been armed. What would they have done anyway, I asked. They were trying to get control of the centre of communications, radio, television, newspapers. The fact that so many radio stations had been in counter-revolutionary hands demonstrated this.

The extraordinary thing was not that Kostia believed this version – he knew no other facts – but that when he explained about this fantastic overflow of armed German tourists, I began to believe him. 'Really?' I asked, thinking that had I known about all those Germans, I would have come to a different conclusion myself.

A Czech explained to me: 'They believe everything because they are peasants, ignorant and stupid.' This is not true. Certainly not of Kostia. But propaganda is a wild tiger, pacing its cage, repeating the same gestures and movements.

The odd thing was that many of the 'officials' I met always asked me what I felt about Soviet intervention in Czechoslovakia. When I answered: 'It was a nasty business, but I don't see what else you could have done,' they generally answered knowingly: 'A good way to put it.' Some would go on to explain the dangers of such a drastic ideological change as Dubcek's which could influence not only the Eastern bloc, but also young people at home and some of the more independent-minded Soviet republics.

The City

I began to feel at home in Irkutsk. Although the place is very isolated, and one feels as though one is on an island in the middle of the Siberian ocean, the island is very graceful.

I couldn't have agreed more with what Chekov wrote in 1890 in one of his letters: 'Among all Siberian cities Irkutsk is certainly the best. Irkutsk is a superior sort of place; music is played here in the municipal gardens and there are interesting theatres and museums, there are even good hotels.' He lived in Irkutsk before going as a reporter to Sakhalin.

Sakhalin at the beginning of the century was used as a penal colony and criminals of the worst class were sent there. The island, in the latitude of Lombardy, is today described as a dream, as paradise on earth. I met a girl who had been born in Sakhalin who enumerated the varieties of vegetation and the richness of animal life of that dream-island. Books published at the beginning of the century give a completely different picture, but today Sakhalin is referred to as 'the treasure island'. Coal, oil, gold and timber and one of the Soviet Union's main paper mills, make the island precious. Besides beautiful mountains covered with forests, there are imposing cliffs, rivers with rapids, sheltered lagoons on the coast, which have become a great holiday attraction. In the South-West there is a warm current, the *Tsishima*, which makes it possible to grow fruit and vine. On the northern coast and on the Tyuleniy island there are marvellous bird sanctuaries and countless seals spend the winter there.

Irkutsk is the capital of electricity, furs, and industrial machinery. There is gold, iron ore, asbestos, graphite and over seventy million acres of wood in the area.

The first dam to provide electricity was built at the city-gates, it was followed by the immense Bratsk Dam – the biggest in the world – and more dams are under construction all along the fast-running Angara' before it joins the Yenisey river.

Although it has often been swept by fires, most of the city is still built of wooden houses. Some of these are very attractive and, if well-built, can be ideal for the Siberian climate, warm in winter and cool in the short hot summers, though they often lack any plumbing or electricity. This architecture with its carved shutters and ornate doors is not in fact Siberian at all, but was brought to Siberia by the conquering Cossacks in the seventeenth century. Most of the shutters are painted according to an old tradition: when a family has a girl who reaches marriageable age, the parents paint the shutters blue to let the neighbours and suitors know.

These houses usually have three rooms; in the main room there is a large brick stove which heats the house and is used for cooking and providing hot steam baths. Russian expansion in Siberia began with Ivan IV who allowed the rich merchant family of Strogonov to explore it. The Strogonovs used a mercenary army of Cossacks, first led by the legendary Yermak. They sailed rivers, conquered mountains and plains in the pursuit of new lands, glory, gold and furs. The conquest of Siberia was less easy once the local inhabitants – nomadic tribes, Mongols and Tartars – discovered that the guns used by the Cossacks were not magic monsters and that they could manage them too. In many ways, the Russian colonization of Siberia has parallels with the Americans' conquest of the Indian territories. When the Cossacks had exhausted one area, they moved to the next in search of more furs, gold, minerals. The Russians reached Tobolsk in 1587 and the Kamchatka peninsula in 1697. By 1725, the end of the reign of Peter the Great, all Siberia was under the Russian empire. In 1890 the Trans-Siberian railway was built, covering 5,800 miles from Moscow to Vladivostok.

In the old days the rich merchants of Irkutsk were allowed to build wherever they pleased and they often chose the middle of main streets. Most of these buildings, which blocked the way, had to be pulled down, but there are still some grand houses left, like the ex-Governor's white colonnaded residence ('The White House') and the house of a merchant who, when the Bolsheviks came to power, gave his fur factory and services to the revolutionary cause.

Irkutsk is very hilly, especially on the new left bank. Its many churches break the skyline of wooden roofs. Some of them are in the process of being restored. The most attractive is the Znamiensky Monastery, the seat of the local patriarch who lives in an attached graceful white building. The monastery was built in 1759 and is surrounded by some interesting and beautiful tombs. Under a neo-classical obelisk (built in 1800) is buried the writer-explorer-scientist Grigori Ivanovich Shelekov, a Siberian scholar. Until 1948 the Znamiensky still housed a nunnery.

The interior of the church which does not 'vaut le detour', was restored in the nineteenth century and services are still held there. When I went with Nadia, I was delighted to see that she too enjoyed architecture and did not mistake my interest in the church for malicious curiosity, a constant suspicion of all unintelligent guides.

17

An old lady was cleaning the floor with the usual abundance of effort and water. Nadia and I removed our boots and discussed the architecture. The exterior of the church, built in white stone and interrupted by the grey roofs, was particularly graceful. There were two main towers, rather solid in structure and the windows were embellished with stucco ornaments, as if the architect had wanted to repeat the carvings of the wooden *izbas*. The simple country monastery was surrounded by white walls and faced the Angara'.

There are several other churches in Irkutsk, including the functioning Lutheran temple and a synagogue (Irkutsk contains the sixth largest number of practising Jews of any city in the Soviet Union).

There are also still services held at another large church, the Krestovosdvishenskaya, begun in 1718 and finished forty years later, on the main road to the Baikal. I went there with Kostia on a Sunday afternoon during one of the services. It was fairly crowded, but most of the young people there had gone just to have a look, like Kostia and myself. The old faithfuls were rather angry at these comings and goings and an elderly *babushka* reproached me for turning my back and leaving after a very short time. In fact I find the Orthodox Church, its oily atmosphere, its decadent richness, very oppressive. As we were leaving the church, I gave money to several beggars who sat on the steps outside the church. Kostia said nothing but, when later I jokingly told him that I knew how much he disapproved of that kind of charity, he told me that in fact everyone had good pensions and that certainly nobody in the Soviet Union today needed to beg. 'It might help them to buy the extra bottle of vodka, but they are well looked after by the State. If I had told you this at the time you might have disbelieved me.'

The boom on the opposite bank of the Angara started with the construction of the railway bridge for the Trans-Siberian railway and with the building of the railway station. The *vaxál* (the word *vaxál* (station) comes from the English 'Vauxhall') preserves a kind of pioneering magic and fascination; it is alive with crowds, sellers of *pierachki* (a meat pastry), and full of newspaper kiosks. Although Irkutsk's development was always dependent on its position on the trade routes connecting Russia with the Far East, the railway also linked the city to Mother Russia, to Central Asia and to Tiflis. When it was first built, the journey from Moscow to Vladivostok took forty-seven days.

However most Siberians today use air communications. When a Siberian describes a place as 'very near, only half an hour away', he almost always means thirty minutes by plane, and which would in fact be at least 600 kms. 'A thousand miles, a thousand roubles, a hundred girls and a hundred bottles of vodka, are nothing for a Siberian,' they proudly say of themselves.

In spite of the great distances and perhaps to avoid feeling isolated, the Siberians travel a great deal by plane. Air travel is cheap and is used almost as casually as buses. After the railway was built, factories and whole districts began to spring up: the population of Irkutsk is now almost half a million.

Irkutsk's air has a reputation for its purity.

'... The air is good; it is easy to breathe,' wrote Lenin to his mother from his Siberian exile, not far from Irkutsk.

I also found that I could breathe in a more relaxed rhythm than I could in Moscow.

The People of Irkutsk

When I went out on my own, people used to come up to me and say: 'You are a foreigner and I am a Siberian, that's why I would like to meet and talk to you.' No nonsense about finding excuses, or asking the way. All kinds of people used to speak to me; and girls in particular tended to start conversations with such questions as: 'What is your name? How old are you? Why are you alone? Why? Why? Why?' All these 'potchemŭ' – why? – reminded me so much of the despair and amusement of Edward Lear on his Calabrian journey, when he was constantly asked 'Perché? Perché? Perché?'

I would be shown round the town or offered coffee, bars of chocolate ('They tell me the English love Russian sweets'), sweet Georgian champagne, and offered badges featuring Lenin as a baby.

'Tell me, please do you like our Siberia?'

Russian and Siberian men have a great weakness for female looks; they don't think twice about kneeling in front of a woman and offering her their future, their possessions and their life. After a little while in Siberia I realized that the kinds of melodramatic and rhetorical scenes that take place in Russian literature and in the theatre, are not in fact exaggerated. Men in Siberia sometimes propose marriage two minutes after they have met someone. 'I have been waiting for you all my life, please will you marry me?' The extraordinary thing is that they really mean it and if one answered 'yes', one might easily be taken straight off to a 'wedding palace'. Nor did the fact that I was already married and had children seem to present an obstacle. 'You can easily bring your children to the Soviet Union to live with us.'

Every time I went with Kostia to a restaurant, elderly ladies expressed their pleasure at seeing a foreigner with 'one of our Siberian boys'. Although the mixing of Soviet citizens with foreigners is officially frowned on, the people of Irkutsk were proud of it.

In Irkutsk one can see many Mongol-faces: in the region there are 250,000 Buryats, once a nomadic hunting population of Mongol origins. They preserve many old traditions and are skilled in medical preparations with herbs and roots which they gather in the *taiga*. Although many of them now live in Irkutsk, their capital is across the Baikal in Ulan Ude'. They are Buddhist and they have their own Dalai Lama there. The most free of all practising Buddhists live today in the Soviet Union: in June 1970 there was a world congress of Buddhists in Ulan Ude'.

But the Russian population of Irkutsk either descends from political exiles of the Tsars, the intellectual section of pre-revolutionary Russia, or from Stalin's political outcasts, the most intellectual section of Soviet society. The 'Decembrists' from St Petersburg were exiled here; Trostky,* Dzherzhisky, Stalin (1914–15), Frunze and Kubishev were here too and in 'The First Circle' this area is one of the sites of forced labour camps.

This means that the average population in Siberia – and especially in Irkutsk where the proportion of forced residents was higher – is more interesting than in other parts of the Russian federation. Whether they told me or not I often met people who had spent several years in labour camps, and once they were liberated (presumably after the 20th Congress), they lingered on in Siberia, far from Moscow's bureaucracy. In this belt of silence nature is generous, the atmosphere is peaceful and there is a new world to build. It is the Soviet potential, the exciting and rich land of the future.

Many of the enlightened Communists who want to return to Lenin's ideas and fight the Stalinist infrastructures live in Siberia. There is a pioneering enthusiasm, a thirst for knowledge and a desire to be linked to the West rather than to the East. It is possibly due to this and to their origins, that the Siberians are more European than the Western Russians.

Situated at the trade-route to the East and to the North, Irkutsk is a commercial centre.

---

* During his Siberian exile Trotsky, then known by his real name, Lev Davidovich Bronstein, got a job as a clerk from an illiterate but wealthy trader in Irkutsk. While still in exile he started writing for the 'Eastern Review', signing the pen-name Antid Oto (the Italian for 'Antidote'), and he built up a great reputation in Irkutsk.

The Irkutsk Fur Centre is a treasure house. Treated skins arrive from the whole of Eastern Siberia. Then the skins are sorted by expert eyes and hands into groups of the same quality and colour. Siberia is so rich in fauna that there are skins of almost every kind in the Fur Centre, a tall building just outside the city. When they have been divided and catalogued, the furs – about five to six million – are sent to Leningrad where the famous annual sales are held; fur merchants from all over the world go there to bid and, regrettably, all the furs are exported.

Kostia introduced me to the Centre's director whose first name and patronymic – Vladimir Ilyich – he shared with Lenin and who told me how it was organized: 'We employ about a hundred people, 80 per cent women. The work certainly requires specialized skills and there are many technical courses available. Near Lake Baikal we have a new sable nursery of about five thousand animals, though it is still in the experimental stage. Artificially-reared sables present more of a problem than minks as they cannot be kept in cages but have to live in the open. Sable is a difficult animal,' said Vladimir Ilyich with respect, 'not like the fox and the mink which are as easy to rear as dogs.'

He was a big, tall man dressed in a serious black suit, and he obviously enjoyed his job. He then showed me round the Fur Centre. Every floor contained a vast hall where various kinds of skins were stacked separately. It was like walking through a furry labyrinth, avoiding walls of white fox skins, bumping into mountains of mink and just missing piles of sable. In each room several girls were at work along wooden counters, packing, separating, choosing. One of them showed me the best kind of sable skin in the world, the Borgusinsky. 'Worth a hundred roubles to the hunter,' she said, though obviously when it reaches the market, the skin is far more expensive than that. I looked at the small blonde fur, shiny and golden like a baby's head. As I went along, I collected little presents from smiling ladies who worked there: a lynx's tooth, an ermine tail, a mink's paw.

Vladimir Ilyich's secretary wanted to know, as usual, how old I was, why I travelled alone, where I had bought my clothes. After satisfying her curiosity, I sent regards to the manager Vladimir Ilyich and went home.

Siberia

Although there are regions like Yakutia where life is very hard, it is not true of the whole of Siberia. The lowest temperature ever recorded in the USSR, minus 88.3, was in Olekminsk, in Easter Vastok, Yakutia, and this was also the lowest temperature ever recorded in the world. Most of Siberia is under *perma-frost* and the coldest pole of the world lies east of the Lena river. The city of Verkhoyansk is the coldest in the world, with an average temperature of minus 49.5 and peaks of 69.8. The citizens of Yakutsk have to put up with minus 50 but Irkutsk is not really much colder than Kazan or Kharkov, although its winter temperature reaches minus 40. When I was in Siberia, it snowed frequently in April, and I always wore winter clothes, but it was so dry that I could bear the cold easily.

But when the wind blew, it was a different matter. This is what the Siberians really mind. They can stand minus 40, but they cannot protect themselves against the cold northern winds.

On cold days, they wear special felt boots (*valenki*) made of several layers of wool, since leather disintegrates in really cold temperatures. Nose, ears and hands must always be covered since they would be the first to go, if exposed.

Siberian summers are very short and hot: in the southern belt 30 degrees of heavy humid heat revives thousands of insects, including ferocious midges, the pirañas of the Siberian air, which can draw blood in a matter of minutes. Autumns are short and splendid: the birch trees are golden and the ground is covered with mushrooms and berries; in

October, winter is back again but, unlike Western Russians, the Siberians welcome it. They like their winters.

They always say that the nastiest season of the year is spring, but this is because they do not really have spring as we know it. In April and May, rivers and lakes are still covered with thick ice, the *taiga* is deep with snow, the trees are bare and the roads melt in torrents of water and mud which turn into black ice at night. But the sky is clear and the sun begins to warm up. I like this season in Siberia because it still has the exotic beauty of the Siberian winter, with the sun reflected in the ice, but the cold is not so severe.

Siberia is not really as beautiful as its inhabitants think, but there is a certain fascination in its uniformity. The eternity of the *taiga*, the monotony of the white birch trees against the dark gigantic pines fill one with a sense of grandeur and power. Most of Eastern Siberia, though, is swampy and horrible.

Rich on the surface, Siberia is also rich underground. One only has to push a finger into the earth to find oil and if one picks up a stone, it is more likely to be malachite.

Siberia contains 75 per cent of the Soviet Union's timber, 80 per cent of its water power, 65 per cent of its tin, as well as many other mineral resources and raw materials. New cities grow out of nowhere rather like the Siberian mushroom which covers the *taiga* in the autumn. Industrial development in Siberia was greatly stimulated by the events of the Second World War, when so many factories were moved to the East to keep them out of German hands.

Although they lead to the Arctic, Siberia's rivers are all navigable when they are not frozen. They are real routes and are used as a major transport network. Otherwise communications are kept up by planes; aeroplanes fly everywhere and the pilots cope somehow with the icy and stormy weather.

But the Siberian sky is sunny for three-quarters of the year and agronomists are experimenting with crops which could be grown under plastic. There are also projects to build whole cities in Northern Siberia under a plastic cupola, like Mirnyy, the diamond capital.

The Taiga

When Kostia goes to the *taiga,* where he spends weeks at a time alone on holiday, he only takes with him some fuel, a few onions, a gun and something to sleep in. When he is hungry he cuts himself a spear and catches fish in the clear streams; if he is on the lake, he uses a fishing rod. When he feels like eating meat, he uses his gun: the choice in the sky or in the underwood of the *taiga* is immense. He cooks over a wooden fire.

He spends a lot of time reading, writing, thinking or just contemplating nature. He loves observing animals and plants. Once he surprised himself singing; it was the first time in two months he had heard a human voice.

When he takes his little boat with him, he sails on the rivers or explores the Baikal. Once he sailed right up the Barguzin river, which is one of the wildest and most beautiful natural places in the world.

Kostia knows Siberia, lake Baikal and the *taiga* better than the city or the street he lives in.

In Siberia they have found a new way of attracting the longed-for American dollar in these areas, Kostia told me: for 1,100 dollars – plus travel and accommodation – Americans can come and bear-hunt here. There is no danger of this animal becoming extinct in Siberia; on the contrary they are almost teeming in the *taiga.* The dogs rouse the hibernating bear and drag it towards the American gunman who shoots it before it has time to wake up properly. The rich American then tells his stupefied friends back home that he has been bear-hunting in Siberia.

The *taiga* reminds one of a Gothic cathedral, like Chartres, when the light streams through the trees as though announcing a celestial miracle. The trunks are so straight, tall and close together that one soon loses one's sense of direction as one forces one's way through the lower branches and the beech trees, almost deprived of light by the gigantic firs. The *taiga* seems unending and at any moment one might come across foxes, sables, birds and bears. The fascination of the *taiga* near Khabarovsk is that it combines Northern and Southern vegetation: a perfect natural botanical garden, it contains bears and tigers, trees which grow in India combined with birches and fir trees, and there are lianas, lotus, kivka berries and wild grapes. The woods are full of fossils and of immense petrified trees, trunks of unimaginable size, branches twining in fantastic shapes.

Khabarovsk

I had reached Irkutsk from the city of Khabarovsk; the whole area of which this town is the capital, the Far East of Siberia, covers a territory which is equal to half the European side of the Soviet Union. In the north the Chukotsk and Bering, in the east the Okhotsk and Japanese seas. The whole area is covered with mountain ranges that run parallel to the coast.

Khabarovsk, the capital, situated upon a promontory at the junction of the Ussuri and the Amur rivers, was founded as soon as the territory came under Russian rule in 1858, after the treaty of Aigun. Apart from the Russians, there are native populations consisting of Tungusis and Mongols.

With the exception of the Chukotsk peninsula which has an arctic climate, the Far East comes under the influence of the monsoons. The winter monsoon blows from cold Yakutia and brings a dry frost. The summer monsoon blows from the ocean and carries moisture, mist and rain. This is why there is such a fascinating variety of plants and animals in the area.

In the lower Amur region Iceland moss grows and there are plenty of reindeer; near lake Khanka there are lotus flowers and Siberian tigers. Around the southern area of the Amur and Ussuri rivers grow creepers like the Amur vine, two famous medical plants, the 'gin-shen', the root that the Chinese believe has the power of rejuvenation, the schisandra and actinidia creepers.

In Khabarovsk I met Vsievolod Pietrovich Sisoyev. He is famous in Eastern Siberia, one of those who can trap the Siberian tiger without a gun. A long white beard makes him look like Lev Tolstoy; and although nearly seventy he was still a great explorer of the *taiga,* and he had written books on the flora and fauna of Eastern Siberia.

He was sitting in the little office of the museum of which he is the director, his brilliant blue eyes looking at me with a tiny mocking glint in them. 'There are laws to prevent some animals being killed except at certain times of the year, and some territories are national parks where nothing can be touched.'

Vsievolod Pietrovich, who spoke fluent Chinese, had been awarded a prize from the Soviet Society for his work on the preservation of nature.

'We protect the Siberian tiger and the leopard in particular, since these were beginning to disappear,' Vsievolod Pietrovich continued. 'I have been protecting the tiger for fifteen years, and now we have about a hundred of them in this area. A few months ago a man killed a tiger, eighty kilometres from here. He said that the tiger was going to attack him and that he had been forced to kill it in self-defence. But I know tigers: they don't attack men unless they themselves are about to be harmed. So we punished the man with a very high fine; it was a good example.

'The tiger,' Vsievolod Pietrovich added, 'is the gentleman

27

of our forests.' His blue slit-eyes smiled with pride. 'The
only way to get to know our country is by foot. I am sometimes dropped in the *taiga* by helicopter; I often sleep in
the open air, even when the thermometer is under 0.'

'How do you manage?' I asked.

'Don't the fish live in the rivers when the surface is
frozen? I take some food with me, and something to sleep
in, but weighing no more than 30 kilos altogether because
30 kilos can seem very heavy if you suddenly realize you
are being chased by a bear.'

Vsievolod Pietrovich travelled abroad sometimes, but
always to see animals. He had been in Japan to check that
the Russian black swans, who spend the winter there,
were well treated. He was pleased to see children feeding
them, and people looking after them properly, and he came
back satisfied. He had also hunted black and brown bears
in China. Politics don't interfere with Vsievolod Pietrovich's
life.

'You know,' he said, 'bears have characters rather like
Russians. They never begin a quarrel unless they are angry
but once they are aroused they can even kill a tiger and
eat it.'

He smiled, and I knew he was about to tell me a story.

'One day I saw an enormous Siberian tiger with its cub
in the forest, a superb specimen. It had killed an antelope
and was about to eat it. I was, of course, hiding, but
I felt a bit nervous when a bear came on the scene, as it
was obvious that it wanted to eat the antelope too. The
two giants started fighting over it. Can you guess what
happened?'

I didn't want to spoil his story, so I said, 'The tiger won.'

'Listen,' he said, 'the tiger leaped at the bear but it failed
to kill it in the first few rounds. You know, tigers win as
long as they can slit the enemy's throat immediately. But
bears are strong, they have great stamina. So the bear got
the best of it; he killed both the tiger and its cub.
Although the bear was wounded and bleeding, it started to

eat the antelope. Then it ate the tiger and the cub as well, and went to hibernate. It must have needed a long sleep to digest that meal.'

Russian children's stories often feature friendly bears which are to Russian mythology what dolphins are to the Greek. In some villages I saw bears dancing in the streets while their masters played the harmonica. But it is a rare scene, nowadays.

'Young bears are playful and curious, like children,' said Vsievolod Pietrovich, 'and each has a distinct personality. Bears do not move clumsily as most people imagine; they are very agile. When they used to dance in Russian villages, people put money in their masters' caps according to their grace and skill.'

The flora and fauna in the Amu-Ussuri area is spectacular. Vsievolod Pietrovich told me of fish five metres long caught in the Ussuri, of sturgeon from the Amur carrying a hundred kilos of caviar. He described the Himalayan bear which lives in a hole in a tree which it carves during the summer. He told me about the bright red wolf which Lenin decreed should be protected; the sabre-toothed black and brown bears, strange kinds of antelopes, sables and minks. There are birds which seem to have come from a Chinese watercolour, many kinds of insects and plenty of fish.

Apart from the monsoon period, the Siberian Far-East has almost constant sunshine, 260 cloudless days a year.

The Siberian Tiger

Although tiger-hunts are rare nowadays, they do take place whenever a specimen is required for a circus or a zoo. But the methods of hunting 'the gentlemen of the *taiga*' are the same as they always have been; nets, dogs and human strength are used. Early spring is the hunting season when the snow still covers the forest. It is not too cold, but the snow shows up the tiger's tracks and impedes its progress.

'We meet early in the morning, five or six of us, in a village about a hundred kilometres south of Khabarovsk,' said Vsievolod Pietrovich. 'The dogs are excited and they look like devils with their heavy breath forming clouds in the cold air. The *taiga* is very dense, at times almost impenetrable. Little light filters through from the high tree tops. We walk silently in the snow. It is very beautiful there: in the summer the ground is covered with flowers and in the autumn a special berry colours the hills a deep cobalt, as if Nature had suddenly decided to turn the landscape blue.

'Anyway, we finally find the tracks of a tiger. The dogs run forward and we follow them. At last we see the animal, a big, regal creature strikingly elegant against the white of the snow. It climbs a tree in its search for shelter, hoping that the dogs will lose its tracks. But when it hears the dogs approaching it jumps down from the branches onto the snow. It is generally then that the dogs manage to surround the animal. We must be prepared or the tiger will kill them. One of us throws a cord around the tiger's neck, while someone else does the same to its front paws. The tiger roars; it is a beautiful animal. Another man now grabs the tiger's neck from behind and when we have subdued it, we bind its four paws to a strong stick and bandage its muzzle tightly. The poor tiger looks a little ridiculous now, staring with its large eyes as though amazed to be alive and in such a ludicrous position: head hanging, its paws towards the sky. We all drink vodka and have something to eat.

'One day we went hunting with a photographer. After we had caught the tiger, he wanted to take some pictures and asked if we would remove the bandages from its muzzle. When we had done so the tiger regained its dignity and strength; in a flash it escaped into the *taiga*. It took six hours to find it again. But the photographer . . . he ran away faster than the tiger and only emerged two days later. . . .'

The greatest tiger hunter in the region is Ivan Pavlovich Bagachiov, who does his job like an artist, a man who has never used a gun in his life. He is as well known here as El Cordobes in Spain.

'After that the tiger is sent off on the Trans-Siberian railway, like an elegant lady in a cage. It is no longer the "gentleman of the *taiga*",' concluded Vsievolod Pietrovich.

An Evening Out

Kostia and I were having dinner rather late that evening. While I lingered in the cloakroom, where I was leaving my coat, Kostia went to look for the non-existent spare table.

'Are you Polish?' the *babushka* in the cloakroom asked me, looking for the loop in my overcoat collar.

'Not Polish, no hook.'

I had two coats with me; the one I was wearing that evening was red, and tended to provoke strong feelings. Russian girls used to criticize me for wearing either boots or flat shoes. Especially with my red coat, they said, I should make an effort and wear high heels. But how could I walk in the snow? I would enquire. Well, they would say, I could either be careful or bring my best shoes in a parcel, so that I could slip them on whenever I got indoors.

'It is a beautiful, beautiful coat,' said the old woman in the cloakroom. 'It is very nice to see you with one of our Siberian boys, very nice. What is your name? Gaia? Just like Gala, a very popular name in Russia. We have Gaias too, I have a friend who was married to a Gaia; but then they divorced . . .'

'There is a Russian poem called "Gaia",' I said.

'Oh, yes. That's almost right . . . it is by Andrei Voznesensky. It goes Ia-Goia . . .'

Extraordinary, I thought, to find an elderly lady in charge

31

of coats who knew modern poetry. Like finding a waitress in Monza who read Montale or a cloakroom assistant in Ullapool who knew W. H. Auden's poetry.

However she saw it differently. 'It is extraordinary to find a foreigner who knows our poetry,' she said.

Loud notes sprang up from the shaky orchestra in the restaurant. A man came and asked me to dance.

'I am sorry,' I said, 'I cannot, I am waiting for somebody.'

'She is with her Soviet husband,' said the *babushka*. 'Besides, I enjoy talking to you,' she added when the man had disappeared. 'Why do you Czechs wear your wedding rings on the left hand?'

It was too late to explain my real nationality and matrimonial status. So I just asked her: 'But why do you Russians wear it on the right?'

'Ah,' she answered, 'but you must know that the right hand is the hand of "forever"; the left is only for short term relationships, like engagements. Also, if your husband dies, you move your wedding ring from the right to the left hand as a sign, I suppose, that you might want to get married again. But I hope your husband will live for a long time,' she said, nodding towards where Kostia had been.

'When I was young,' she continued, 'Soviet men didn't wear wedding rings, but now it has become fashionable.'

I always got on very well with old ladies in the Soviet Union. Although I don't look like a child, they always treated me like one. In fact Russian women generally look older than they are because of their diet and the hard lives they lead and that's why people thought that I was much younger than I am. The *babushka* in charge of hotel floors used to spoil me, bringing me flowers, sneaking away dirty linen, bringing it back clean the same evening, and refusing to be paid. For my sake they broke strict hotel regulations.

Some old *babushkas* used to stop me in the streets, pleased to see that my skirts were considerably longer than Soviet girls wore. In fact my 'midi' clothes were a great success.

'That's the way,' one old lady would say to another, 'our girls show too much of their legs these days.'

Feeling totally excluded by the conversation, I would say, in defence of my Soviet sisters: 'Oh, but if you saw some girls in the King's Road . . .'

'Where?'

'In London, you would think that your girls wear their skirts very long indeed.'

'That might be all right for English girls who are thin and have long legs, but we have large, stocky legs. It's nice to be solid and well-built, but you can't make a show of it. Imagine me – ' she would say, pulling her skirt over two fat knees, ' – imagine me with a skirt as short as this.'

I love these tough Russian women. Sometimes they are rude, but they melt in a moment . . . You see them every-where, looking older than they really are, brushing streets, buildings, airports. A good friend of mine, a poet, says it was the Russian women who won the war against the Nazis.

'And you know, I like your hair.' Kostia hadn't appeared yet and I was beginning to get impatient.

Soviet girls have begun to spend money on their looks. It was different the first time I went to Russia, ten years ago. Now a large number of girls seem to be keen on dyeing their hair yellow; 'bee-hive' hairdoes are the thing and hair-dressers are open until nine in the evening almost anywhere. I visited one of them one day in Dushanbe, but, menaced with perms, tiny hair-rollers and bleach, I rushed out, drying my wet hair in the hot Dushanbe air.

At last Kostia came back. I felt secure, watching him walk towards me with his large honest smile. Not only had he found a table, but he had had it placed as far away from the orchestra as possible.

He wasn't hungry, but I was. I ate marinated herrings while he watched, and we drank warm champagne. A friend of Kostia, another engineer, was serving us; he had come to help the girls in the restaurant.

'Tell me,' Kostia asked, 'what do you do when you arrive

in a city and you don't know anybody? Whom did you see in Khabarovsk for example?'

'I always manage to meet people. Anyway, people speak to me in the streets.'

'That's bad.'

'Why? It's very good: I have to meet people, different kinds of people. That's why I am here – and it's the best way.'

'Do men pick you up?'

'I meet some girls, but I suppose that it would be truthful to say that most of them are men.'

'And what do you do then?'

'Talk, walk . . . in Moscow I had some friends, anyway. Besides, I went to the theatre a great deal and spent a lot of time in offices fixing things up. In Khabarovsk I met a nice journalist, who took me around a bit. I spent a terrible evening listening to Soviet songs . . .'

'Why do you say that?'

'Can't Soviet songs be bad, sometimes? They were terrible, a man and a woman dressed in sequins and singing "Oh sole mio".'

'It sounds good. You and I would not like it, but most people would. What is Khabarovsk like?'

'Have you never been? It's not that far from here in Siberian terms. You should go. The city is ugly, there are too many institutes and, out of masochism, I saw every single one. I was somehow moved by the Amur: I used to look at it on the map, and think I would never get there. I also met some nice girls who stopped me in the street and wanted to talk. I had an imbecile guide. But I prefer Irkutsk, by far.'

'Do you? Really? Why?'

If one wasn't careful, Kostia would ask thirty-two questions a minute.

Kostia once explained how the medical service works in the Soviet Union. Doctors who work for the State generally have no time for private practice, because they work

34

until 6 p.m., but if they want to, they can take on private patients after then. Those who deal entirely with private patients give a percentage of their earnings to the State. 'Private dentists are all Jews.'

We talked about Russian literature and then about Soviet writers. 'Even if you disapprove, I love Bulgakov. Anyway, he is back in favour now, there was even one of his plays on in Moscow,' I said.

'What do you think of Kuznetzov?' Kostia asked.

Everybody asked me that question: his defection had obviously made a strong impression on people.

'He didn't cause much of a stir in England,' I answered, 'but we all respect Solzhenitsyn, he is truly great; probably the best writer living today.'

This was taken as a provocative remark by Kostia, although it wasn't intended as such. I knew that he disapproved of Solzhenitsyn, of Daniel, of Siniavsky. 'Soviet writers,' he had told me one day, 'should write within the frame-work of the system; it is unpatriotic to do otherwise. If they really want to, they can publish everything they want to here.' I looked sceptical.

'It might mean that they have to spend one or two years persuading the authorities to publish, or they might have to cut parts of their books. But if their work appears in the Soviet Union, they will have helped to build a better society and to correct mistakes. But to criticize from abroad, that is negative and unproductive. They belong to the community, they exploit the advantages they receive from the State, and they have a duty to work for it. All the exaggerated fuss made by the foreign press is as damaging for them as it is silly.'

A writer's work is to criticize, to judge society, I thought. But I said instead: 'Mayakovsky thundered against bureaucracy.'

Mayakovsky is a national demi-god, he has a square, a tube station and a theatre all to himself in Moscow. Some of his lines on Lenin were printed and used triumphantly during the centenary celebrations. But Mayakovsky's suicide, obviously provoked by the anguish and disappointment of witnessing Stalin's rule, is not so openly talked about.

'What would have happened
if that revolver had missed?
What if to live until then he was fated?
Would he have humbled himself?
Become cautious? . . .'

Yevtuschenko wrote in his 'Mayakovsky's revolver'.

'I am glad you know Mayakovsky. Do you read him in Russian?'

'Too difficult,' I answered. 'One can't even find the words he uses in the dictionary.'

'Of course not, he coined many of them.'

'You know,' Kostia said, 'I shall not let you go back, I'll keep you here.'

'Really?'

'Of course.'

'I shall run away.'

When he took me back to the hotel that night I said 'No'. 'Why?' he asked. 'It would be too easy,' I answered. Besides I was terrified of getting involved with a Soviet citizen. It was most discouraged by the authorities and I had been warned at home that it might easily mean trouble.

The Baikal

Kostia took me to the Baikal; it was a perfect day, cold but sunny. The road from Irkutsk runs parallel with the river, going through wooden villages, and large frozen bays. Otherwise it was a strip of asphalt wrested from the thickets of the *taiga*.

We stopped near a large loop of the Angara, walked over the ice towards the tiny dark shapes of the fishermen squatting on the frozen river. We walked round a ship which was frozen into the ice like a beautiful prisoner. The black shapes increased in size as we approached.

They were fishing for *omul*, one of the many fish which are unique to this part of the world. Its rounded body has a bright orange belt, and, although it looks too beautiful to be good to eat, it is a great delicacy.

We walked for miles along the bay, from one group of fishermen to another. They all had small drills for making holes in the ice. A little boy, muffled by furs and woollens, was fishing next to his severe-looking father. There was a very large pile of *omul* beside him.

'Fish and children understand each other,' his father told me. 'Look at me, I haven't caught half as many as him, though I have been fishing only a few yards away.'

The few roads that led away from the one we were on were guarded. Soviet citizens either need a special permit to go down them, or they have to prove they live in the area. A foreigner who wants to explore them would do better to forget about it. If he persists he might be the first to find himself in one of the Soviet secret cities. These are always centred around secret military factories. Soviet citizens who work there have to remain for at least three years; they cannot bring any member of their family with them and they cannot leave under any circumstances. Even Soviet citizens are not allowed to visit these cities unless they are connected with them.

But there are compensations for living in these cities. People are given higher salaries, and also better quality food and clothes are sent to the secret cities. Apparently fur hats, vegetables and caviar are all available there: things that ordinary citizens find it difficult to buy.

Since the Russian stories often illustrate situations very well, here is a rather vulgar, but revealing 'anecdote'.

An unfortunate engineer who had been working for a year in a secret city, went to see his boss: 'Tavarish Piotr Ivanovich, please could my wife join me from Moscow? I cannot bear it any longer.' Tavarish Piotr Ivanovich answered: 'Engineer tavarish, you know our regulations: no wives are allowed here. But if you really cannot survive without sex, we have at our disposal Nikolai Nikitin, the cook.' Appalled at the idea of making love to a man, the engineer went away, but after a month he returned to Piotr Ivanovich's office. 'Tavarish, I have decided to make love to the cook. But besides the two of us and Nikolai Nikitin, nobody else must get to hear about this.' 'I'm afraid it will have to be five,' Piotr Ivanovich answered. 'Five? But why?' 'There's you and myself, there is the cook Nikolai Nikitin and there are the two soldiers who will have to hold him down.'

I didn't let Kostia know that I knew about the secret cities. He might have started asking me how I had heard about them. I didn't want him to suspect anybody.

As we arrived at Lake Baikal, 'the pearl of Siberia', as Chekov called it, a strong wind began to blow frozen clouds towards the mountains. Kostia and I walked on the pack-ice near the banks and then on the flat iced surface of the Baikal which reflected the glowing light. Even Kostia was cold. We walked to Koti, a tiny village which could not be reached by road. At every window of the wooden *izbas* there were lace curtains and indoor plants. As we walked, guard dogs protested at our arrival; the melting snow from the mountains had transformed the street into a torrent.

We lunched at a restaurant near the lake where Kostia had booked a table that morning. The Australians duly appeared, accompanied by a Buryat Intourist guide.

At another table one man was toasting Lenin. His friends filled their capacious stomachs with more and more vodka. After a while the first man collapsed and fell off his chair; he was taken away by a couple of waitresses.

'His birthday,' said Kostia.

Every time we saw someone drunk, Kostia would jokingly

say that it must obviously be the man's birthday. The Russians had many birthdays every year. Girls too have many birthdays these days.

Russians have an ambivalent attitude towards their propensity to drink; they are proud of the amount they can hold, but at the same time they are ashamed that there is such a high proportion of alcoholics in their country.

The German scholar, Adam Olearius, who was in Moscow four times between 1634 and 1643, wrote: '. . . there is no place in the world where drunkenness is more common than in Moscovy. People of every condition, ecclesiastics, the laity, men and women, young and old, drink strong water at all times of the day.'

The Soviet government has tried to stop heavy drinking by doubling the price of alcohol but many Russians told me that if there were not such a shortage of bars and restaurants, people would not feel compelled to drink as much as poss-ible whenever they finally managed to find a table. On their way home from work many Russian men stop at a food shop and perform the 'na troich'. One man waves a rouble, asking 'na troich'? (amongst three?). Two generally totally unknown persons join him with a rouble each and so they share a bottle of vodka, drinking it there and then. 'For one rouble each one can get warmed up, make an occasional friend, be in a good mood for one's wife and yet it isn't quite enough to get drunk on.' Very recently, though, a bottle of vodka has gone up from the proverbial three roubles to 4.85: 'An impossible number to share. I bet it was done on purpose . . .' But what is new and cheap is Sovietsky or Hungarian whisky.

'I'd like some champagne,' said Kostia, 'but a whole bottle would be too much at lunchtime; it would make us sleepy. Do you think we might try to persuade your Australian friend to share one with us?'

I welcomed the suggestion.

'Champagne at lunch time?' said a genteel voice in a genteel accent, 'we never have champagne for lunch.'

'The answer is no,' I said to Kostia.

Another table filled with soldiers from the Red Army. I made some jokes about exchanging their army fur hats for my Scottish cap, and we all laughed. Then Kostia and I went out again into the cold, and wandered along the lake.

Lake Baikal, called by the Mongols 'Bai-Kul' (the lake of Fortune) is the deepest in the world. The volume of water it contains corresponds to one fifth of the world's fresh water supply. The Baikal is surrounded by high mountains, which contain deposits of rare metals and lapis-lazuli, jaspers and amazonite. Eight hundred of the 1,800 different species of flora and fauna found here are unique to the area, for example the brown seal, the *omul* and some side-swimming cray-fish.

On the Baikal there are more days of sunshine than on the Black Sea and the water is famous for its purity. But recently there has been some concern about pollution in the Holy Lake, which would also mean the end of so many unique species of fish. When I was in the Soviet Union there was a film about pollution. 'It is a Soviet film and all Soviet films are good.' This is usually meant sarcastically. When I asked another friend about a play, I was told: 'It is a Soviet play, my dear, you know already what it is going to say.'

The Buryats, the mongol hunting tribe that were the only inhabitants of this part of Siberia before the arrival of the Cossacks, have a charming legend about the Baikal:

Father Baikal had 337 daughters (336 rivers feed into the Baikal, and one flows from it: the Angara'). Father and daughters lived together happily until one day the beautiful Angara' ran away while her father was asleep and went to join the lonely warrior Yenisey, who was hunting miles away. As she broke away, cutting a deep cleft in the earth, her father Baikal realized what she was doing and threw a rock in her path to block her way. But he could not stop her and the violent Angara ran over a thousand kilometres to join her beloved river Yenisey. Her married life must be increasingly disturbed by the dams which are constantly being built to exploit her 'impetuous' flow.

The rock thrown up by father Baikal to block his daughter's way can still be seen. It is called 'Shaman' and considered a sacred symbol by the Buryats.

Encounters

Near the Chersky peak, where the Angara runs out of the Baikal, there is a rest-home; what the Russians call a 'sanatorium'. Kostia once spent a month there walking, sailing, eating and resting. He was proud of it and wanted to show it to me. A large *babushka* barred our entrance through the main gates but Kostia rang the director and in a matter of minutes, we were inside. The buildings had been designed to catch as much sun as possible and to blend in with the surrounding countryside, a rare quality in new Soviet architecture.

'I like it very much,' I said.

'You know, it's wonderful. I have never felt so well in my life and it was all paid by my Union; anyone who needs a rest can come here, and it is all free.'

Later I was told an odd story about the complex of buildings which had been built to house President Eisenhower on a scheduled visit to Premier Khrushchev. The visit was cancelled and Eisenhower never saw Irkutsk, the Baikal, or Nikita Khrushchev. But the place was turned into a 'sanatorium' and Kostia amongst many others had stayed there.

Next we wandered round a fishing village. The harbour was frozen and the boats were stuck in the ice, but the beautiful view of the lake was interrupted by large posters carrying Lenin's face.

'Poor Lenin,' I said.

It was sad to have to resent him as much as one resents *Panettone Motta* or *Martini and Rossi* blocking one's best views of Italian landscapes.

Then Kostia and I walked to Listivianka, a small village near Listienichnoye. We wanted to visit a wooden church but it was difficult getting to the village because of the thawing snow. When we finally got there, after jumping torrents and splashing through gigantic pools, a very old woman came out of a wooden *izba* adjoining the church. She had a deeply wrinkled face and was wrapped up in coloured shawls. After hearing my accent and having a good look at me, she almost embraced me.

'I am Polish too,' she explained radiantly.

But since she was about to talk in a language that would have left me paralyzed, Kostia disappointed her: the happy look faded from her face and I felt guilty for not having been born in Poland.

I wondered how a Pole had come to be living in that tiny lost village near the Baikal? I could not ask her, but anyway she would not have answered in Kostia's presence.

The old Polish woman told us that she had the keys of the church but could not open it. At the moment it was used as a hospital and a sick woman was lying inside. I thought the story very odd, but accepted it.

As we were leaving I was seized by touristic fervour and asked a tall old Siberian who was brushing the snow from the entrance of his house, whether I could take a picture of him.

'Go ahead,' he said. He had narrow blue eyes and high cheek-bones.

He offered us cigarettes; but Kostia had given up smoking two years earlier.

'I would like you to send me a copy,' the old man said to me. He was called Simion, wore a black fur hat and a thick woollen jacket.

42

'Certainly, if it comes out. Otherwise I shall send you a postcard.'

He wrote his name down on a piece of paper. I couldn't help thinking that it was a miracle that this man who lived in a remote corner of the Siberian *taiga*, could read and write fluently. In Italy, a man of his age and doing his job would be illiterate.

After the usual little chat, smiles and hand-shaking we parted.

A group of people were building a wooden house.

'How long does it take?' I asked.

'About two months altogether.'

The Mir and the Russian spirit of community never fail: a group of friends were combining forces to get the house built quickly.

The old Mir, or village commune, whose origins are very old, is the great unofficial nucleus of the village.

The German Baron von Haxthausen, who travelled in Russia in 1830, wrote: 'The family is the national microcosm; in it reigns a perfect equality of rights. The Commune, or Mir, is an enlarged family. The land belongs to the family or Commune; each individual has only a claim to usufruct to which all persons born in the Commune have an equal right. The land therefore is equally divided among all who live upon it, to be temporarily occupied by them. The children have no rights of inheritance from their father; every one gets an equal share by virtue of his individual right as a member of the Mir.'

When building a house they would seal the logs together with moss and with a plant which looks and feels like rough wool. The windows and doors, they explained, are cut out when the main structure of the house is finished.

Did they mind if I took a photograph?

They did not, and lined up next to the house they were building, their handsome eyes gleaming under their fur hats, jackets which looked as if filled with cotton-wool, trousers disappearing inside their black leather boots.

Kostia told me that geologists are of the opinion that Lake Baikal was fairly recently formed. The rift that started in Siberia, cutting through Central Asia, the Caspian, and the Red Sea and ending up in Kenya, reshaped the crust of the earth with cataclysmic upheavals. Some think that Baikal was once connected with the sea and such a hypothesis seems startling if you look at a map. Certainly, this is the only lake where seals live (if we consider the Caspian a sea), about 40,000 of them, 3,000 of which are harpooned by the Buryats every year. To have seal-colonies at over a thousand miles from the ocean is indeed surprising. They live off a transparent oily fish which lives at all levels of the Baikal, precious to men and seals alike.

The bears come down from the *taiga,* searching the iced surface of the lake for holes made by the Buryat fishermen. They often get better results fishing from these holes than the fishermen do.

Occasionally the Baikal is still shaken by earthquakes. In the nineteenth century many Buryats were killed by one. Their priest, the Shaman, told them that the earthquake had been sent to punish them for their misdeeds but even as he was preaching, a rock fell on the Shaman himself and he was killed instantly.

Apart from the earthquake, the Baikal is a violent lake; tempests are frightening, waves can be gigantic and the sunsets reflected in the pure deep waters are violent in colour. Kostia sometimes drives all the way from Irkutsk to watch the sunrise on the lake. And the lake is violent in other aspects: in winter 1919 the defeated Whites, 20,000 of them, ran away from Irkutsk, Eastbound, setting out to cross the frozen Baikal. But the immense procession, dragging with them families and possessions, struggling against the Arctic wind, was frozen to death. Their iced bodies survived

44

the winter in a grim *'tableau vivant'*, until the spring came, dissolving their flesh; and when the summer released the waters from the ice, the macabre procession disappeared forever in the deepest lake in the world.

Because there are warm springs at the bottom of the lake, all the water that gathers in Baikal is drawn to the bottom and it is calculated that every drop of water that arrives in the lake will take 400 years to reach the surface again and rush out through the Angara to the distant Yenisey.

It was getting dark when we started back.

'What shall we do tomorrow?'

'Well,' I said, 'I would like to be allowed to visit Irkutsk's synagogue.'

The Jews in Siberia

Some people admit that they are Jewish, others disguise the fact, but there are many Jews in Siberia.

The Soviet Union follows the Jewish law of considering a Jew anyone whose mother (and not father) is Jewish. But if people want to avoid having 'Jew' on their passport they can call themselves 'Russian'. Or they can, and often do, change their names altogether. This anecdote is very telling:

'Osip Sternberg went to the police and asked to have his name changed to Ivan Ivanovich. All is easily done, but after a week he's back at the police station, asking to have his name changed to Nikolai Burtov. "But why?" asks the same policeman who had seen him the previous week. "Ivanov is a Russian name." "Well, yes," answers the new Ivan, "but when people ask me what is my name and I answer Ivan Ivanov, they want to know what was my name before changing it, so I have to say Sternberg. Now, when they ask, I shall be able to say that before Burtov, I was called Ivanov."'

When I asked some people where they came from, they would answer quite firmly: 'I am Jewish. Others whom I knew to be Jewish tried to avoid the subject or said: 'I am from the Ukraine', or wherever it was. An acquaintance of mine whom I liked was continually making anti-semitic remarks. After a while I reproached her and told her that my father was Jewish. She was ashamed of having offended me and apologized at length. I answered that I did not feel offended when she made such abusive remarks as I knew them to be false but that I really minded for her as she was an intelligent person. I told her that generalizations of the kind she was making were made by Hitler, Mussolini, Stalin and Mosley.

A few hours later she confessed a secret, something that very few people knew about her: her father was Jewish too. While I was in the Soviet Union a new novel came out, whose main theme was anti-semitic, stressing again that Trotsky was on the payroll of the imperialists. Although there are occasional outbursts of anti-semitism, it would not be fair to say that the attitude is universal. There are six Jews at present in the supreme Soviet and I met a number of Jews who held high positions in the bureaucratic machine.

Israel's victory made the Russians feel differently, though unofficially of course, towards the Jews in general. The usual accusations of cowardice and fear have been withdrawn: there is nothing that the Russians admire more than technical progress, organization, toughness and courage. All this is Israel. Moreover, not only do the Arab countries appear chaotic and cowardly, but they absorb much-needed Russian money, something overwhelmingly resented.

One night, when I was in the Soviet Union, I was taken to a club. It was late, people had drunk quite a lot and everybody was gay. Suddenly one person got up from our table proposing a toast: 'To the victory of Israel.'

The glasses of vodka were emptied.

'Do you know what the cultural exchanges between the Soviet Union and the United States are like?' somebody asked. 'We send Jews from Riga and Odessa to America to play the violin and they send Jews from Riga and Odessa to the Soviet Union to play the violin.'

But this is the enlightened class speaking.

All the Jews in Siberia are there because at one time or another they or their families were sent there as a punitive measure. The same can be said of the Jewish Autonomous Oblast, a small and remote region 250 kilometres from Khabarovsk, near the Manchurian border. In 1928, this territory was chosen by the Soviet Government as a national home for the Jews. The plan to give the Jews a national home came from Lenin, who had died four years earlier, although I am sure he himself would have chosen a region less reminiscent of exile and punishment.

In the event the republic was never a success: during the anti-semitic period of Stalin's regime, those Jews who would have liked to flee to a remote place, were not allowed to go there at all.

Now there are about 157,000 people in the area, which was given an 'autonomous' administration. Half the population is composed of local Manchurian inhabitants and the rest are Jews. The capital is Birobidzhan. As always people feel that the Jews are better at their occupations than the local population and they resent this imposed arrival. So anti-semitism has developed on the Chinese border.

Russian anti-semitism however has been prevalent since the beginning of its history. From Ivan to Nicholas, the Tsarist system needed scapegoats and provided the population with purges in the form of huge pogroms. In 1903 the Minister of the Interior Plehve instigated a number of pogroms at Kishinyev on Easter Sunday, at Gomel in August and September, in the hope of '... drowning the revolution in Jewish blood'.

Nicholas II, and his father before him, had a particular hatred for the Jews. When Stolypin, the chairman of the council of ministers 1906–11, proposed to relax certain restrictions imposed on the Jews, the Tsar replied that he preferred to follow 'his inner voice' (generally the one of his German wife Alexandra Fiedorovna). The Tsar was a member of the anti-semitic union of the Russian people

47

and he was a friend of its President, Dubrovin. He felt that pogroms were justified as a measure against 'the impertinence' of the socialists and revolutionaries.

The State is anxious to populate Siberia and to fill the border territories. I once said to a Soviet friend that his country had on its Eastern borders a problem very similar to Israel's: with land which it took from another people (the Chinese, in this case), colonizing it, enriching and transforming it. It was as though I had compared the Blessed Virgin to Brigitte Bardot when talking to the Pope. But he came round to my point of view. Those cities now look Soviet; and the people there are Russians. It is inconceivable that the Chinese should get the land back.

The Jews who ask to emigrate to Israel are considered 'traitors' but a minority is allowed to go, with a visa costing the overwhelming sum of 400 roubles. They are not allowed, either, to take with them any possessions. But allowing Soviet citizens to leave (or, worse, to make demonstrations and protest) is a dangerous precedent; many others, who are not Jews, would like to do the same.

Tsarist Russia in 1914 had about six million Jews. Due to German exterminations, the re-division of Poland and Stalin, there is about half that number today. In Israel they seem to think that there are four million Soviet Jews, but it would be difficult to give a precise number, because many have changed their names and there are no precise data. It is interesting to note that Israel's leaders at the time of writing, Moshe Dayan and Golda Meir, are either Russian or of Russian origin.

The Irkutsk Synagogue

I finally reached the synagogue half an hour late, with a small delegation headed by Alieksandr Andrievich Vsiesielkov, minister for religious affairs for the Irkutsk region. Two other people came with us.

Aliexsandr Andrievich was a tall thin man in his fifties, with a wrinkled Siberian face and unofficial manners.

Our car stopped in front of a large wooden building painted in turquoise. One would never have guessed that the tall, pretty building housed a synagogue.

We climbed some wooden stairs on the side and entered straight into the upper part of the synagogue; it looked clean and in good condition, and it gave no indications of the poverty of its religious community.

Alieksandr Andrievich introduced me to Moisiei, a short old man, wearing a cap, who looked just like a character painted by Chagall. The local Rabbi had died, so he was temporary head of the community. They were waiting for a new Rabbi to be sent to them from Moscow.

It wasn't easy to find out precisely how many Jews live in Irkutsk: nor do I know whether the whole community is religious and whether there are other synagogues in the city. But from my observations I would say that young people do not attend the synagogue any more than young Russian gentiles go to church.

Moisiei led us into a room where twenty people were sitting on wooden benches. They had large empty bags with them: they had in fact brought their flour to have it made into matzo 'for the coming Passover'. Women wore black scarves around their heads and long skirts; it was like finding oneself in an old Russian peasant community. People greeted me very cheerfully, not at all resentful of my intrusion. On the contrary they seemed grateful for the visit and for the attention.

In the next room, several people were at work. Two women dressed in white, their hair held back by hygienic caps, were mixing the flour into a dough. The flour was first weighed on an ancient, highly polished brass weighing-machine: it had to be precisely five kilos. The flour was then mixed into a hard dough with a very small amount of water from a brass cup. With a slow and careful rhythm dictated by old laws and traditions, the women kneaded the flour into dough with their large hands.

When the dough was ready (the women aching with fatigue), a young man also dressed in white, started to flatten it with a long wooden stick. This procedure was obviously hard work too and the muscles of the young man's arms showed the effort involved.

Meanwhile in the third room, a large brick oven was blazing continually fed with pine-wood; the heat from the red-hot bricks reached us as we entered to witness the last stage of the preparation. The flattened dough was carefully transported and fed into a rustic machine worked by six women. First the dough was put between two rollers which transformed it into a long ribbon. This procedure was repeated at least ten times, each time the space between the rollers getting a little smaller until the dough was as thin and dry as a piece of material. It was amazing that so little water had actually coagulated the flour in the first place.

The workers then cut the strip into squares and a man at the oven pushed twenty of them over the hot bricks. The actual cooking took only a few seconds; little bubbles appeared on the surface of the matzo and, as they burst and became golden-brown, the expert shovel drew them back again.

There is nothing more delicious than warm fresh matzo and even Alieksandr Andrievich, at first reluctant, tried some and agreed.

When the rite was over, the people sat down to rest before starting work on the next five kilos. Their faces were like Rembrandt's biblical studies; they looked exhausted.

The Jews do not have separate cemetries. In the old days they used to dress their dead in white and lay them directly in the earth. Now they use wooden coffins, but they still dress their dead with strips of white linen, and cover each eye with a stone. But Russians are beginning to use crematoria, and one is at present being planned in Leningrad.

Yes, the Rabbi was in Moscow, Moisiei told me. Did he keep a Talmud-Torah* school in the synagogue? I asked. Yes, he said vaguely, keeping a cigarette in the corner of his mouth. And were children given Jewish names like his own, nowadays? It depended, he answered.

I was clearly not going to get anything but careful answers. There were too many people with me. Or perhaps, those Jews had no particular complaints. But if they had, he would not have told me about them: I was there as a foreign writer.

But had I been allowed to visit the synagogue by myself, I would have had fewer doubts about the community's well-being.

Bratsk

As I looked out of my window at the snow and the 'sea' beyond, created by the barrage of white spume thrown up by the dam on the Angara, I knew what Yevtushenko must have felt like when he was sent for a 'purifying' visit to Bratsk, after time spent abroad.

'... As I stood at the base of Bratsk power station
Mayakovsky came to my mind
as if he,
             that hard-boned
                 wide-eyed creation
was resurrected in its mighty expression.
Like Bratsk he shines
             over the peaks of the eras,
far over your head,

* Sacred Jewish texts on which children are taught.

51

academic-parasites,
over petty generators of poetic careers,
cracking
on the greasy fuel of lies . . .

Why had Nadia (Intourist) come along to Bratsk with me?
Couldn't I go anywhere alone? Why did I have to inspect
the great power station, anyway?

I am incapable of being moved by machines; I don't
understand them, I don't see the beauty in them. If I do,
it is only by comparing them with Nature: turbines that
look like enormous red spiders, electric poles, man-made
taiga.

When I was in Cairo, the Egyptian Minister of Guidance
asked me whether I had been to Aswan. I answered I was
planning to go to Luxor and spend as long as possible
there, so I would not have time. A big dam, I explained, was
for me just a huge piece of cement holding up a lot of Nile.
My reluctance intrigued him. 'You must go there, we have
worked so hard to build the dam, you must at least have
a look at it. We can arrange it all for you.' However, I
assured him that it would be a waste of everybody's
time.

Although he finally managed to persuade me to visit
Aswan, I certainly responded more promptly to the temples,
to the Nubians, to the delegation of Syrians and Iraquis and
to the Russian family flying in the same plane as me.

Yes, as I stood at the base of Bratsk power station, I
resented the presence of Nadia, and of the Australians (they
were there, of course). I felt imposed upon. I felt I was
expected to describe Bratsk as the Soviet shop-window,
the miracle-city. I envisaged hours spent visiting turbines
and factories and I knew that I would be expected to ask questions about technical details I did not know or understand.

Although Bratsk was one of the first places conquered by
the Cossacks – an attractive wooden structure built in 1631

emerges from the *taiga* to witness their arrival – Bratsk as it stands today, is only fifteen years old.

Our hotel was in the 'older' part of the city; a charming, small wooden building. Apart from the district where the hotel was situated, several other nuclei had sprung up around the factories and the dam, all separated from each other: it was like a mini Los Angeles.

The first engineers who had come to Bratsk to build the dam, had had to work their way from village to village. A straight way through the *taiga* was then impossible. Now there are roads, taxis, and a good airport. Bratsk is a large city of about 150,000 inhabitants, all carved out of *taiga*, a wonder place which has sprung out of nowhere; a sort of Las Vegas which, instead of having vice as its image, is offered to travellers as the capital of virtue, of man's determination to conquer nature at all costs, at any sacrifice.

Bratsk is, in fact, an ugly city, composed of ugly new buildings, of ugly empty roads, a city where the distances between the various districts are gigantic, taxis are rare and private cars almost non-existent.

Although it is only 600 kilometres from Irkutsk, Bratsk is considerably colder: in winter the thermometer sinks to minus 58 and the maximum temperature in the summer is a damp 35 plus. There are only about eighty-four frostless days a year. Bratsk has no Baikal to temper the climate.

'Do you *really* like Bratsk?' I asked Kostia.

'Why not? It's nice. There is nothing special to do there, but it makes a change.'

The nice hotel had been Kostia's choice: at last not a gigantic cement box; I had pleasant rooms with an adjoining kitchenette. We often ate with friends, or went across the snow-covered meadow into a nice wooden *izba* where, according to pamphlets, one could eat Russian specialities, '*pelmeni*' (a Siberian version of the *tortellini*, kept in snow and cooked in boiling broth. Kostia once ate fifty of them), and bear steaks. The reality was cruder and more realistic.

While I was there, it started to snow. That night we were

going to have dinner with Alieksiei and Natasha Martuk. They were friends of Sasha, an engineer-journalist friend of Kostia's.

Sasha was a plump man of thirty-four. Under a perpetual woollen cap, he looked much older. With the help of a Cuban engineer who had worked in Bratsk, Sasha had learnt Spanish, which he talked fluently and incessantly, much to Kostia's consternation. He had never been outside the Soviet Union, nor had he travelled much within it, apart from his native Ukraine, but one felt as if he knew the world well: he had a touch of the cosmopolitan. His two heroes were Castro and Che Guevara and he knew many Latin-American songs which he frequently sang, whether in the silence of the *taiga* or in the smallness of a car.

He was pleased to have met me, there was no doubt; I was somebody with whom he felt he could talk about foreign poetry, music, painting. In fact, it was obvious that he was going to monopolize me.

'Castro is marvellous . . . his face . . . He came to Siberia and was given a baby bear. I wonder if he took it back to Cuba . . . I suppose you are right, Guevera was a romantic, but so pure . . . tonight we shall sing many songs.' He had energy and enthusiasm and the will to survive; I liked him.

Kostia was ambivalent towards him: Sasha was too noisy and chatty for his taste. Besides, he was a Jew.

'Don't tell Sasha you have visited the synagogue; he is Jewish and does not want to be reminded of the fact.'

It was getting dark. I put my embroidery on the side-table and switched the light on. Kostia liked to see me stitching away and he even wanted to learn to do it himself.

'You know,' I said to Kostia, 'I would like to walk in the *taiga* and meet people. But no dam, no factories, no institutes, please.'

'I prefer the *taiga* myself, but a meeting with the director of the dam complex has been arranged for you. You are a foreign writer and you have to accept these kinds of honours.'

'I am sorry for that director. Imagine how many foreigners he has met, all asking the same questions.'

Besides, I was over-sceptical. I was told that if the concrete poured into the construction of the dam (127 metres high and more than 5 kms long) were to be used to build a wall two metres high and half a metre wide, it would reach all the way from Bratsk to Moscow. I wondered if it had really been built by enthusiastic pioneering heroes flocking from every Soviet city in a spirit of self-sacrifice to create the State, as Lenin had dreamed. Or was the construction of the dam the result of forced labour, as one might rationally conclude and as is suggested in the anonymous book 'A Witness from Moscow'? And why were the officials themselves so anxious to state that no forced labour had been employed in the building of the dam? There is a story that Harriman had taunted Khrushchev with this who then sent him to Bratsk to see for himself. As if forced labourers had it written on their chests! But I suppose there is no other way that Siberia can be built up . . .

'. . . Thomas More, the old geezer who wrote 'Utopia'. He had the decency to admit there'd always be manual jobs nobody wants to do. He thought about this and found the answer: even in a socialist society there'd be law-breakers and they would be made to do all the hard manual labour. In other words, there's nothing new about labour camps – they were thought up by Thomas More.'
(*The First Circle*, A. Solzhenitsyn.)

When we reached Martuk's address we climbed to the second floor of a shabby-looking block of flats and a tall thin black-moustached man came to open the door.

Martuk had dark hair cut short and jet-black almond-shaped eyes; he had arrived in Bratsk fifteen years earlier when there was no dam, no district, no Bratsk; only the *taiga* and a tiny village which was now under water.

Alieksiei Nikolavich Martuk had graduated from Moscow University, engineering faculty, belonged to the Komsomol and had chosen to devote his life enthusiastically to the transformation of Siberia. He was another perfect Soviet citizen.

The same reasons had led Natasha to Bratsk; she had almost the same background as her husband; they had both been to Moscow University although they had never actually met there. The University is a ferociously large building where, it seemed to me, a student is lucky if he ever meets his teacher.

Life must have been very difficult in those early days.

'Midges in the summer?' – the director of the dam, Alieksandr Borisovich, had answered my question. 'When we started it was impossible to work: the mosquito larva only takes five days to develop and there are a thousand of them in every cubic metre of water. Now we use chemicals and things have improved. Then we longed for winter but when it came with temperatures of minus 45, and minus 55 degrees, even the crane got stuck and we couldn't unfreeze it.'

Yet Alieksandr Borisovich had found those days exciting; it was a great challenge and only people at Bratsk felt confident that they would really succeed.

At the Martuks'

We took off our coats; in the hall there was a profusion of boots, hats and plenty of brushes, essential in Siberia, for cleaning off snow and mud.

We entered the living-room; there was a sofa on one side, and a television set facing it. Apart from a rather attractive semi-figurative wooden sculpture, there was no attempt at decoration, either in the form of pictures or books. Natasha asked us to sit down and moved the table opposite the sofa

where Kostia and I sat. There were two bedrooms, a kitchen and a bathroom. This couple of high-powered engineers lived in a flat exactly like most of the others I had visited.

It is difficult to find a flat with good interior decoration because objects and pictures are difficult to find, so people don't really bother and do not try to appear different from each other.

Flats are small but almost free: only ten to twenty roubles a month. On the other hand, there are privately owned flats which are let at higher prices. You find these advertised in weekly publications. The value of a rouble is untranslatable. In the Soviet Union education is free and students pursuing higher education are actually paid thirty-five roubles by the State. We foreigners buy a rouble for one dollar, which doesn't help us to understand its value. The cost of living for foreign travellers in the Soviet Union is another matter again, the Russians try to extract as much as possible of the much-needed foreign currency from them.

The Soviet Union needs foreign exchange to buy foreign goods, especially machines, tools and industrial machines. If it were not for this, I am sure tourism would not be encouraged at all.

Natasha began to lay the table, bringing out dishes of dried meat, smoked fish and sweets. One of the desserts looked like the dam I had visited and had the same consistency, but it tasted delicious. Bottles filled the table: Italian brandy, Algerian and Russian wines, and vodka.

The three Martuk children – eleven, eight and three – had stayed up to see the foreign guest. They had a good look at me and shook hands and then Natasha begged them to go quickly to bed and switch off their light.

She was a handsome woman: high cheek-bones, slanted blue eyes, a long severe face and a rounded body; she must have been thirty-seven or thirty-eight. But she had

57

made no effort that evening; her hair was parted in brown waves which softened a tired face undefended by make-up; she wore a pullover and her woollen skirt hardly covered her knees.

Alieksiei spoke very little, but when he did, his rather gloomy expression would give way to an agitated smile, which stretched his moustache almost up to his eyes.

Obviously Sasha was at home there, Kostia was his usual silent self and Nadia was pleased to be out of her Intourist routine. I liked her in spite of her Intourist duties and even though I knew she was going to make a report on the people I had met while in Bratsk. She was well-read and pretty.

Conversation was on the scarce side. I had difficulty speaking Russian in a group and the children kept peeping round the door. They slept in the room adjoining the one we were eating and drinking in.

Natasha was shy. Sasha seemed to be the most lively and toasts were many: to Siberia, to Bratsk, to Alieksiei and Natasha.

Sasha complained if my glass was full for too long, requiring that I should empty it with one gulp with every toast.

I always find this rather a bore in Russia as toasts are many and can easily lead to a point of no return. Sometimes I found that I had to spill the glass on my knees; vodka doesn't smell, or stain and it dries quickly. In this way I managed to keep half-sober.

At Sasha's insistence, Alieksiei brought out his guitar and they both started to sing. Sometimes Natasha joined in: they sang many Russian folk songs very beautifully, one on the Hussars who spilled their blood for the Tsars, many written by Alieksiei himself about Bratsk, the dam, Latin-American songs (Sasha's speciality) and 'Bandiera Rossa' in my honour.

One child started to cry; I was wondering how the children could sleep in the middle of the songs and talk. Natasha reproached them, but there was no attempt to stop the singing.

I was handed two little albums: they contained photos, autographs, notes: the story of Natasha and Alieksiei's life together, their life in Bratsk. There was a younger Natasha and then the first baby, the joy of having a second child, and then a third one. 'I do the writing,' said Alieksiei, 'I am tidier than Natasha.'

'Exactly the same with us. If I dared to write in our photograph-album my husband might shoot me,' I remarked.

Natasha gave me an understanding look. People are really the same the world over, she said with her eyes. I silently conveyed my agreement.

There were more photographs of Alieksiei singing and playing the guitar in the *taiga,* with the dam workers, tall Yevtushenko and the Martuks, the poem Yevtushenko had dedicated to them, pictures of Alieksiei singing cut from *Paris Match.*

Was I there because the Martuks were part of the Bratsk show-case, I wondered, or had they really asked me as a friend of Sasha's? But I had met Sasha only a few hours before and I know how reticent Russians are about asking people to their flats. They often say that their house is too small for you, and you all go to a restaurant instead. Were they part of the sight-seeing tour for foreign writers, a symbol of the virtue of Bratsk? A loving couple with three children, engineers who helped build the dam, dedicated to the State and hardworking, hospitable and gay . . .

Perhaps I had just missed meeting the Australian couple at the Martuks'. But I didn't tell Kostia what I felt as he was sensitive and realistic and he might have found it difficult not to agree with me.

As I Stood at the Base of Bratsk Power Station...

I woke up early and went for a walk alone in the *taiga.* It was very cold but sunny, the crust of the snow had iced over and it cracked under my boots. At times I sank

into deep snow and, feeling utterly undignified, I would pull my knees out slowly, looking for the nearest iced surface where I could lean safely – only to find that it too would crack and my legs disappear in the white trap.

The light of the early sun was on the other side of the Angara on the low rounded hills covered by black *taiga*.

I was glad to be alone, to be able to reflect in peace.

I had intended to describe the country I was visiting during Lenin's centenary: the Soviet Union one hundred years after his birth. But I was beginning to wonder whether Lenin was still the spiritual protagonist of Russia or whether a new dummy had been pushed on the stage to take his place. Or was the Lenin I loved different from the Lenin who had been? No, Lenin's Soviet make-up today is as heavy as the cosmetics on his waxy face under the glass of his granite Mausoleum.

This was what Lenin had said:

'We must not be embarrassed by the fact that the voices of political arraignment are so weak, rare and timid at the present time. The reason for this is not in the least a universal reconciliation with police arbitrariness. The reason is that people who are able and ready to arraign have no tribune from which to speak, no audience passionately listening and encouraging the orators, they do not see anywhere in the people a force to which it would be worth their effort to turn with a complaint against the "all-powerful Russian government" . . .'

('What Is to Be Done?')

Lenin still speaks: his words are still valid today, but it is not the same Lenin that is pictured on the millions of posters distributed all over the Soviet Union today.

Lenin is like the Bible, in the sense that one can always find somewhere in his writings a sentence to support any action. But one day (after talking to some Soviet children) he said to Gorki: 'These children will have happier lives than we had. They will never know many of the things we

60

had to go through. There will be less cruelty in their lives.'
(From Wilson's 'To the Finland Station'.)

But those children had Stalin round the corner.

Now there is still 'no tribune from which to speak', but
there is food and education. They learn how to think and
speak, regretting even further the lack of a tribune.

Anyway, I was in a bad mood, fighting my way through
the snow. What a mistake it had been to travel with Kostia,
since 'they' disapproved. On the other hand I was able to
know one version of the truth really well – to learn what
it is like to be a Soviet individual which was certainly better
than trying to get to know 270 million versions of the truth.

I had also behaved badly: I had not spent long enough
over the interview with the director of the dam plant.

After the director, I had to visit the turbines, the central
control board – worked by a lonely girl at the computer
centre – and I had met, guess who? – the Australians. I
couldn't understand how there could be such a paper shortage in the country with the biggest power station in the
world – 22,000 million kwh. of electricity annually, and more
acres of woods per inhabitant here than in any other part
of the world. But this is not the kind of question you can
ask in the Soviet Union.

I had refused to see some documentaries on the building
of the dam, although the studio and projector had been
made specially available. I had sat gloomily in the back of
the car, exchanging not a single word with Nadia, Kostia or
Sasha, who was still singing Latin-American songs.

Then they had taken me to visit a 'rest-home' on the
immense lake created by the barrage, the Angara *morie*.

'You'll see bears in the *taiga*!'

I revived. 'But will they be caged or free?'

'They are Soviet bears,' Kostia had answered, 'they must
be free.'

When we got to the shabby rest-home, we found the
bears were behind bars.

'That's Soviet freedom for you,' I said to Kostia, delighted to be able to annoy him. And out of the corner of my eye I noticed the arrival of the Australian couple, cameras in hand, rushing towards the two prisoners.

It had been a bad and moody day, I was thinking to myself on my early morning walk. Then Kostia came out from nowhere and joined me in my solitary progress through the wood.

'I was looking for you. Are you angry? You disappeared.'

I had no reason to be angry that I could explain, so I said there was nothing wrong.

'But you look angry.'

Poor Kostia, he was sweet. I would have liked to tell him, but my Russian wasn't good enough to explain that I was being shown lots of things I was supposed to be thrilled about. There are things I like about their society, but those are the most inaccessible – like their houses. I also admired the egalitarian distribution of social assistance that prevented anybody from starving, and the system of free education.

Most people in the Soviet Union seem quite happy today, I thought. Whatever 'happy' means, this is the only way of judging a country; comparisons with other countries don't have much meaning. People now ate, even too much. They had clothes, they had a sense of purpose. For writers – good writers – and scientists, things were different, but their values were also different and they are a minority anyway. Freedom? What is it? They have never had it, Russians don't know what it is. People do not trust each other: radios are switched on to cover up conversations just in case. I found this horrifying but to the Russians it seemed quite natural. The Russians haven't known freedom of speech since before and after the Varangians.

How could Kostia know what I was talking about?

Three Conversations At Random

'One of the difficulties in this country,' he said, 'is that we all have money now, but there is little to spend it on. Our economy is still as it was in the post-war period when we had to produce fixed quantities of items to last over long periods. Now nobody wants to buy these strong and ugly goods; they remain in the shops, unsold, and we even have to have clearance sales sometimes. Goods arrive from Yugoslavia or England, and hours before the shop opens, people start queueing to buy them. Foreign goods are very expensive and often they are not suitable for conditions here: the shoes wear out easily, the coats are too thin: but the design is good, and new. Even if we have money to spare, we have never learnt to invest. You can see how we spend it – on food and drinks and drinks and food. Once only the intelligentsia (in the Soviet Union 'intelligentsia' means all those who have had higher education) went to restaurants, ate caviar and drank Armenian brandy. Now everybody has the money to do so and everybody has learnt that caviar is better than *seliodka,* the popular marinated herrings. As you can see for yourself, it is now difficult to find a table in a restaurant or find a jar of caviar anywhere.'

He went on, explaining that if a certain number of suitcases had been programmed as the output of a five-year plan, nothing could be done to change this if by the third year demand was much higher than production. No more suitcases than planned could be produced. This is because other factories had been planned to provide exactly the required amount of leather, straps, et cetera. If more suitcases were planned in the following five-year plan, people who had been yearning for that product would buy a stock of them, terrified that they might suddenly disappear from the market for the following three or four years. When I was in Moscow there were bras and stockings in one size only and no tea-pots.

The new Kosygin economic laws aim to de-centralize, to provide incentive and to give the managers more responsibility. The new regulations have been tried out in some factories and State farms, though, as my friend explained, there are few men yet trained to take responsibility and make decisions. If a clever manager wants to produce, let us say, twice as many pairs of shoes as scheduled, there would need to be equally energetic managers in the factories supplying the leather.

'Nobody wants to work nowadays: there is no incentive. However hard you try, you don't get paid any more, and there's nothing really worth buying anyway.'

Indeed in Moscow taxi-drivers stop for you only if they feel like it. Usually they prefer to cruise alone; why bother with passengers, after all?

'It is a pity about bureaucracy,' he went on, 'it's an old Russian disease and we'll have to fight against it. But you are wrong to condemn Stalin so harshly; he made mistakes, but he won a war. Nobody else could have done that.' 'Have you read the text of Khrushchev's speech at the 20th Congress? You should not talk about Stalin without knowing it.' 'We need a strong hand, otherwise corruption develops and production falls off.'

'Stalin was a great source of corruption because he recreated bureaucracy.'

'We are different from you; many of us have been in concentration camps. When we come out and see nobody doing anything, we feel that there is a strong wish for a Stalin to be back in power.'

Conversation with several people around a dinner table:

'Why is Khrushchev so unpopular in the Soviet Union today? We, in the West, liked him so much,' I said.

'We probably disliked him for the reason that you liked him. He was too much of a *kulak*.'

'Nobody forgave him for hitting the table with his shoe, during his speech at the United Nations,' somebody else said. 'He also made big mistakes like Berlin and Cuba.'

'To think that he might have been in power during the Six Days' War . . . God knows what he would have done.'

'Khrushchev used very coarse language. *"Cushkin's mother"* is vulgar in Russian; he used the expression in all his speeches.'

'He certainly deserves credit for "relieving the Russian soul". Not only were millions of human beings liberated from the camps, but we were suddenly able to talk and to breathe freely: there was a change in the atmosphere, in the emotional climate: you could see it in everybody's faces in the streets. It's hard to explain what it was like. He did his best things at the beginning and made his mistakes at the end: and people only remember the mistakes.'

'But why after Khrushchev's time has Soviet history, as re-written by Stalin, remained the same? I mean, Trotsky is still a rude word, isn't he?'

'Certainly. But remember that Trotsky had served his military purpose: he would have been a disastrous leader, more cruel than Stalin.'

'The very fact that Stalin managed to get rid of Trotsky even before Lenin's death proves that Stalin was the stronger, was the man for power. Eventually, remember, it was Stalin who was right about industrialization and collective farming. We know what the cost was, but Stalin was right to oppose Zinoviev and Kamenev who both wanted to move forward step by step. He was convinced that war would be unavoidable and that the Soviet Union would not be in a condition to face it without an effective industry.'

'Stalin had "presence". People here really adored him and would do anything for him. There was a real Stalin personality cult.'

'Well, there was a cult of Ivan the Terrible in his time,' I answered. 'In fact I see why Stalin rehabilitated Ivan iv historically, forgetting that Russia was left in total chaos after his death.'

'But there was no chaos after Stalin. These three who rule today are respected. The odd thing is that when Stalin was in power there were many hushed-up anecdotes about him. Later there were plenty about Khrushchev, but now there are almost none about Brezhnev and his colleagues.'

'Why is that so?'

'Kosygin, Podgorny and Brezhnev are anonymous: they keep distant, and they rarely appear in public. It is really a reaction against Khrushchev.'

But once a friend told me that while he was waiting in a Leningrad tube-station, he passed a man on the stairs who looked like Khrushchev who was Prime Minister at the time. Turning to have a second look, he realized the man *was* Khrushchev. My friend was amazed that Khrushchev walked about so casually. Stalin, he told me, only went out in bullet-proof cars, surrounded by militiamen.

'In the West people talked about changes at the top, but I gather it was only Western press speculation and nobody heard anything about it here,' I said.

'You must have been talking to officials, we have talked about nothing else for months. But we are rather conservative, you know, we don't like changes because we don't know where these changes might lead us. And we live quite well, now. We have enough to eat, we have larger houses, and good salaries. In fact, we never had it so good.'

'It is true,' said another, 'but what must be explained too, is that our system is so bureaucratic that any change might mean that whole battalions of civil servants would lose their jobs. None of them has the slightest inclination to see a change in the leadership.'

'But the West doesn't understand that the leadership doesn't count so much in Russia as the immense bureaucracy: the machine. Even Khrushchev's reforms did not have any effect. Leaders are as restricted by the complexity of bureaucracy as we are.'

'There are many who would like to see younger men

at the top. In others there is a desire to return to Lenin's principles and ideas, to a more direct form of Communism.'

'That would mean eradicating many of Stalin's innovations. With the revolution Lenin had abolished medals and epaulettes; there was real equality in the army. In '39 Stalin had to face the war: there were two ways of waging it: either the Soviet Union could be seen as a symbol of socialism versus the Fascist Nazis, or it could be seen as a war between Mother Russia and Germany. To appeal to the masses, he rightly chose the second. Anyway the name "Nazi", then, did not yet have terrible connotations. After signing the pact between us and Germany there had been quite a lot of pro-Nazi propaganda. Patriotic words like "Motherland", tons of medals, all Lenin's *bêtes noires,* were dug up again by Stalin.'

'Many people notice the corruption and the slackness at work in Russia. Now, everybody is paid whether they do their job or not. The young who have not experienced life under Stalin, like the idea of a tough presence. This is the reason for Brezhnev's popularity. But it was also a mistake to erase Stalin's name all of a sudden, after the 20th Congress. This aroused people's curiosity, and they became fascinated by him. Why did the young have to whisper the name that once had been shouted? After all, Stalin had carried the country further, had won the war.'

'Apart from the purges, Stalin was really respected: he had a fantastic presence. He had magnetic eyes and a strong Georgian accent. Like Lenin, he was tiny.'

'What do people say about Brezhnev?' I asked.

'Here is a nice story, which illustrates what we think about him and Khrushchev. Brezhnev is working in his study. His private telephone rings. "Leonid Ilyich, in ten minutes you are going to die, prepare yourself for a horrible end." There is a click and the communication is cut off. Leonid Ilyich continues to concentrate on his work. After five minutes, the telephone rings again. "Leonid Ilyich, you are going to be killed in five minutes." Again the voice rings off and again Leonid Ilyich Brezhnev goes on working as peacefully as before. After another couple of minutes: "Leonid Ilyich your end is approaching . . ." "Will you stop bothering me, Nikita Sierghievich and let me work in peace?" '

'Lenin's centenary? It has been a bit mismanaged, hasn't it? It has almost put people off Lenin: one can't walk a step without seeing his face. People do really love him but they are bored by the platitudes. We are now making extra-large matrimonial beds. You know what we call them? "Lenin's bed", because there is room for the husband and wife and extra space for the omnipresent Lenin.'

'Would you like to live here?' I was asked one day.

'In the Soviet Union?' I asked. In fact I hadn't thought about it until then. Could I live in the Soviet Union? People have a cheerful stoicism, a detachment from money, which I like.

'But I couldn't be a writer or journalist,' I answered.

'You could certainly learn Russian well enough.'

'That is unlikely, but what I mean is that I would end up in the salt mines of Siberia. There isn't much room for criticism here.'

'Criticism? Of course you can criticize – look at the letters printed in *Pravda*.'

'That's not what I mean.'

The waiter brought a bottle of beer. My host poured a little into his glass, and tasted it before filling mine. Then he filled his own. It's odd how this absurd habit has caught on in the Soviet Union, for vodka, wine and even beer.

'Moreover,' I said, 'life for women is very hard here. Your girls have to work full time as well as doing all the house-work. The fatigue of buying food and necessities for the house is abominable. If I had to do all the queuing, I'd let my family starve.'

'How do you yourself buy the food for the house? Does

a servant do it for you?'

'No, I have a woman who comes in to clean, just like you. But I order food on the telephone and the milk is delivered every morning. And here, these poor girls have to look after their children as well as everything else.'

'Their child,' my friend corrected me.

He was right. Although statistics show an increase in population, it is mainly in the southern states (Armenia, Georgia, Tadzhikistan, Uzbekistan, etc.) that families are large. Otherwise, and although people marry very young, the tendency is to have just one child because life would be too difficult with more.

The State tries to encourage larger families, especially in the more sophisticated and truly Russian sections of the population: Siberia needs many more people.

Birth control and abortion are legal, of course, but not really encouraged. As far as I could understand from the several girls I spoke to (not the easiest of subjects, though Russians are generally very relaxed about these matters in spite of the puritanical cover-up of the regime) – they know about the coil, but can never actually acquire one. Pills are rare and foreign-made (generally from Finland) but now doctors are discouraging their use. The girls I consulted had never heard of the diaphragm. A popular method is to go to a nursing home and 'to have chemicals put in. I don't like this, I am sure it is not good for one's body and it is not absolutely safe, either, as you can well imagine'.

Abortion is free and is a popular 'remedy', although girls are evidently reluctant to resort to it.

'So you would not live here?'

The Soviet Union is one of the few Socialist countries I know: there's more or less no class distinction, there's medical assistance, more or less adequate housing for everyone, pensions, education available to all, work is the duty and right of all citizens: unemployment is not an economic necessity, as in the capitalist world and to fire somebody from his job is almost impossible.

Turgenev writes in *Smoke*: '... The Government has freed us from serfdom, all thanks be to it, but the habits of slavery are too deeply ingrained in us; it will take us years and years to get rid of them. Everywhere and in all things we want a master; as a rule that master is some actual person ...'

I finally answered: 'I could live here, but I would be a difficult customer. This regime is rather impatient with unconventional citizens too. I know that Communism is going to arrive here eventually. But at the moment what the Soviet Union needs is a brilliant theorist to develop doctrines. But this is impossible without freedom of speech and thought. On the other hand, I feel more at home here in the Soviet Union than in most other countries. Still, everything is forty years behind the times here and the idea of "change" is suspect to most people. The trouble is that Stalin took you back a century, and it still seems difficult to erase his presence. That's what I think. But when I go to Moscow I will try to meet theoreticians of Communism, and I'll go to the Marxist-Leninist Institute.'

'Ha, ha, that should be interesting!'

That friend knew his country well.

Irkutsk Again

It was time to be on my way. Kostia and I spent some sad meals knowing that we were soon going to part. I was going to miss having someone looking after me, always anxious that I should find everything interesting, that people should not upset me. I was going to miss, I knew, his tender expression and deep blue eyes, and his Soviet convictions. People in the West had stressed that I should try to meet critical voices, but on the contrary, I wanted to meet convinced Communists, people who believed in the system ... my eye is critical enough, anyway.

I wanted to visit Shushenskoye, the village south of

Krasnoyarsk, where Lenin had spent his Siberian exile.

'I bet you'll never get there,' Kostia said.

'Nonsense. I especially asked for permission in London and in Moscow; I was promised that it would be quite easy. Why shouldn't it be? Lenin's houses are all open for the centenary, except Kazan, which I am having some difficulty with.' Kostia withdrew into a deep gloom. I felt very sorry for him, for I knew he was very lonely.

'When shall we meet again?' Kostia asked.

'I don't know,' I answered.

'Couldn't I join you somewhere? You could write and tell me where you are going to be.'

'I can't promise you that.'

'Why not?'

'Well, you see, I might have forgotten you by tomorrow.'

'It is honest to say so, but it is not kind.'

Nadia and Kostia came to the airport and the Australians were also there. They were, it goes without saying, flying in the same plane as me.

'Are you going to Novosibirsk?' I asked alarmed.

They were going to Tashkent.

We waited a long time in the special hall reserved for foreigners, Generals, and special Soviet citizens. In Soviet airports, factories and restaurants, the spirit of equality tends to disappear.

A delegation of strong men with large muscles joined us.

'If you guess what kind of delegation that is, I shall give you a present. Actually, I'll give you one anyway.'

'So I don't need to try. Anyway, I can't guess.'

'Mongolian wrestlers.'

'Really? How could I have guessed that?'

We had a quick breakfast in the restaurant. As usual waitresses greeted Kostia and served him first. He ordered a double portion of caviar for me as he knew I liked it.

Just before I was off, an Aeroflot plane landed for refuelling; it contained an amazing number of Chinamen, all dressed identically in pale blue denims, some holding the

71

little Red Book. As they walked, everyone stopped talking and a deep silence accompanied their progress through the hall into another remote enclosure, separate from us, uncontaminated by Soviet people and foreigners.

'Do these planes land here often?' I asked, interrupting the suspense after they had all disappeared.

'Yes, for refuelling on their way to Peking.'

'What do the Mongolians feel about the Chinese?' I asked, indicating the delegation.

'The same as the Russians.'

'And where does the plane come from?'

'Moscow.'

'Do you have diplomatic relations with them?'

'Only just. There is a consul here in Irkutsk.'

It was time to say good-bye on the tarmac.

'What will you write about Irkutsk?'

'I shall say that I have been constantly followed by two Australian spies, that Irkutsk is inhabited by Chinese and that people in Bratsk speak Spanish.'

'It will be a very interesting book.'

I knew then that I would never see Kostia again.

China

For about a month it seemed to me that I had been courting China, touching its frontiers from Khabarovsk to Alma Ata. And on these borders, China is the constant subject of conversation.

'What do you think about China?' is the question which at one stage or another all Soviet people will ask.

'We were friends . . . we used to call them "brothers" once. But it is enough to look at our history to see that brothers, we could never really be. I'll tell you a story which illustrates how we felt even five or six years ago.

'Four people were travelling together in a train: an American, an Englishman, a Russian and a Chinaman;

they were arguing about which of them loved his national leader the most. "For President Kennedy," said the American, "I would make a great sacrifice. I would even throw the letters of my beloved fiancée out of the window. Look." And he threw them all away.

' "Just watch me," said the Englishman, "for Macmillan I'll throw away this precious watch given to me by my father, God bless him."

' "For Nikita," said the Russian, "I will do more. I will throw my brother out of the window." And out goes the Chinaman.'

Peter the Great developed the silk and fur trade with China, leaving unchanged the good relations between the two countries based on the treaties of 1647 and 1689. A treaty with China in 1896 gave Russia the right to build a railroad through Manchuria. In the middle of the nineteenth century, Russian policy towards China was in the hands of Muravyov-Amursk, Governor-General of Eastern Siberia, Admiral Putyatin and General Ignatiev. These three did not pay much attention to the various treaties signed with China, nor would they follow directions coming from St Petersburg. Muravyov occupied the area on the north bank of the Amur and reached the mouth of that river. This area was then organized as a Russian province and the Chinese, who came under attack from France and Britain over Canton and Tonking, had to recognize this new Russian province.

Meanwhile Russia had acquired land on both banks of the Amur and a strip of extra coast where a new city was founded in 1861. This was Vladivostock, which in Russian means Commander of the East. This harbour had indeed a most strategic position, commanding the approaches to Japan, North Korea and China.

In 1894, when Japan had defeated China, Nicholas II, backed by Germany and France, forced Japan to relinquish the Liao-Tung peninsula – on which stands Port Arthur. A new secret treaty of 'friendship and non-aggression' was negotiated between China and Russia and they also arranged to build the railroad through Manchuria to Port Arthur 'to protect China from the aggression of Japan'. The Dowager Empress of China was so pleased by this treaty that she hung the text above her celestial bed. The Chinese Eastern Railroad was really under Russian control and industries were built up in Manchuria. Later the Russian Navy gained control over Port Arthur and forced the Chinese to agree to a twenty-five-year lease of the base. At this point, the Dowager Empress of China tore up the framed document that she had kept in her bedroom. Simultaneously the British, the French, and the Germans seized other long 'leases' from China; these events not surprisingly, led to an anti-foreign revolution, the Boxer Rebellion. Now all these Powers had a splendid excuse to move their armies into China but although everyone else moved out once the rebellion had been crushed, the Russians did not.

'The Provisional Government,' Lenin wrote in July 1917 in one of his strong accusations against Kerensky, 'has not even published the secret treaties of a frankly predatory character, concerning the partitioning of Persia, the robbing of China, of Turkey, the annexation of East Prussia, etc . . . It has confirmed these treaties concluded by tsarism, which for several centuries have robbed and oppressed more peoples than all other tyrants and despots . . . disgracing and demoralizing the Great Russian people by transforming them into executioners of other peoples.'

One of Lenin's first acts after he came to power, had indeed been to renounce all claim to those areas of Iran and Turkey which had been annexed by the Tsarist imperialism. By so doing, he gained the friendship and alliance of those nations.

'What do you think of the Chinese?' Most Russians are extremely curious to know what 'we', Westerners, think of China.

It is, of course, a very difficult question to answer: China seems as remote to us as it feels close to the Russians. Only by talking to many individuals, can one understand what a bogey China is to them. Russia feels menaced from the East, as it so often has been in the past. In this light the importance of the new pact between Germany and Russia is seen by the simple citizen, for whom West Germany still has Nazi overtones, as a protection on the Western frontiers, leaving the danger only on the Eastern borders.

'I don't know what they want from us,' some would say. 'This is a political war, they probably don't know what they want themselves.'

Others would say: 'They want territory, but that is now ours. Before we arrived there was nothing here, we have done everything ourselves.'

Certainly cities like Khabarovsk or Komsomolsk-na-Amure don't even remind one of the East and couldn't look more solidly Soviet, in their buildings, town planning, monuments and with their pink inhabitants.

In the modern section of Khabarovsk museum, which is by the way, a very attractive building in stone on the right side of the Amur, photographs of Soviet soldiers, 'hero-victims of the war against the Chinese', were displayed. The date of their deaths was 1969.

'I was there once,' somebody told me, 'in an island on the Amur, last March. After what I saw I'm not afraid of the Chinese any longer: the Russian army is technically and scientifically so superior. On one side of the hill was the Red Army, the other was literally covered with Chinese soldiers. Suddenly a red flame covered that side and not even the bones of the Chinese were left.'

'Was it napalm?' I asked.

'I don't know; I don't know what napalm is anyway.'

'China? It's a very sad business,' somebody in Dushambe told me. 'You see, their cultural revolution doesn't mean anything: just to read a newspaper they need to know

3,000 signs; they haven't even reformed the alphabet.*
All they think about is war.'

On another occasion, someone told me: 'The Chinese
are not dangerous although they certainly want war.
They are a stupid and undeveloped people. The Jews are our
real danger, they want to get in everywhere, into the Party
machine, into the administration . . .'

The next thing I heard was that the Chinese had just
launched a new satellite. I understood then why the news
had not been released to the Russians – apart from three
lines in *Izvestia*. The Russians are worried, the Chinese
leaders have too often stated their belief in the revolutionary
necessity of wars. The Russians really don't want a war;
they have had enough, their country was overrun by the
Germans in the most appalling way. The State takes infinite
trouble to teach the young what war really means; children
are taken to museums, shown in detail, lectured about
the horrors of human destruction. 'It is not enough to say
that war is bad. We have to show them.'

I also get the impression that border incidents between
Russians and Chinese happen more often than we are told
and certainly the Chinese have also often attacked on the
Kazakhstan front.

Those Soviet intellectuals who have made contacts with
the West are alarmed to see that some Western Left-Wing
sympathizers are pro-Chinese. 'Really,' a well-known poet
told me, 'the Chinese Cultural Revolution was a terrible
event and Mao is just a tyrant; the purges at the top of
the party were exactly the same as Stalin's. Can't they see
that?'

They also refer to the Italian Communist Party and to
Yugoslavia as 'the Left', China, and part of their own political
structure as 'the Right'.

'Do you know when there will be a world famine? When
the Chinese learn to eat with forks and spoons.' There is a
telling line in this *boutade*; 'If they eat, we can't.'

* The Chinese alphabet has in fact been reformed.

76

Another anecdote:

The steppe is infested by wolves. Two Russians and two Chinese are travelling in a horse-drawn cart. Suddenly they see a famished pack of wolves behind them. 'Our load is too heavy: they will catch up with us and kill us,' says one of the Russians and he decides to throw out one of the Chinamen. The wolves stop, eat the Chinaman and, in a few seconds, are again behind the cart, snapping menacingly at the back of it. The second Chinaman soon shares the fate of the first. When the wolves are again behind the cart, one of the Russians presses a button and switches the motor on.

Novosibirsk

'It is the Chicago of Siberia.'

Chicago! That would be like comparing a beautiful woman with Margaret Rutherford. Perhaps one day, it might become like Chicago – after all Novosibirsk does share with Chicago a certain masculinity and toughness – but it's unlikely that a Sullivan, a Mies Van Der Rohe or Frank Lloyd-Wright will leave his mark on the capital of Siberia.

I took a preliminary walk through the city; behind the large unattractive modern main roads, the wooden city stretched into the distance. I looked at the lace-carvings around the roofs and the windows and noticed an old woman sitting on a bench outside her wooden gate. This was carved in large, rose shapes, something I had never seen before.

'Could I take a picture of your house?' I asked.

Not much interested, she nodded. She was enjoying the warm sun, like any old person in the world, a brown cigarette glued to the corner of her wrinkled lips. This was actually a *papiroski*, an old Russian cigarette made half of cartons which the peasants prefer to the new and more expensive innovations.

A man emerged just as I took the picture.

'Why are you photographing her?' I knew what he meant.
'I like the pattern of that wooden carving. It is beautiful.'
'Beautiful . . .' He went away grumbling, not believing me.
I said good-bye to the old lady and, as I was walking away,
a militiaman, tall, plump, his Red Army colback menacingly
proud, stopped me. His voice was ferocious.

'Why are you walking here? Why are you taking this
kind of picture?'

'Why not?' I asked.

'I know you foreigners . . . at what hotel are you staying?'
Go and take pictures there, of the theatre, of the
monuments; don't come here. GO AWAY.'

He bullied me back towards the foreigners' ghetto: the
main streets, the new squares.

And yet, I had only been walking three hundred yards
from my central hotel. Those houses were so obviously
attractive and it made me very resentful to be told what I
could and could not look at. People always seemed to be
trying to keep me away from the best side of the Soviet
Union.

The journalist I had been looking forward to meeting in
Novosibirsk was ill. But I met Nellia, another APN journalist, a charming girl, rather fat with intelligent eyes and sweet
manners. She was going to introduce me to people in the
Akademgradok, a place she adored.

Meanwhile in Novosibirsk the sky was grey.

The Question of Shushenskoye

'Shushenskoye?' Mikhail Shimkarienko, the man in charge of
visas and permits repeated, looking at me from behind his
wooden desk. 'Impossible. It's not ready.'

'Not ready?' I repeated, equally amazed, looking at him
from the other side of the desk. 'Impossible. It can't be. It
was ready for Lenin, why not for me?'

'It is not included in your passport visas.'

'Let's telegraph Moscow,' I said. I was, naively, sure of the positive outcome of such a procedure. 'I have been told many times that there would be no problem getting to Shushenskoye.'

'It takes a long time, so you must count on at least three days.'

'All right, I will.' It had become a point of honour.

'You will have to take a plane to Krasnoyarsk, then catch a bus which takes six hours to reach Shushenskoye. You'll need a guide, and you will have to pay her fares and accommodation.'

'Is there a plane to Krasnoyarsk tomorrow morning? Of course I don't need a guide, whatever for?'

'We have prepared your programme for your stay in Novosibirsk. Here it is.' Mikhail Shimkarienko had certainly done a beautiful job – only he had been expecting a man.

He handed me a carefully typed piece of paper headed 'PROGRAMME FOR THE ENGLISH CITIZEN MOSTYN-OWEN'. He had drawn up a list of engagements and appointments, interrupting meetings with one optimistic hour for lunch or dinner, as though he didn't know that one cannot eat in one hour in Russian restaurants. A telegram arrived from Moscow: Mostyn-Owen was to stick to the visas issued on her passport and forget about Shushenskoye.

'It will be for next time. You can come back to Novosibirsk and also go to Shushenskoye,' said Shimkarienko smiling.

I was furious. I had made a point of visiting places associated with Lenin in the Soviet Union and I had been particularly insistent about Shushenskoye.

Clearly it wasn't Shimkarienko's fault, but my Italian temper got the better of me and the little office shook with insults to the bureaucracy. I accused them of lack of faith, dishonesty, stupidity, and so forth. As I was to discover later, an outburst of temper pleases the Russians. 'You are a woman, but you have guts,' Shimkarienko said smilingly.

Ideological War

Some Soviet citizens who had travelled abroad – especially in Britain – told me that they were rarely left in peace by the Secret Service; I wonder whether this is true or if they imagined it.

They say that they are always shadowed when in the West and generally finish up sharing a bottle of vodka with the man who had been silently following them for days.

The Russians have, understandably enough, an *idée fixé* about spies and take for granted everything they do, say, or think might be registered by the KGB, MI5 or CIA. The British intelligence, by the way, has a fantastic reputation. Having belonged to the Italian Communist Party, I myself once had some trouble from them. But the truth is that I despise spies and I would rate prostitution as a much nobler profession. I don't believe that there are ideological spies (except for Fuchs, perhaps). If Philby, for example, had really been a convinced Communist, he could have worked towards his ideological aim in his own country. As it turns out, Philby was a clever man, intellectual and romantic, inoculated with the Lawrence-of-Arabia virus, with a strong attraction to alcohol and a contempt for women.

In the Soviet Union, sometimes, one finds traces of him, places he has been to, eternally accompanied by a 'guide' – in fact a necessary presence to see that, after his third bottle of vodka, Philby goes out of the restaurant without causing too much trouble. He is now a broken man, not because of ideological disappointment, but because – I think – he can no longer do what he really likes: spying.

One's Soviet friends' alertness for 'planted' people is infectious. I certainly have no doubt that telephone calls between one Russian city and another are controlled. Before making the call one has to give one's name and the name of the person one is calling. I noticed that if the other person is telling one what happened somewhere, a 'click' and silence follows for a few seconds. 'They' are jealous about the secrecy of their cities.

What constitutes a risk? For the Americans it is to have a situation where there are ten people, ten bottles of whisky and ten cars to drive home. For the Russians it is to have ten people, ten bottles of vodka and to get into a conversation about politics. One of the ten persons is bound to be a KBM agent.

Once in a plane from Alma Ata to Tashkent – where I was getting a connection to Dushanbe' – a large man came to sit next to me. He settled down and opened a paper printed in German.

By then, I knew, in Soviet planes, I would be made to sit either next to elderly ladies, Red Army officers or empty seats.

The arrival of this gentleman made me very suspicious. I knew he must have been a Volga-German, a group which was removed 'en bloc' from the Autonomous Republic where they lived and resettled in Siberia and Kazakhstan.

They have a strange history. Catherine the Second (Catherine the Great) issued two manifestoes in 1762 and 1763 inviting the Germans to settle in her empire. They were promised freedom of religion, exemption from taxes and from military service, and they would receive financial aid. Catherine the Great was pursuing Peter's policy of westernizing Russia and encouraging as many skilled artisans as possible to come to Russia.

Prosperous German colonies settled in different areas, but mainly around Saratov on the Volga. Even during the Tsarist regime, in World War One, the community was, probably rightly, suspected of being more pro-German than pro-Russian and there were plans to move them all to Siberia.

The Russians never liked this injection of Teutonic blood: 'As for the Russian Germans, I don't need to mention them – we all know what sort of creatures they are . . .' (Turgenev, *Fathers and Sons*). Although one Russian German woman

81

was to give birth to their most beloved citizen, Lenin.

It was Lenin who made the area into a strict Autonomous Republic with four hundred thousand citizens, but when the Germans attacked Russia in 1941, Stalin decided to follow up the Tsarist plan. To test their loyalty Soviet planes disguised as German ones dropped pamphlets; many inhabitants rose to the bait and many were shot. Stalin was probably justified in his fears: more than fifty thousand Soviet citizens of German descent living in the Ukraine and many again in the Caucasus joined the German army. Then the territory of the former autonomous republic was carved up, between the cities of Saratov and Stalingrad (now Volgograd).

Because of this interesting background I was longing to talk to the fat German who had come to sit next to me. Could I start the conversation? There was no need to stress that I was a foreigner, but I opened a book printed in English and started to read. Perhaps he spoke only Russian and German and it was up to me to make a remark about the weather in Russian. But if, after the first sentences, I were to pass on to more interesting items, would I be risking some of my visas?

The German was unlikely to think that I was 'planted'; foreigners are dangerous to them for other reasons, but not on chance encounters. I came to the conclusion that there was a fifty per cent chance that my neighbour just happened to be sitting next to me, and fifty per cent that he had been asked to sit by me. It would be wiser to wait for him to talk to me.

He never did and when we got to Tashkent's airport, seeing me picking up my coat, he remarked in perfect English: 'That coat will be far too warm for you in Tashkent.' Indeed, Tashkent was hot.

I must say, I prefer a more civilized form of ideological warfare as fought in conversation. Kostia was convinced that Communism was the only solution for the future and that the Western way of life was doomed, based as it is on colonialism and the exploitation of others. But since I agree on this point, there wasn't much room for discussion.

'All Western foreign policy is based on exploitation and it is planned and implemented by the rich.' The Russian concept of Western capitalism coincides with the posters one sees in Soviet streets: fat little men, their pockets bulging with dollars walking over the poor who are about to break out of their heavy chains. It is difficult to explain that capitalism is no longer as it was in the days of Marx, Engels or Lenin; that it has become more paternalistic.

One girl who did not belong to the Communist Party and was very critical of the regime, nevertheless told me one day: 'But you know, if Russian Communism was threatened, I wouldn't hesitate to fight for it.'

Apart from the 'secret cities' I have already mentioned, there are whole areas in the Soviet Union closed not only to foreigners, but to Soviet citizens too. Those who live in such places must carry special papers. All the peninsula of Kamchatka – apparently a paradise of beauty – is closed and so is part of the Crimea, Balaklava, Alupka. 'The mountains over the sea are guarded by the police, but there are always ways of getting there. One can pretend to be a friend of a family who lives there.'

Spying

In Leningrad, near the Admiralty, near the the Neva there's an anonymous building, inconspicuous between two greyish pre-revolutionary structures. 'That's where the CHEKA was first set up.' I looked at it with fascination; that was where Felix Dzherzhinsky had first started to operate. Looking at it, I was almost run over by a bus.

'It nearly claimed another victim,' my friend commented. 'Be careful.'

In the same flat voice several people had pointed out the Lubyanka palace, a previous insurance office in

Moscow. In the middle of the square a very realistic bronze monument to Dzherzhinsky surveyed his creation. The legendary Felix Dzherzhinsky came from a quite well-off Polish family and like Stalin had been drawn to the priesthood. He was a tall, big man, sometimes described as one who loved children and helped the poor, and sometimes as a monster. He had neat regular features, a dark moustache and beard and slightly sad eyes. Dzherzhinsky was always close to Stalin and sided with him on the question of nationalities. Near the Lubyanka, the tube-station named after him contains another bust of Dzherzhinsky, one of the few men who, although he had been part of Lenin's Politburo, escaped physical and historical elimination by Stalin.

'It is not all that large,' I once said, indicating the Lubyanka palace, as I walked towards Sverdlov Square.

'My dear, it takes up the whole district. Behind that building it stretches on and on, with prisons and offices.'

'What is the district called?'

'Don't make a note of it. Leave them in peace, don't write about them.'

Lenin was responsible for the creation of the CHEKA, the *Chrezvychaina Kommissia,* whose full name is: 'All Russian Extraordinary Commission for Combatting Counter Revolution and Sabotage' (Lenin went in for long names). This had been the official political police of the Bolsheviks. It had full powers: it acted as police-force, judge, jury and executioner. It was ruthless enough but not as terrifying as the organizations which followed, (in 1922 the CHEKA was reorganized as the GPU and later as the OGPU). There is now a tendency in the Soviet Union to make out that the CHEKA was a good body which defended all honest citizens.

In his biography of Stalin Trotsky wrote, discussing the year 1916: 'Stalin derived a sense of impunity and safety from the friendly influence he exerted over the head of the CHEKA ... One was conscious of the obvious intrigue behind this episode and of the invisible presence of Stalin behind Dzherzhinsky.'

When Dzherzhinsky died of a stroke in 1926, two years after Lenin, he was succeeded by another Pole, Vyacheslav Menzhinsky, who was later poisoned.

'Menzhinsky,' wrote Trotsky in the Stalin biography, 'head of the GPU, had been involved in all the opposition movements in Lenin's day . . . But towards the end of his career he was carried away by the machine of police repression. His only interest was the GPU . . . Once during the Civil War, Menzhinsky unexpectedly warned me about Stalin's intrigues against me . . . He transferred his loyalties to Stalin when the Triumvirate fell apart.

'In the autumn of 1927, when the GPU began to intervene in the internal disagreements of the Party, a whole group of us – Zinoviev, Kamenev, Smilga and I, and I think someone else – called on Menzhinsky . . . "Do you remember, Menzhinsky," I asked him, "how once you told me on a train at the Southern Front that Stalin was conducting an intrigue?" Menzhinsky became embarrassed. At this point, Yagoda, who at that time was Stalin's inspector, over the head of the GPU, intervened.'

Genrikh Yagoda, the notorious poisoner, succeeded Menzhinsky. Again, in Trotsky's words: 'The office in which the investigators of the OGPU carry on their super-inquisitorial questioning is connected by microphone with Stalin's office . . .' Yagoda had a long chin under his Hitler-style black moustache. After a terrible term of office from 1934–36 Yagoda too was tried and executed. Trotsky writes: 'A special place in the prisoner's dock was occupied by Yagoda who had worked on the CHEKA and the OGPU for sixteen years, first as an assistant chief, later as its head, and all the time in close contact with the General Secretary (Stalin) as his most trusted aide in the fight against Opposition . . . During the great "purge" Stalin decided to liquidate his fellow culprit too, because he knew too much. In April 1937, Yagoda was arrested. As always, Stalin thus achieved several supplementary advantages: in return for a promise of pardon Yagoda assumed personal guilt at his trial for crimes which rumour had ascribed to Stalin. Of course the promise was never kept: Yagoda was executed, demonstrating once again how Stalin didn't let moral concerns interfere with his legal decisions.'

The name of Nikolai Yezov, the dwarf who succeeded Yagoda for only two years, is even today synonymous with terror and criminal madness; the period is referred to as *yerzhivshina.*

'When Yezov became chief of the OGPU,' Trotsky wrote, 'he reformed the toxicological method (Yagoda who was a chemist, was interested in poisoning) of which in all justice Yagoda must be recognized as the originator . . .'

It is impossible not to admire the beauty of Yezov's face, an Angel of Evil with clear large eyes over high cheekbones and well-designed thick lips over his long chin. With his short blond hair he looked like a handsomer version of Yevtushenko.

In 1946 Stalin reorganized what had become by then the NKVD (the People's Commissariat for Internal Affairs) and in 1950 made it into a Ministry, the MVD, mainly in charge with GULAC, the body administrating labour and concentration camps.

Yezov was succeeded by Beria.

'Beria was also a rather short man,' writes Djilas in *Conversations with Stalin,* 'in Stalin's Politburo there was hardly anyone taller than himself. He too was somewhat plump, greenish and pale, and with soft damp hands. With his square-cut mouth and eyes bulging behind his pincenez, he certainly reminded me of Vujkpvic, one of the chiefs of the Belgrade Royal Police, who specialized in torturing Communists. He even had the same expression – self-satisfied and working – but at the same time obsequious and solicitous like a clerk. Beria was Georgian like Stalin, but one would not have guessed from his appearance.'

Stalin, who by this time had Beria on his death-list,

conveniently died on 5 March 1953. Beria then became, after Malenkov, number two at the Kremlin. But after Khrushchev seized power, he was arrested and shot, in December 1953. After Beria's disappearance, the MGB turned into the KGB (Committee of State Security which did not have ministerial rank) while another new body, the MVD, became the Ministry in charge of the police, frontier patrols, and registration activities (birth and marriage certificates, internal and external passports, visas for Soviet citizens and foreigners, etc.).

Serov, who had been a chief deporter for Stalin, was made the head of the KGB, but in 1958 the young and bright Alexander Shelepin, a protégé of Khrushchev's, took his place. And when Shelepin became more powerful his friend Semichastny took over. But again, after the 23rd Congress of April 1966, when Brezhnev, Kosygin, Suslov and Podgorny took power, and ousted Khrushchev, Yuri Andopov, an ex-ambassador became head of the KGB, and remains so today.

When people talk about 'they', it is to the KGB that they refer. This body, whose headquarters is in the Lubyanka palace, is the secret police.

Russians are constantly anxious about the KGB, whether they say so or just show it. Often whatever they tell one, whether it is a cookery recipe or a comment on the weather, takes on the air of a State secret. 'Please don't say I've told you.' The Russians have learnt a great deal from living in this perpetual state of suspicion.

In some hotel bedrooms, Soviet people point significantly at the lonely painting hanging on the wall, asking for silence, although I have often looked and never found a microphone.

On the other hand, one develops, just like the Russians, a kind of *laissez-faire* attitude towards the KGB. A first night in a city must be spent out 'just to let them have a look at your suitcases.' One Soviet person said to another 'So you were followed? Why complain? How else could those poor people justify their wages?' At other times I myself made

87

no mystery of the fact that I knew whom I was talking to; the joke is generally answered by another understanding joke: they are pleased one has got the point.

'Would you like to smoke?' a semi-official who had taken me out to dinner in Moscow asked me. I counter-offered my Virginia tobacco cigarettes; I knew he liked them.

'No, I mean the real stuff, hemp.'

'Goodness,' I said, knowing how forbidden drugs are in the Soviet Union, 'and how did you get it?'

'Some American tourists gave it to me.' Not very likely, I thought.

'And do you smoke it often?' I asked. Fearing that I might use it against him or devote a chapter of this book to hemp-smoking in Moscow, he cut me short.

'If you want to smoke some, I have it at home.'

I didn't go in for drugs, I told him truthfully. It doesn't interest me at all.

On another occasion the same man asked: 'Do you like gang-love?'

I had never heard the expression.

'What is it?'

'Sex in a group.'

Risking being judged square by my dinner-companion, I told him I found the idea totally ridiculous. The sight of all those white bottoms and pink legs would either make me laugh or put me off sex for life.

'It's difficult enough with two persons, anyway,' I said. 'Do you engage in it often yourself?'

'Sometimes,' he said.

I wondered if he was trying to trap me and if so why? I wondered what he would have done with photographs of a foreign blonde smoking hemp and making 'gang-love'?

Novosibirsk Opera House

I went in from the stage entrance, through long corridors and vast halls which would have been the envy of Covent Garden. In his sumptuous office I met the Director who told me about the opera in Novosibirsk.

'The ballet is more popular than the opera in Novosibirsk. For Lenin's anniversary we are staging a new work, the ballet "Sebastopol". Also "Laurentia", the ballet I am taking you to tonight, is a new work by Krein, a Soviet composer.'

The theatre was opened on the 12 May 1945, three days after victory. It is extraordinary that this immense building was erected during the war years, during famines and when people were sacrificing themselves in overwork. Building a colossal opera house during the war was a tremendous act of faith in peace and victory; it must have been a symbol of so many hopes and for that reason I came to like the giant cupola, a superb example of Soviet stubbornness.

'Yes, we are totally self-contained, we have our own orchestra, singing school and ballet school and our soloists give concerts as well. Salaries are given according to profession and talent. Everyone here works full time: if not actually performing, they either rehearse or train.'

Vladimir Kirsanov, the vice-director, wore on his chest a medal he had just received bearing a golden portrait of Lenin. At that time this kind of medal was given to citizens in all walks of life to mark Lenin's centenary. My congratulations pleased him.

The great theatre can hold three thousand people. It had been conceived by its architect as a multi-purpose hall. The stage was movable and could be used 'in the round', the floor could be flooded for water performances, the cupola had been conceived for *camera obscura* effects. But half-way through the administration changed its mind and the theatre was finished in the conventional manner, although it still shows signs of its many potential uses.

The vice-director asked me after the performance of 'Laurentia': 'How did you like it?'

'Lovely,' I lied.

The performance was certainly not to my taste; its grandiose scenes were designed to appeal to the masses. The music in 'Laurentia' was very conventional and so was the plot: in a poor village a good boy and a pretty maiden, Laurentia, plan to get married. Everybody is happy for them. But a rich brute comes from his castle and energetically seduces every girl in sight. He has designs on pretty Laurentia as well. After the loss of many ballerina virginities and after many of them have been tortured by the rich lord and his team, Laurentia starts a revolution. The good ones win, and the bad perish.

'Of course ballet is the most pornographic art in the world,' a sophisticated Soviet friend once said to me. 'Why don't they just "do" it on the stage? Strip-tease must be far more innocent.'

Someone else told me in a very matter-of-fact way that their male corps-de-ballet was almost without exception homosexual, whereas the official line of the regime suggests that there are almost no homosexuals in Russia. There are in fact fewer than in the West, but there are queer meeting places in Moscow just as in any other capital.

The Georgians and the Armenians certainly have a great reputation for being queer even though they are Soviet citizens.

Some people asked me about avant-garde ballet in England. Of course 'avant-garde' to the Russians still means the early '20s, in architecture, poetry, films and music. People still look back at that time as a blessed age of self-expression. Eisenstein, Mayakovsky, Bulgakov, Shostakovich, Stanivslavsky, Pasternak, all demonstrate what a climate of intellectual freedom can produce in Russia.

The night following the performance of 'Laurentia' I went

to 'Prince Igor' on my own. It was a lovely performance, well sung, and beautifully designed.

During the first interval, I went to have a snack at one of the many cafeterias in the theatre. The room was vast and richly decorated with chandeliers. Every single table was full. People had obviously just had time to change before the performance – which started at seven. The men wore suits and the women woollen dresses, nylon stockings and high heels. It was unlike the kind of crowd that one sees at a Western opera house largely because this is a popular audience and not an audience composed of the élite. It reminded me of an Italian crowd listening to a political speech sixteen or eighteen years ago.

While I was strolling in the foyer, people asked me where I came from, whether I liked their Novosibirsk opera house, the performance and their city. When I was in the Soviet Union the first time, ten years ago, people used to stroll around the foyer in an orderly circle, leaving a curious empty space in the middle, each following the rhythm of others, but this habit has now died and the audience at Novosibirsk behaved just as any audience waiting during the interval. By chance I met the vice-director who was pleased to see me there as a proof of my interest in the opera house. I asked whether he always worked at night and he answered that of course he did. They had to be there during performances. He took me to see the *maquettes* for the future production of 'Sebastopol' and I noticed how many of the public knew him, but how relaxed their attitude towards him was . . .

At the Akademgradok

I find scientists attractive as people and I was looking forward to visiting what is probably the most important scientific centre in the Soviet Union, the academic citadel of scientific research (Gradok means little city) near Novosibirsk.

Although it is only one hour away from Novosibirsk, the journey seemed very long. The countryside along the road was flat and monotonous, wooden houses dotted the landscape, the sky was low and ice-coloured.

In 1958 the Soviet Government decided to set up a Siberian department of the Academy of Sciences of the USSR. Finally Novosibirsk was chosen because of its good communications network, its many factories which could provide building materials, its central position in Siberia, its good hydro-electric resources. They had to create a new road and then a new city. Every single stone came to the Akademgradok carried by lorries which often sunk in the deep snow, or slipped on ice. 'Of course the difficulties of creating the city were immense,' the President of the Akademgradok told me. 'I remember in the autumn when the road was not yet asphalted, more than a hundred lorries got stuck in the mud. Winters were fierce and the cement broke with the cold.'

But the city was built; it now covers an area of ten square kilometres, includes twenty-two institutes, living accommodation, shopping centres, botanical gardens and university schools. Of its fifty thousand inhabitants, fifty are members of the Academy of Sciences of the USSR, about a hundred are Doctors of Science and a thousand are researchers. Besides this there are the students of the university and schools, the administrative staff and the shopkeepers.

Mikhail Laurentiev

The mathematician Mikhail Alieksievich Laurentiev, a Soviet Academician, is the President of the Akademgradok.

I was lucky, for Mikhail Alieksievich is usually too busy to see anyone, but that day was his birthday ('His seventieth,' a professor specified. 'Why did you have to say how

old I am to a young woman?' Laurentiev answered jokingly.)
A large camera crew was filming 'a typical day of the
President of the Akademgradok'. So, sitting in the boardroom under strong film lights, the gentle and charming old
man told me a lot about the Akademgradok.

The principles upon which the science centre was
planned he explained, were based on Soviet and foreign
experience of scientific development.

'A centre of this kind,' he said, 'had to include men from
all branches of science. So we set up institutes of mathematics, physics, chemistry, geology, mechanics, biology,
economics and a computer centre. And of course the
Akademgradok had to justify itself economically by offering valuable advice to factories and by getting scientific
discoveries incorporated into the national economy.'

The Akademgradok is not only a centre for pure research
but also includes a university of three thousand students
(small in Soviet terms) who are strictly selected.

'We decided to build the Academy here so we could give
special help to Siberian industry and explore and develop
the natural resources of the area. We wanted to develop
science in the Eastern part of the country.

'You ask which institute I am most proud of; it is difficult
to say,' he went on. 'The Geophysics Institute played an
important part in mining the resources here, but I am also
proud of the Institute of Nuclear Physics.'

Mikhail Laurentiev was very popular in the town of
Novosibirsk. I discovered that he was loved by all sections
of the population, by the shop-keepers, students and professors. He had informal manners, he was simple and he
liked to walk for hours every day. 'It is the best exercise in
the world,' he said.

'Yes,' he went on, 'this is a very international place. In
our kind of work scientists from all over the world co-
operate; people make a combined effort not only between
countries, but between different branches of science. Of
course we have scientists visiting us from all over the world

and we also attend scientific congresses abroad.

'The most serious problem,' he continued, 'is the question of youth and how future scientists should be educated. Our teaching system differs from others because the laboratories and research institutes are attached to the university; from the start students enter the world of science and the scientists themselves enjoy the nearness and the ideas of young people.'

The union between research in science and education of the young is the trade-mark of the Akademgradok.

'As usual in the Soviet Union, students receive a grant from the State; the salaries of professors, assistants and teachers are geared to their qualifications. I would like to see professors in physics and mathematics receive still higher salaries,' added Laurentiev, who had been head of the Akademgradok since its foundation. I asked him whether the Siberian staff were paid more to attract them to a place where the winter temperature could drop to minus 55 degrees centigrade.

'No, we receive exactly the same as, let us say, a scientist who works in the Ukraine even though life is in fact more expensive here. Food costs more and so does travel. We also need more expensive clothes like furs, woollens, etc., because of the climate. But people are attracted to the Akademgradok because the equipment is new and scientists here enjoy total freedom of research. People who like nature and are tired of large cities, come here happily and never want to leave. I, for example, worked in Moscow, but would never go back. My childhood was spent close to Nature. Until I was twenty-one, I lived near Kazan in a settlement located in the forest. During the cold weather I went to work on skis and in the summer I boated and fished on the Volga which, near Kazan, is like the sea. The Akademgradok resembles the Kazan of my childhood. The new Kazan is an industrial city, but here we still live close to nature. It is very nice to have one's grandchildren here rather than in big cities. In the summer we swim in the lake, row and fish. It is a good place for summer holidays.'

The streets of the flat city were wide and empty, leading to the different institutes: solid, rectangular shapes, flanked by fir trees and by the pink Siberian pine, the *sasna*, a brother of the Scottish pine, which imparts a welcome variety to the Novosibirsk landscape.

The *morie*, the large lake, was visible from most parts of the city. There is an artificial beach with huts and merry-go-rounds. When I saw it, the beach was covered with snow, the lake was frozen and the merry-go-round looked like part of a forgotten piece of theatrical scenery, dripping icicles and rusty rain: it was hard then to visualize children in bathing costumes. But the odd Siberian climate transforms the landscape with the warm spells of summer. The elegant district, the *Zalatoi dalmini* (the golden valley) away from the modern shopping centre and glassy culture house of the Akademgradok, is the only undulating valley which breaks the flatness of the countryside, flaming gold in the Autumn. Top scientists and foreign visitors live there, in very attractive *dachas*.

All over the city, and on the edge of the forest which flows into the citadel itself, little wooden boxes are suspended on the branches of the trees to feed the squirrels during the winter. People really love and preserve nature in this corner of the world.

I passed along the *Prospiect Nauki*, the Boulevard of Sciences, flanked by flats for married students, passed the hospital and arrived at the scientists' club, the *Dom Uchonih*, a very attractive building lit by large areas of wall-to-ceiling windows and standing on a terraced base. I was meeting Nellia for lunch.

Spartak

All I knew was that I was going to have a talk with the head of the Akademgradok University, Spartak Timotievich Byeliayev.

'Are you going to meet Spartak?' 'I wonder what she'll make of Spartak.' 'Laurentiev and Spartak . . .'

Also Nellia told me: 'I shan't say anything about him, you'll have to judge for yourself.'

Of one thing I was sure: they were all proud of 'their' Spartak.

My first reaction to him must have been the same as that of hundreds of others. I had expected him to be ancient and white-haired and I couldn't stop myself saying: 'I didn't expect you to be so young.' He smiled a cold patient smile as if hearing an obvious remark on the weather.

Spartak spoke excellent English. He was dry and lean, dressed in a dark, rather elegant suit; it was immediately obvious that he lacked the warmth of Laurentiev. He seemed very English in appearance and attitudes.

'Have you any experience of scientific institutes?' he asked.

'I know Berkeley and MIT a little but I know the Weizmann Institute* quite well.'

'Do you really? When were you there?'

'Two years ago; I was a guest there for a week; have you been there?' I asked.

'No, but I know some of its scientists. I met Amos de Shalitt . . .'

'Did you know that he died recently?'

'Yes, it is very sad. He was such a brilliant man. He had marvellous ideas which he was just developing. We worked in the same field.'

From this I understood that Spartak was a nuclear physicist.

'Does the Akademgradok resemble the Weizmann at all?' I asked.

'Not really; although we too have fields in pure research. But our teaching staff and our scientists work with the students; I believe we are quite unique in adopting this system. Let me describe the general structure of the univer-

* The Weizmann is in Israel.

sity and the schools which were established and conceived at the same time as the Akademgradok. Since our main purpose was to educate the young, we needed above all to find scientists who could teach; we needed the right environment for teaching, and good students. The most important thing is the selection of students. The standard of education here in Siberia is not as high as in Europe, nor is it so widespread but we do want to develop really first-class science here.'

Seven years ago the Akademgradok established a rather complicated system of selection.

'We send a group of problems to all schools in Siberia asking the children to solve them in writing. Those who answer correctly – about fifteen thousand of them – are given a second set of problems to solve. The children who solve these, about eight hundred, are then invited to spend the month of August at the Akademgradok for a combination of holiday and summer-school. These children are given daily lectures by our leading scientists and they attend seminars in physics, mathematics and chemistry. At the end of the month 250 are chosen in what is called "the Olympiad", and they stay and pursue their education at the Akademgradok. Equal numbers are chosen from each city. These children aged about thirteen or fourteen, live in boarding-houses and attend an ordinary secondary school which has, however, a special emphasis on science subjects and is conducted under the supervision of our professors.'

All these younger students later enter the Akademgradok university, Spartak explained, and join the scientists in team-work, in close collaboration. This mixing of generations and qualifications seems ideal, although the 'Olympiad' has an Orwellian tone.

'If a student wants to,' Spartak went on, 'he can change his subject and switch from Mathematics to research in Physics. He can also follow two subjects at the same time and later choose the one he wants to specialize in.'

'Do you think there is a greater attraction towards science

subjects in the Soviet Union than in the West?'

'There used to be, but recently there has been an increase in young people wanting to study the Humanities.'

Spartak's eyes looked distant through his spectacles; he had fine bone structure and delicate features. 'Our university is very popular because it is small and because it gets good results.

'About a hundred foreign visitors every year come to the Akademgradok for short periods. We haven't established many relations with foreign scientists so far, but we hope for more.'

Spartak's eyes looked less metallic when their owner at last removed his spectacles. They were cold, technocratic eyes which had obviously been made to work too hard.

Spartak had been professor at the Akademgradok since 1962 and he was made head of the university in 1965. A little Russian warmth came through when he asked if I would like to visit the Department of Physics. This was an honour.

The undergraduate schools and some institutes

The University was huge and attractive. The school for those thirteen-year-olds, the future scientists chosen at the 'Olympiad' was modern and co-educational. I was surprised by the ease with which professors, teachers and pupils of both school and university mixed in the classrooms. It was particularly unexpected in the middle of Siberia.

'Siberia will add to the might of Russia,' wrote Mikhail Lomonosov, who in the eighteenth century founded Moscow University.

Every child was taught to type and to drive a car. The latter was perhaps a little pointless considering how scarce cars are on the huge empty roads of the Akademgradok.

The lavatories were surprisingly primitive, although clean. Pieces of *Pravda* cut into neat shapes were used as lavatory paper. The partitions were flimsy, but I didn't see, on this journey, what I had seen previously: communal lavatories, rather like the ones the Romans used, where people apparently sat and chatted to each other. Russian and Finnish villages have them, and the mayors are proud of their sixteen- or eighteen-seaters. I often wondered whether the need for privacy in the lavatory was perhaps unnatural, yet the sophisticated cream of technological Siberia must have felt the same as I did.

I liked the fresh approach to teaching there, the concept of mixing the ages and capacities; old scientists teaching children, students working with researchers. I also admired the view of the lake from the school: the high trees touching the window-panes of the classrooms, the silence, the monotony of a landscape which must encourage concentration.

Some of the institutes of science in the Akademgradok are of particular importance to the development of Siberia. The Geological Institute, for example, carries out research on the composition and history of the earth's crust, the conditions in which minerals were formed: Geochemistry and Seismology. The results have helped to discover deposits of gold and diamonds. The Soviet Union is one of the main sources of both these.

By using mathematical methods, the institute has been able to assess geological reserves of oil and gas in remote areas of the West Siberian lowlands.

The Institute of Mining, led by Nikolai Chinakal, designed pneumatic drills which were used in the construction of the Aswan Dam.

The effort to integrate economic and mathematical investigations is vital to the Soviet Union during this period of economic troubles. The Siberian Department of Economics is said to be the leading one in the Soviet Union, although decisions are still made in Moscow.

There is, of course, a very important Institute of Nuclear Physics which dominates the centre of the citadel. New methods of accelerating elementary particles, the principles of treating high temperature plasma and the problem of controlled thermonuclear fusion are being worked on there.

There are institutes of Hydrodynamics – very important in Siberia – an institute of Catalysis and a Computer centre.

One preparation invented by the Institute of Biochemistry at the Akademgradok particularly interested me: a preparation for curing infections of the eyes, nervous system and skin caused by the *herpes* virus, still considered incurable by many in the West, which attacks my nose twice a year regularly.

Introspection

'This is the dream – you do not sleep but dream
you thirst for sleep, that there's a fellow dozing
and through his dream from underneath his eyelids
a pair of black suns break and burn his lashes.'
(Pasternak. *In the Wood.*)

It was already dark. I prepared my bed – in the Soviet Union beds are made like envelopes – and tried to draw the flimsy curtains as tight as possible. But the cord snapped and they tumbled onto my table which was laid out with stamps and envelopes in preparation for letter-writing. I switched on the television and after a few minutes of a film about the Great Patriotic War – the Russian name for World War Two – I turned down the volume and went back to my table. I watched the images reflected in reverse in the dark window-panes – a succession of war scenes seen against the Siberian night.

I stared into the darkness, behind the grey images of soldiers whose mouths worked in a silent frenzy.

Russia is a country which forces introspection on one. The sense of space gives one a feeling of monotony, and a feeling of the certainty of death. Spending evenings by myself did not make me lonely as travelling alone often has; on the contrary, it offered me a soft longing for solitude when unlimited spaces and the snow outside my window compelled the self to come to terms with the other selves.

I had begun to realize that behind almost every Russian's smile there was a tragedy of such proportions that one wondered how they managed to cope and to go on living. (It was estimated that, at the end of Stalin's days, one family out of three had one member in a concentration camp.) Yet the Russians have learnt to accept suffering both in the past and in this last century of civil war, famine and war against the Nazis (twenty-five million people lost their homes, two factories out of three were either burnt down or bombed). Their skins have doubled in thickness, but the soul inside is still the soft melting Russian soul.

Contemplation is an Eastern heritage, something that comes from the Orthodox religion rather than from the Catholic. Our spiritual stress has always been in Jesus, humanitarianism, and cultivation of the intellect. But the Orthodox has always stressed the Almighty, on the sublimation of the soul, something nearer Buddhism. This search for abstraction, for the 'better', is always present in their literature as much as in their lives. '. . . No, the Russians are not what you imagine them to be. They hold traditions sacred, they are a patriarchal people. They cannot live without faith . . .' (Turgenev's *Fathers and Sons*.)

Even the purest Russians* have a background of Tartar occupation, of Orthodox religion, of acceptance, of cataclysm, of gloomy mythology, which makes them different. They react, they think, they behave differently from us. In character they are more European than Asian but, unlike us, they have faith in a Utopian and forever distant paradise. They dwell in Purgatory and some of them have had a long experience of hell.

The sunlight was casting a faint light on to the border of the flimsy curtains, or what remained of them. The tele-

---

* i.e., not the Kazakh, the Tadzhik, the Armenian, etc. The Soviet Union is not one country, it is a solar system. It is so big and complex, its people are of different nationalities, cultures and languages.

vision had long since interrupted its grey reflections while I had gone on with mine. Even my letters had remained unwritten.

Siberian Archæology and History

At the Akademgradok Institute of Siberian Archaeology and History I was expecting to meet Mr Rusakov, head of the institute, Yuri Serghievich Pastov, the editor of a monumental encyclopaedia on the history of Siberian literature and David Konstantinovski, 'the' Novosibirsk writer. I had gone through a book of theatrical essays given to me by the author and I had noticed a strong official line in Konstantinovski's writing. He was a rather good-looking man but I cannot have much respect for the regime's writers; it is a contradiction in terms.

I was surprised when Yuri Pastov told me that he was working on a biography of Shelley. There was something incongruous about Siberia and Shelley, but Yuri Pastov was obviously a man of letters. He asked me to send him a book on Shelley since he had few sources of information. Poor man, working on Shelley near Novosibirsk, surrounded by the *taiga*. I did send the book, but I doubt that he ever received it.

'Shelley is my hero,' said Pastov and asked me who my hero was.

I have had many heroes. Mozart, I said, and Ekenaton and Voltaire.

'It's a pity that Voltaire was a friend of your Catherine the Great,' I said, following my own train of thought.

'In those days the liberals liked to be close to the sources of power.'

'Just like now. Look at the court surrounding the Kennedys.'

'Oh, but I loved the Kennedys.'

Strange how Russians did. Perhaps it was their beauty or

the similarity of the two Kennedy assassinations with the violent deaths of so many tsars.

'If you don't like Catherine the Great, you are not a typical Westerner.'

Catherine was a tyrant who opened the way to a few reforms but later undid her good work by clamping down on the people as harshly as ever. On the other hand, although she was German, she could also be described as a great Russian patriot. She annexed a great deal of strategic territory to her empire.

'But she also destroyed her son,' I said.

'Paul? He was mad, but perhaps a genuine reformer. But you know . . . he had relationships . . .'

An homosexual ruler, ruled out.

'We are preparing an encyclopaedia in several volumes devoted to the history and traditions of Siberia,' Pastov said. 'Siberia became the country of political convicts, and they started writing, like the Decembrists. At the same time peasants were not as badly exploited here as they were in Russia.'

'Siberia is so large,' Konstantinovski went on. 'The scenery and environment are so varied that it is impossible to generalize about our character. I made a trip to the Far East of Siberia. Well, it was like going to another planet.'

'We have a reputation for being reserved and firm. But again the variety of people is so great: what do the northern Yakuti and the Russians from the Kamchatka peninsula have in common?' Pastov went on. 'The kind of life we lead in Siberia makes for strong ties; social groupings are closer because they are isolated. Some villages are only linked to the outside world by boats when the river thaws.'

Groups of Soviet, American and Japanese scientists are working on the problems of the primary Siberian populations, of the first appearance of man in the Far East.

'It was not Columbus who discovered America, but the Siberians.'

There are theories about the migration through Alaska

down the American continents; there are connections between the Northern Siberian populations and the Aztek, Maya and Inca civilizations, both in their physical characteristics, style of clothing, ornaments and sculpture. It is also interesting to note that these civilizations never discovered the wheel, unnecessary in a land of snow and ice.

The original nomadic populations of Siberia are small, brownish-yellow in complexion, with tiny noses and mongol eyes. These ethnological groups who have settled down in specific areas, have characteristics and languages which differentiate them.

The department of the Institute of Archaeology which is in charge of the museum and of archaeological expeditions also works to preserve these languages, many of which have no written form. But although the scientists assured me that these original languages had had an influence on spoken Russian in words like *taiga, tundra* and *pielmeni,* I could not see any other signs of influence. The Russian colonization has certainly been overwhelming. In cities like Khabarovsk, the local population – the Nanais – have lost their cooking traditions and their way of dressing and it is very difficult – indeed impossible – to see their beautiful embroidery, needlework, pipes made of bone, leather shoes coloured with ornaments, belts, and head-covers, except in the museum.

There are many such populations and I am told that in the North their traditions have been maintained; the Yakuti who live in part of the immense autonomous region of Yakutia, in north Siberia, the Ani, the Kamtchatki, the Sakkali. Stella, a Nanai girl I met, was extremely pretty, tall, slim, long-haired and she taught in a high school. Liena, a girl who came from Yakutia, was instead Russian in origin. She was tiny and was horrified at the thought of going back to live in one of the coldest cities in the world.

For centuries travellers reported seeing rock drawings and sculptures along Siberian river-banks which are now being studied at the Institute. The Siberians call them *pisanitsy.*

They were found along the Yenisey, the Amur, the Angara and Lena rivers. The drawings were painted with red ochre mineral-paint and portray animals, symbols and stylized figures of men. Scholars not only try to determine the age of these drawings but to establish which pre-historic civilizations lived in Siberia before the arrival of the Tartars and the Russians.

The earliest known pre-history drawings were found near the village of Shishkino, on the southern point of the Lena river. Their style is curiously similar to those found in France. At the institute we looked at reproductions and the original object. As the ice age waned and the land changed, so did the animals painted by the first Siberians. Again at Shishkino, super-imposed on the figure of a bison of the Upper Paleolithic period, there is a reindeer stag drawn in the period which followed. Later still when the *taiga* had replaced the *tundra* and steppes, in the Neolithic age, the Siberians drew elks which became not only the main source of food, but also a constant presence in religious rituals. Drawings of elks were found on rocks near Bratsk, and the Lapps, the Samoyeds and Tungus tribes picture the soul of the world as a big elk with gold antlers.

In the Neolithic age the human figure, always in profile, appears in rock drawings; sometimes elks are shown being hunted by men on skis. With the Bronze and Early Iron Ages, human figures and monsters appear on paintings along the Angara and in the east Baikal.

The so-called 'cosmic monster' is a strange animal drawn with a secure hand, its spine covered with spikes and the long muzzle open in the act of swallowing the symbol of the moon or of the sun. More than a thousand drawings on the rocks have been found in the area.

There are also a number of sculptures generally carved on sandstone along the rivers; several along the Yenisey portray human faces. In the Transbaikal and in Mongolia the dominant feature is the eagle which, in their mythology, was connected with the sun. The cult of the sun survived until the time of Ghengis Khan and remained the central figure of the Buryats' religion of Shamanism, up to today.

Professor Oklandnikov has been studying a different area, the lower Amur region in the Neolithic age and its connections with other cultures in Asia. He found that 5,000 years ago there was a fully developed Neolithic culture in what is today the Soviet Far East.

The drawings and sculptures found in the Amur-Ussuri area, many of which were discovered 130 kilometres from Khabarovsk, at the village of Sakschi-Alyan, show a different culture from the ones found in Central Siberia, which tend instead to depict men and animals. Here the tendency is mystical: ducks and snakes form entwined motifs, mysterious stylized masks appear on the rocks; the figure of man is only represented by his skull.

This style which is always drawn in attractive curved lines can still be found in ornaments of the Nanai tribes. Indeed in the Far East I bought children's books designed by local painters which combined all the elements of the rock drawings and mythological legends of the Amur region.

In the Altai mountains, another civilization, that of the Scythians, who then moved on to the Black Sea, left marvellous vestiges in their tombs, gold ornaments actually manufactured for them by the Greeks. All these are to be seen today at the Hermitage Museum in Leningrad.

Part Two
Central Asia

Alma Ata

I left Novosibirsk and Siberia behind. After three hours on
the plane we were over Kazakhstan, one of the largest of the
Soviet Republics.

Suddenly the clouds that had obscured the view lifted and
I saw the mountains of Tian-Chan, the mountains of the
Sky, locking Alma Ata in a snowy bastion. The highest
point is the Khan-Tengri, 6,955 metres high. I stared ecstatically at the blossoms covering the trees, at the green leaves
and the shiny tender grass waking up to spring. Spring ...
it was another world. I couldn't get accustomed to the
absence of snow under my feet, flowers looked like miracles
and I felt the warm air with surprise: it was the South,
it was spring.

And indeed my hotel bore the characteristic signs of
southern chaos. It looked as if an earthquake had shaken its
foundations: beds in the hall, chairs stacked in a corner,
piles of carpets, crowds waiting, just waiting ... People's
attitudes were also more relaxed and southern: there was
no danger of being taken on forced guided tours.

After I had been led through Kafkaesque corridors where
beds were accumulated and people in pyjamas wandered
casually, I arrived at the gigantic bedroom and private study
that had been allotted to me and I was left to myself.

The information I got at the hotel desk bore a southern
trade-mark as well: not only was 'Kovanchina' not on at the
opera house that night as had been indicated, but there was
to be no performance at all for the following three days.
The theatre, too, was not performing Chekov that night,
nor was it in fact performing at all as I found out when
I checked there; the following day it offered a modern play
in the Kazakh language, a treat I was anxious to avoid.

About half of Alma Ata's 660,000 inhabitants were
Kazakhs: round, brown fleshy faces, Mongol eyes and

straight shiny black hair. To my alarm they spoke Kazakh a language which has Turkish origins* and shops had notices both in Russian and in Kazakh. When I switched on the television, I was startled to see a Kazakh film, with Kazakh actors all looking like Ghengis Khan. The Kazakh's alphabet has been Russified and changed from Arabic to Cyrillic lettering but the language is totally different. Here people spoke about 'Russian colonialism', an expression I had not heard in Siberia.

The flower market was a triumph of colours and variety: lilies-of-the-valley, violets and plenty of those red tulips that cost half a rouble each in Irkutsk. Here a big heavy bunch costs the same.

Alma-Ata lies on the south-eastern edge of Kazakhstan, only about a hundred and fifty kilometres from the Chinese border and on the old silk route between China and Byzantium. In 1854, Russian Cossacks founded two *stalniza,* Russian Cossack village fortifications, at Alma Ata and that is why the town is built in colonial style, with no oriental flavour. Tsarist penetration in Kazakhstan did not start until 1890 when Alma Ata was renamed *Dvierni* (Loyal) up to 1920. One year later the first train connected Alma Ata with Moscow.

Alma Ata was a difficult place to cultivate the revolution: in 1918 there had been a counter-revolution against the Bolsheviks as much of the land belonged to the Cossacks, mercenaries of the Tsar, to whom the crown had been generous. The Cossacks were always the element the most faithful to the crown and during the civil war tended to join the White rather than the Red Army.

Finally the city reverted to its original name (Alma Ata means in Kazakh 'father of apples') and the name *Dvierni* was abandoned forever. In 1929 Alma Ata became the capital of Kazakhstan.

* The heirs of the original Mongols speak languages related to Turkish. In fact the tribes which pushed towards Turkey from the Far East have the same origins as the Crimean Tartars, the Kazakhs, the Kazan Tartars (and, of course, the Hungarians and the Finns).

The city is superbly situated, and the richness of the vegetation gives it variety. The climate is continental, hot summers and cold winters, but long warm springs and autumns.

In the city there is a peculiar nineteenth-century wooden cathedral built without the use of a single nail and covered with stucco to make it look as if it were built in stone. 'I turned the corner and saw the famous cathedral. I had heard so much about it, but what I saw was absolutely unexpected. Very high, a forest of cupolas, decorated with arabesques, painted in different colours, it has extremely complicated cornices and roofs of undulating sheet-iron, a steeple and a staircase, or rather a whole complicated system of staircases, corridors and galleries.' (From Dombrovsky's *The Curator of the Museum*.)

Today the magical building created by Zenkov houses a museum of the Republic. Russian artisans were very skilled in inserting wooden panels and tree-trunks without using nails, the most beautiful and famous example being the churches at Kishi, in northern Russia. This talent was encouraged partly because nails were expensive and rare.

This Alma Ata wooden building survived many violent earthquakes. There are – how could there not be? – a huge statue of Lenin and a new opera house. This has just been repainted a bathroom-blue. It is huge and decorated inside like a provincial ballroom. The first government house of Kazakhstan is a surprise; it was built to a design of Le Corbusier's. It is a rather small cubist affair left today in a battered state of decay; cubism, modernism – all that belongs to Mayakovsky's and Lenin's age. Today Soviet architecture is just turning away from the wedding-cake style of Stalin's era to the sublime heights created by the Hilton hotels.

If one sneaks off Alma Ata's modern central boulevards ('This one was called after the students, then after a hero of the Soviet Union, now its name has changed again; I

111

can't keep up with it,' somebody told me), into the side roads, the wooden houses looked richer than the ones in Siberia.

Apart from this, there isn't much of interest to see. Indeed, from a tourist point of view I feel ambivalent about Soviet Central Asia: on the one hand I long for the old colourful folklore which is no longer there, while on the other I delight in the lack of poverty and the high standards of living. The capitals of Kazakhstan, Uzbekistan or Tadzhikistan are rather sparing with local colour; they have been intent on obliterating links with a backward past. Only recently a desire to return to some of the old ways has become more accepted. But it is easier for the Russians to revive their old traditions than for the 'Autonomous' states, since it is feared that in so doing nationalist feelings could revive, and they do. Strong desires are stirring in some republics for actual independence from the excessive grasp of Mother Russia.

So the Sentimental Traveller had better forget about bazaars, exotic materials, scents. People laughed at me for wearing a practical Afghan sheepskin coat, saying that only the *kulaks* would have worn that coat, and many years ago.

Many political exiles have been sent to Alma Ata and Kazakhstan from Tsarist times onwards. The Volga-Germans were exiled here and so were some Ukrainians and those Yugoslav Communists who happened to be in Russia at the time of Stalin's wrath against Tito. Trotsky, expelled by the Party in 1927, was exiled to Alma Ata until January 1928. One year later he was banned from Soviet territory altogether.

In a previous visit to the Soviet Union I remember meeting, in Tashkent, an unfortunate man who had been exiled there while his father had been sent to Alma Ata; their separation repeated the pattern of tragedy suffered by those Russians who had already been in German concentration camps.

The valley of Alma Ata was white with flower-blossoms when I was there. It is the highest apple-producing area in the Soviet Union. I was often told that I should come back in the autumn to eat the *aport* apple of which the Kazakhs are very proud. Alma Ata is situated on a plateau 900 metres high and is built on a seismic area; earthquakes are common here and all new houses are built with reinforced concrete to a limited height. It has a Seismology Institute and an Observatory, though if one listens to the official dates of the great earthquakes and natural calamities, one will find that the Soviet regime has even been able to stop the crust of the earth from shaking! The great care taken in erecting new buildings in Soviet Central Asia is in painful contrast with the equally dangerous earthquake area of North-East Iran where mud huts fall at the slightest seismic provocation, burying their occupants.

I was in the Meshed area in Iran in 1968 during an earthquake in which 20,000 died and it was terrible to see hundreds of wounded being removed to present an orderly sight to the visiting Monarch.

In Iran, where there are different rules – and houses – for the rich and the poor, the mud villages disappeared but the few well-built houses stood.

Indeed to appreciate Soviet efforts in Central Asia, one ought to approach it from the South; on that side illiteracy is almost total while the opposite is true in Soviet Central Asia, and while people in Iran starve and lead a medieval life of deprivation, on the Soviet side people have enough to eat and to clothe themselves.

One of Alma Ata's hazards is a beautiful torrent, the Alma Atinka, which gushes down from the steep mountains. When the ice on the mountains melts, the torrent becomes a swelling river of stones and mud, and is often in danger of bursting its narrow banks. In 1902 (note, before Soviet times) the city was flooded and destroyed. Now an artificial mountain is being bulldozed to bar the rocks and the mud;

113

towards Alma Ata two dams of earthquake-proof design make sure that the city is well protected from this menace in the future.

Kazakhstan

Kazakhstan is eleven times as large as England, a gigantic piece of land bordered by the Caspian Sea, the *taiga* of the Altai, the Urals and in its east-south borders, China's high deserts. A finger of Kazakhstan stretches into Europe while the rest of its body and soul belongs to Asia.

Most of Kazakhstan's steppes are undulating, unlike the flat steppes of Southern Ukraine, while the Khan-Tengri, at the borders of China and Kirghisistan, is one thousand metres higher than Mont Blanc. The deepest depression in the Soviet Union is near the Caspian Sea, 132 metres below sea-level. The Republic is also famous for its nineteen million hectares of Virgin Lands which were cultivated between 1954 and 1960 in the notorious Khrushchev efforts to produce more wheat for the Soviet Union.

Near the Aral Sea there is the missile base of Baikonour, where the Russian cosmonauts are launched into space. Near Alma Ata, towards the mountains, a very attractive villa secluded by high walls and an elaborate iron gate houses the cosmonauts during their rest-periods and when they want to ski. When I passed it with a friend, I was told: 'This is for State visitors and for the cosmonauts. There is no longer any mystery about the fact that cosmonauts are launched from near the Aral Sea.'

Officially cosmonauts are considered symbols of wealth and security, rather like Sophia Loren's bosom for the Italians, although many Russians think that far too much money is being spent on space research, when it is badly needed on the ground.

Kazakh culture is limited by the fact that the population has been nomadic for centuries, living mainly off the land and divided by tribes.

A plump Kazakh reproached me. 'We study English at school and read Shakespeare. You don't even try to speak Kazakh or read our great poet Abai Kounanbayev.' This is quite true. On the other hand Kazakh only became a written language in the nineteenth century and Abai – the man who gave the language a literary shape, more of a Chaucer than of a Shakespeare – only died in 1907. Perhaps in five hundred years, I told him, we shall all be reading Kazakh literature, but in the meantime they will have to work hard at it.

The Kazakhs

'No, no, we don't speak Russian at home,' one Kazakh told me, 'for us it is a kind of Latin, a language we speak badly. I myself learnt it when I started to work. In villages people only speak Kazakh amongst themselves. Alma Ata has lost its character, you should come to Karangada. We have more character, we are not like the Siberians who are almost like the English.' The south always advertises itself in the same way.

The Kazakhs were divided into tribes, had territories and demarcation lines, tribal symbols and colours. The riding competition held between tribes, the *kopkar,* is still as popular in Kazakhstan as the *corrida* is in Spain.

There are equivalent competitions for women, the *jorgga-jarys.* These Amazons wear marvellous head-dresses covered with jewels and their saddles are particularly beautiful and ornate.

Their houses are called the *yourte,* marvellous octagonal tents with very elaborate frames, decorated with tapestries, carpets and cushions; the only furniture they have are inlaid wooden chests.

Their national clothes which can still be seen in villages are really beautiful, masculine and tough, rich in fur and leather. In a country composed of steppes where riding was more important than walking, boots were the principal

115

garments for both men and women. Both sexes also wore trousers, the women had long skirts over theirs. Kazakh women don't wear veils or cover their faces but they wear instead rigid conical hats often bordered with fur. Islam came very late to Kazakhstan and it did not interfere as much in their costumes as it did in most Moslem countries.

Most objects were made of leather, even the bottles in which they kept the *kumis,* the Kazakh national drink made from the fermented milk of mares. As it contains some spirit, it is called the champagne of the steppes. I prefer French champagne but *kumis* is said to possess healthy effects which Dom Perignon does not have.

All Kazakh national dishes are designed for a nomad way of life. They are easily transportable, fermented or spiced to prevent them from going bad and they are meant to be eaten with the bare hands. Whereas in most Soviet Republics one is always told about national cooking, but can never actually taste it, in Kazakhstan national food is much in evidence.

The *besbarmak* consists of thin strips of mutton or horse-meat stewed with onions and pieces of pastry; the name means 'five fingers' and it is served in a large bowl in the middle of a tent or in the middle of a table and people help themselves with five fingers; it fills up one's stomach, but takes a week to digest. Cheeses are dry, prepared from sheep or mares' milk and very white. There are many different ways of cooking meat; the *lapsha ocabova,* which I found as forbidding as the *besbarmak,* is a very spiced form of stew.

All meats are accompanied by *baursaki,* a pastry fried in lard, plenty of tea and either *shubat* (fermented milk of the dromedary) or *airan* (fermented milk of sheep). But the 'champagne of the steppes', the *kumis,* remains the most popular of Kazakh drinks. I don't see how one could digest a typical Kazakh meal without going for a three-hour gallop in the steppes. But probably the nomadic tribes didn't have regular meals and only ate once a day.

116

The Tartars also used to carry their food with them. They kept their meat under their saddles so that the salty sweat of their galloping horses would prevent it from going bad. But when they ate it, they minced it and spiced it as much as possible. These are the primitive origins of the 'steak Tartar' we order in de-luxe restaurants in the West.

APN's man at Alma Ata was young: he was tiny and gay and his philosophy of life was southern. He believed that the only worth-while thing in life was to have girl-friends and a cosy wife at home. All of which, he assured me, he managed to do. His idea of social encounter was to eat, so whenever we met, whatever the time of day it was we would go and eat something. Once he drove me to the mountains above Alma Ata. All along the road apricot and apple trees were in blossom: it was as if the lower side of the Tsai-Cheng had been bathed in snow as well as the top. We stopped at a little bar-restaurant; we had climbed to 1,600 metres, we had *shashlik* mutton cooked on coal with onions and red peppers, and a bottle of Rumanian wine. It was four o'clock in the afternoon.

A Georgian in Alma Ata

In the afternoon the centre of the city filled with people dressed in their best European-style clothes, walking up and down, stopping to chat and looking at each other, just as in any southern provincial city. I joined in the procession.

'Where are you going in such a hurry? Do you understand Russian? Why don't you slow down? What are you looking at?' The boys would repeat the southern litany more to annoy the older passers-by with demonstrations of their masculinity than for any other reason.

When another voice said: 'Can I be your guide?' I turned round and accepted, saying that I would like to have a friendly guide to Alma Ata. I was to regret my positive answer for the rest of the day.

The man standing next to me was Georgian. He thought nothing of the Russians and said that all Georgians – Grusini in Russian – are marvellous. Wasn't Stalin a Georgian too?

'The Russians are like this,' he said and showed me a flopping finger. 'We instead are like this.' The finger became erect. I only realized in retrospect what he meant and I felt an idiot for having missed such a vulgar implication.

I must confess reluctantly that I dislike the Georgians, not only because such charming citizens as Stalin and Beria came from Georgia, but because they all tend to be bullies.

'Have you really been to Tiflis?' the man said ecstatically. 'Isn't it a marvellous city?' I didn't like Tiflis with its moustached ladies, but Georgian nationalism being what it is, I was cowardly enough to say that Tiflis was all right.

Had I been in the funicular? Yes, I had, for my sins – high enough over the city to face the other high peak from which a huge statue of Stalin blessed the city.

When I was in Tiflis, Stalin had just been 'exposed' by Khrushchev's secret speech, and plaster statues of the Monster had been shoved in the corridors of our hotel.

Gheorg – as my Georgian guide was suitably called – had a head covered with dark thick hair; he was thirty-two had three children, the youngest of which had had his second birthday that very day. He was a cook and worked in a kiosk where they sold *shashlik* and in another place where he prepared *pirochki,* a pastry which envelops minced meat and onions with a lethal fried consistency and defies any amount of Alka Seltzer.

I said to Gheorg that I wanted to walk and that I would be very glad if he came along to show me around. After trying to pack me into a taxi and 'take me for a round of the countryside', I dismissed him angrily and walked on by myself. But he was soon on my tracks. What did I want to see? Did I really come from Italy? Then I was a southerner, like him. How could I have stayed in Siberia for such a long time? I must have been mad.

Suddenly his unsteady pace and loud voice made me realize what I should have noticed earlier – that he was drunk. I told him so, adding that I preferred to be left alone.

'I didn't drink much, just a bit for my son's birthday. We had a few friends in the house and they insisted that I should drink a toast to the health of my baby.'

'And why isn't your wife taking a stroll with you?'

'Wives stay at home.'

He was in a sparklingly good mood. Laughingly, he showed me all the new buildings along the way, the new Party headquarters where the heads of the Kazakh State work – another source of great hilarity – and he showed me children bringing flowers to the huge statue of Lenin. 'Do you recognize him?' Gheorg pointed to Lenin. 'That's Palmiro Togliatti.'

He laughed and took me by the arm. 'Come and have a *shashlik* where I work.'

I wasn't hungry, I told him, but I would like to see the place where he worked. He led me to a little square, the *shashlik* were being cooked in the open next to a coffee-bar. Gheorg cut the queue standing in front of the kiosk and went straight to the cook. 'Hallo, there. How are you? A specially good *shashlik* with very good pieces of meat for Gala, our Italian guest.' I was thirsty; Gheorg pushed a boiling *shashlik* into my hands. I couldn't eat it, I said, I really couldn't, didn't he understand? More *shashlik* was forced on me.

'Come on Gala, I want to give you a bottle of champagne,' he said, pointing to the coffee-house. Kostia would have so disapproved.

I didn't want champagne, but I would have loved some coffee. All the other tables being full we joined a young couple sitting at the corner table.

The waitress arrived swiftly and was instructed to bring one coffee, one bottle of champagne, a box of sweets and a tablet of chocolate. I protested but Gheorg stated that it was 'for his foreign friend'.

As the massive tray arrived, Gheorg seized the bottle of champagne and shook it violently, so that when he uncorked it, the liquid exploded like a volcano, sprayed all over the ceiling, washed down the sides of the window and splashed all over us, but especially on the lady sitting at our table.

People turned to look at the wet confused foursome; I was furious. I didn't like the attention the episode had provoked. Fearing an explosion of southern temper from the man sitting at our table, I apologized profusely. But nobody seemed to mind much and the waitress rushed to dry the table, the lady and myself.

'I don't like that at all,' I said, sounding rather like a governess, 'that was rude. Apologize to this lady.'

Gheorg did so and filled two glasses with what little champagne was left in the bottle, cut some squares out of the hard tablet of chocolate and immersed them in my glass. The broken pieces of chocolate covered with bubbles looked disgusting.

'That is the best way to drink champagne.'

I had already said many times I did not want champagne, I disliked the brown lumps bubbling away in front of me. I was furious at the way he had dismissed my wishes and I was angry with myself for having got into such a situation.

'I am sorry, you are too drunk. I am going.' I got up and left. I walked down the steps towards the boulevard when his running steps reached me.

'Are you angry with me?' He apologized again.

How was it possible to get rid of him?

'You have spent too much money,' I said. 'Anyway I must go home now.'

'Is your husband waiting for you?'

What a splendid idea. 'Of course,' I answered.

'Are you angry with me?'

'Of course, and stop touching my shoulders.'

'What do you want to do now?'

'Go home.'

It started to rain slightly. 'I'll show you our opera house so we don't get wet. We are very proud of our opera house.

There we were opposite the lavatory-blue building. Gheorg displayed southern cheek in persuading the lady attendant to let us through the locked doors, and in convincing the man in charge that it was important for the Italian visitor to inspect Alma Ata's opera house, and fooling a clerk that he, Gheorg, was my Intourist guide.

'Come here,' he said.

We were out in the streets again, there was the kiosk where he cooked *pirochki* and I suspected that this business was 'private', while the *shashlik* was State *Pirochki* which one finds all over the Soviet Union, are very convenient for the tourist who has no time for proper meals, as they successfully block one's appetite for hours. Inside the tiny kiosk built with pieces of tin, stones and wood there must have been three or four Georgians – how they could squeeze into such a small space it was impossible to guess. Gheorg started to talk to them in Georgian. The outcome of the conversation was three hot *pirochki* wrapped in a piece of brown paper and pushed into my hand.

'You must eat them now, while they are hot.'

'I can't, I'll eat them later.'

'They would be offended, it is a present.'

We sat on a bench.

'You think I am poor,' said Gheorg, 'and that you are higher than me, that is why you laugh when I say I love you. Isn't it so?'

'Yes,' I said. I couldn't play his game and protest about the statement. Gheorg, surprised, must have thought I had understood the question.

'You think I am a fool, don't you?'

'Yes,' I assured him again.

One of the Georgians came rushing from the kiosk and

added eight boiling *pirochki* to the other two which were lying cold and dripping with fat on my knee.

'You must eat them, Gala.'

'I am not hungry, I have told you this again and again.'

'I am not either, but I eat and you must too. Are you thirsty, Gala?'

'Yes, but I am going back to my hotel.'

I got up, but Gheorg pulled me down.

'Don't be in such a hurry.'

'If you touch me, I'll scream.'

'Scream, Gala.'

Gheorg's offers of food, love, drinks, fidelity, *pirochki*, flowers and future followed me all the way to my hotel.

The Georgians

In the Soviet Union nationalities are felt very strongly. Don't say to a Ukrainian that he's Russian, or confuse a Tadzhik with an Uzbek. You'll just get away with it, as a foreigner, but you will have to apologize.

Although I recognize in the Georgians all the ebullience of the familiar south, there is a bullying or Mafia element, a national pride, that I find irritating. The Georgians are the Sicilians of the Soviet Union but they differ in that they are rich and powerful.

'Why have they got so much money?' I asked a Russian friend.

'You know, those high Caucasian mountains . . . the wind of the Revolution never passed over them.'

The Georgians are rich because they have a strong sense of trade. Fruit and vegetables are sold privately at high profits on northern 'free' markets; anything grows in Georgia; vines, rare fruit, tobacco, tea, vegetables.

Georgia, called *Gruziya* in Russian, is perhaps one of the Soviet Union's most beautiful republics, food is good here and well cooked, but it is as related to Russia as Patagonia

A classical example of a large nineteenth-century Cossack house
in Irkutsk. It is built entirely of wood and intricately carved.
(Photo Douglas Botting)

Leopards, like tigers, are caught by hand without being injured.
These animals are generally sent to zoos and circuses all over
the world. *(Novosti Press Agency)*

Akademgradok—the Siberian city of science. The House of the Scientist where the author had lunch. *(Novosti Press Agency)*

The famous Academic Opera and Ballet Theatre in Novosibirsk, built during the war. *(Novosti Press Agency)*

The village of Listivianka in the Baikal region—the author with a Siberian. *(Photo Serghei Ostroumov)*

A Siberian fur trapper in the Arctic region of Siberia with some of his frozen polar fox. *(Photo B. Korobeinikov, Novosti Press Agency)*

Yakuti women making boots.   *(Photo V. Yakovlev, Novosti Press Agency)*

Lenin lying in the house at Gorki, near Moscow, where he died
22 January 1924. (*Novosti Press Agency*)

The Nikalskoye cemetery in Leningrad, the tomb of a Ussar.
The inscription says:
'*Give me your hand, Comrade, and follow
me here; we tasted happiness,
let us taste the flavour of the earth, now.*'

One of the most popular Russian pastimes: old people playing chess. *(Photo Douglas Botting)*

is to England. For me to include Georgia in an itinerary of the Soviet Union, seemed totally absurd, although I had an invitation to a party given by a Georgian 'industrialist' which included a free two-way ticket.

The Russians like to make fun of the Georgians and Armenians. They invent a series of jokes to which everyone contributes. The best series remains the one on the subject of 'Radio Armenia' which was started before the Brezhnev era. There is a real Radio Armenia, but the one featured in the jokes was invented. The series is so famous that at a congress of Radio Workers in Moscow, when the Erivan representative of Radio Armenia got up to speak, the hall shook with laughter. The anecdotes start: 'Do you know what Radio Armenia says?'

For example:

Radio Armenia receives a question from a listener.

'We hear that Communism is already visible on the horizon, but where is that horizon?'

Radio Armenia answers:

'It is an imaginary line which gets further away as one approaches it.'

'Will there still be a need for a police force when Communism has prevailed?'

'Certainly not, by then citizens will have learnt to arrest themselves.'

'Which tea is better for one's health? The Chinese or the Russian?'

'Don't get involved in the conflict between the two Powers, drink coffee.'

'What is Capitalism?'

'The exploitation of man by man.'

'And what is Communism?' the listener insists.

'The other way round.'

'Do people in the Soviet Union read books by Solzhenitsyn?'

Radio Armenia answers: 'Only those who can read foreign languages.'

'What are the conquests of Soviet Agriculture?'

'To sow wheat in the virgin lands and buy the harvest from Canada.'

The Armenians and Georgians are often detectable in a Russian group, they speak with a heavy accent and behave like our *nouveaux riches:* clashing colours, huge tips; they make a show of their wealth and are often accompanied by pretty girls.

At the Astoria restaurant in Leningrad, the lazy orchestra only starts to play full blast when a Georgian comes in. 'A couple of Georgian national songs and silly Western tunes,' a friend explained, 'and the orchestra gets a twenty-rouble note.'

The Astoria restaurant – foul food and slow service – is considered as chic as the Four Seasons in New York or George's in Rome. But it is the exclusive playground of Georgians and foreign tourists who are totally unaware of the situation and would give anything to be able to eat elsewhere at a faster pace – but they are linked to the Astoria by their Intourist coupons.

Leningrad citizens complain little about the situation and I found that I was giving somebody a treat if I took them for a meal at the Astoria.

One, a Georgian acquaintance I made in Leningrad, was a boy of twenty-eight who studied at the Institute of Film-making. He said he was 'a bit behind in his studies', but that his father was supporting him with good money sent regularly from Tiflis. He had a flat in Leningrad and easy entrée to the Astoria restaurant – huge tips to the porter – and he wore a flashy tie.

He had stopped me in the Nevski Prospect telling me he knew I was Polish since he had seen me having dinner with a Russian and speaking Russian. He was tall, looked like a classical Greek statue and dressed in 'mod' fashion. Two years earlier he had met a German girl and after a week they had got married but, he added, he was now thinking of getting a divorce. His wife now lived in Munich

and they had never lived together for longer than a month.
We spoke Russian as his English was poorer than my
Russian and I couldn't understand him.

'I have a baby son, so I am going to get married again.'
I couldn't understand this.

'Is the baby in Germany?'

'No, I have a son by somebody else.'

'And will you go back and work in films in Georgia?'

'Perhaps,' he said, 'but I may stay on in Leningrad.'

This is another kind of choice that no Soviet citizen is
allowed to make. Soviet rules definitely don't seem to apply
to Georgian citizens.

In 1913 Yosif Dzhugashvili, a Georgian ex-Jesuit seminarist
who, after taking the pseudonym of Koba from a celebrated
Georgian guerilla and freedom-fighter then chose the name
of Stalin, wrote: 'There is no serious anti-Russian nationalism in Georgia, primarily because there are no Russian land-
lords there, and no big Russian bourgeoisie to feed the fire
of nationalism among the masses. In Georgia there is *anti-
Armenian* nationalism . . .' (his italics).

But the formation of a Georgian Republic in 1918, the
strong independent group purged by Stalin (a Georgian),
and by Dzherzhinsky (a Pole), the revolt against the Soviet
regime in the '20s and a strong anti-Russian attitude even
today, make one realize how little Stalin knew or wanted
to know about his own country. Stalin spoke with a strong
Georgian accent which many people still like to make fun of
at parties, after they are emboldened by drink.

Georgians are fiercely anti-Semitic. So was Stalin, of
course, though not Beria. 'Not less interesting,' wrote Stalin
from Georgia, reporting on the 1907 London Congress, 'is
the composition of the congress from the standpoint of
nationalities. Statistics show that the majority of the
Menshevik faction is Jewish – not counting the Bundist of
course – then came Georgians and the Russians. On the other

hand the overwhelming majority of the Bolshevik faction consists of Russians, then of Jews – not counting of course the Poles and the Letts and the Georgians, etc. For this reason one of the Bolsheviks observed in jest (Comrade Aliexinsky, it seems) that the Mensheviks are the Jewish faction and the Bolsheviks a genuine Russian faction, whence it wouldn't be a bad idea for us Bolsheviks to arrange a pogrom in the party.' (Stalin, *Collected Works, Vol. II.*)

A Scholar in Dushanbe

The scenery was beautiful; from Alma Ata we flew high over chains of mountains and along the range of white peaks: it seemed as if the steppes stretched forever below the mountains. A tiny train puffed round the elevated railway of the Alma Ata-Tashkent line.

Tanja, an Intourist girl with peroxide hair and Jayne Mansfield breasts, greeted me loudly: 'You are in Dushanbe, the Soviet capital of the Autonomous Republic of Tadzhikistan.' I was too tired to tell her that I was quite aware that the hot night and the tiny airport belonged to Dushanbe rather than Gorki or Arkhangelskoye.

Dushanbe at 800 metres in the Hissar valley, is an attractive new city where the modern architecture has been carefully planned and landscaped; gardens and alleys separate the houses and, walking through side-streets, one sees flowers, fountains and marvellous wild blue birds.

Dushanbe, ex-Stalinobad, means 'Monday' in Tadzhik, as the market came to town every week on that day. A market meant life in such a remote place. Tadzhikistan, even now is one of the most inaccessible places in the world but is geographically the centre of the Asian world: China, India and Russia meet here. There are only two and a half million inhabitants in the whole of Tadzhikistan since the land is largely composed of the Pamir mountains. The indigenous people look different from the Kazakhs, less

Mongol and more Farsi. Their ethnic group was pushed up into the mountains and high valleys by the Mongol invasion and their ancestors the Bactrians, Sogdians and Sakians; their language, of West-Iranian origin, is very old and so is their literature which was, unlike the Kazakh, in written form already in the tenth century. They also wear their national costumes in the streets of the capital. It is less handsome and fierce than the Kazakh's; both men and women wear head-covers, elaborately embroidered caps (the Tadzhiks have been Muslim for a long time), white shirts or dresses covered with a velvet waistcoat and richly pleated white trousers which expand gracefully from their embroidered leather boots. Some dress in the Uzbek fashion, with caftans and silk robes.

After the rule of Ghengis Khan, most of what is Tadzhikistan today was under the rule of Tamberlaine. It was then divided into different states which finally fell under the emirate of Bokhara. The name Tadzhik comes from an Arab tribe which called itself Tadji and then Tas; the name was later transformed into Taj and then Tadzhik.

Tadzhikistan lies roughly on the same latitude as Greece and Southern Italy, so it has a temperate climate. The temperature never falls below zero. Mountains, hills and plateaux make up ninety-three per cent of its territory. Earthquakes are frequent as the mountains are still being formed. The highest peak of the Pamir is 7,495 metres high. It is called 'Peak Communism' and has for its neighbours 'Peak Lenin' and 'Peak Stalin'. Imagine calling Mont Blanc 'Mont Capitalism' and the Aiguille du Midi 'Peak De Gaulle' facing the Pompidou mountains. One has to wait for clear weather to fly to the Pamir. Apparently one can be stranded their for months, waiting for the wind to drop.

I visited Boris Anatolievich Litvinsky, Professor of history and archeology at Tadzhik University, in his wooden *dacha*, situated in a side-street of Dushanbe, shaded by trees. He came to open the door himself, a tall old man, slightly stooped with a tired smile, hair cut *en brosse* and long handsome hands. He led me through a tiny corridor into his small study, whose walls were covered with books. There was just room for his desk and two chairs. Litvinsky knew and loved all the many books that lined the walls. From time to time he would indicate one to me, knowing exactly where to find each volume. He read French and English but claimed that he could not speak the latter. But I suspect this was due more to shyness and lack of exercise than to lack of knowledge.

He was, like many Russians I met, a man of great culture and modesty, whose life had been spent in study. He seemed to enjoy his isolation and retirement. He only went to Moscow from time to time for a few months, he told me, to study at the great libraries. Otherwise he had never left Central Asia.

The west side of the Pamir is made up of deep valleys, while the eastern side is flatter. 'The first inhabitants of the Pamir, who were the fathers of the Scythians, were there about 10,000 years ago; I myself excavated 200 tombs up there,' Litvinsky said. 'Every year the post-graduates go up there for research work.'

In the Pamir the only cultivation is barley. Otherwise the indigenous population lives from hunting and fishing, which is very rich. 'These people have never been afflicted by any viruses or bacteria: so they are very healthy,' he told me.

Apparently they speak a language which is 'as close to Tadzhik as English is to German'. Litvinsky had been working on the Pamir for twenty-five years. One of the most extraordinary excavations he worked on, he said, was a Buddhist monastery of the seventh century, about a hundred kilometres from Dushanbe, towards the Afghan frontiers.

'We found many sculptures well preserved by the clay which had covered the building. The best was a Buddha, twelve metres long; there is a pedestal for the sitting Buddha who takes several postures symbolizing different moments in his life: Buddha contemplating, Buddha thinking, Buddha teaching. In the centre there is a prone Buddha who has attained Nirvana. Sculptures of comparable size have so far only been found in Ceylon.'

Forty-five rooms have so far been excavated, but there are more in the large remains of the Buddhist monastery, elaborately built, with flights of steps and pavilions and corridors. In each room the team found a piece of sculpture.

'Scholars have come to see it from many countries. I am afraid I might become a Buddhist,' said Litvinsky, laughing. It was obvious that ascetism would be attractive to such a solitary person. 'There are records one thousand years old showing that Buddhist pilgrims came here from China. There were many monasteries in this area: it was a holy place of isolation. Many monasteries were destroyed by the Tartars, but the culture survived.'

The archaeological section of the university has contacts with scholars in Japan, East Germany, Iran and England, said Litvinsky. 'In England there are very good orientalists and archaeologists; we read their works more than they read ours,' he said.

'After the Roman Empire fell and the dark ages darkened Europe, there was still light here,' he told me. 'Culture flourished here in those days; there were knights and tournaments; there was a real Renaissance. In the seventh and eighth centuries, travellers who came from Europe found this area much more civilized than their own. Samarkand was a beautiful city of 200,000 inhabitants when Paris had only 50,000. Tamberlaine's ambivalence was that of someone who was both destroyer and builder; he took artists from the places he conquered and brought the best of them to Samarkand, his capital. In 1404 the Spanish ambassador De Clavico, wrote: "Not in Paris, or Madrid are there such buildings as in Samarkand, such artists and painters." Afterwards European culture developed fast but this did not advance.'

Litvinsky quoted everything by heart. He had published one hundred and twenty works altogether, articles and books. Eight volumes were on the history of Tadzhikistan. Although of obviously European origin, he was born in Tashkent and lived most of his life in Dushanbe.

'Boris Anatolievich,' I enquired, 'where do you come from?'

'I am of Jewish nationality,' he answered and stressed it again to make sure I had understood. 'I am *ievriei.*'

After I left him, I met Yuri Chienovi, a writer from the Caucasus, with a long face and green eyes and the sophisticated background of Moscow University. He had come to stay in Dushanbe for a while to write about the Pamir; he was, like me, waiting for the wind to fall so he could fly up to the high valleys. With him was Ghiennadi Adramian, APN's man in Dushanbe, a rather plump gay Armenian, who constantly covered his large blue eyes with dark glasses.

'Did I understand him correctly?' I asked Yuri. 'Litvinsky said he was Jewish.'

'Yes, there are quite a lot of Jews here in Dushanbe, about 10 per cent of the population.'

The result of the combined effort, I thought, of Stalin and Tsarist times.

'Before he died, Churchill said that the British were not anti-Semitic because they didn't realize how much cleverer than them the Jews are,' Yuri added.

The three of us were heading towards the market.

I said to Yuri that, on the contrary, England was rather anti-Semitic though less than Germany, Poland and the Soviet Union.

'Do you really think we are? I am not. You will find people who are anti-Semitic and others who don't even think about it, as in every other country in the world.'

Two Colleagues

We wandered about the market, there were marvellous fruits and vegetables, immense red radishes which had a piquant taste, dried melons, delicious to eat and nuts I had never seen before.

Yuri and Ghiennadi loaded me with presents of dried fruit, pastries and a special creamy cheese which, eaten with the dry melon, was delicious. The market was built in cement and was modern, like all Dushanbe. The different sections – fruit, vegetables, meat – were crowded with men in kaftans and women whose heads were covered by veils, but whose faces were uncovered. It was hot and we were thirsty. Although we had eaten a lot at the market, the three of us settled down in a restaurant, ordered five litres of beer, vodka, coffee and a proper meal of *shashlik* and *plov* (a special rice dish).

Ghiennadi talked rather fast and Yuri kept interrupting him, begging him to slow down and choose easy words for my sake.

Ghiennadi was shortish and handsome by southern standards, but he was too plump for Western taste. Unlike Yuri, Ghiennadi was typically Caucasian. He adored talking about women and love, just like his APN colleague in Alma Ata. Yuri was the opposite, both physically – he was tall and lean – and in his interests.

At the restaurant, Ghiennadi was very alert to every woman who came in. It was like being with an Italian. 'She's rather exotic. I like the one in red, I wouldn't mind the small one on the right. Life without women is no life.'

Both of them treated me as a colleague and talked to me as if I were a man, something I was aware of and enjoyed.

'Tell me,' Ghiennadi asked me, 'do you have brothels in England?' The question was rather unexpected, although he asked it after our second glass of vodka.

'There used to be, but they are illegal now. So there are prostitutes who use their own rooms. The same happens in Italy. Are there brothels here?'

'There are prostitutes as you described.'

131

'Are there many?'

'A fair amount. They walk about at night dressed in a recognizable way.'

'I thought I saw one in Moscow, but I wasn't quite sure.'

'She probably was if she looked like one.' Ghiennadi helped us to more vodka. He was treating me like an old chum. 'And tell me, are there lesbians in England?' Amazed by the equally unexpected question, I gulped down more vodka.

'Some, but it is difficult to tell. But they usually don't look any different from anyone else.' The idea of lesbians obviously excited Ghiennadi.

'Do you have homosexuals here?' I asked. 'Male homosexuals, I mean.'

'Yes, but they are not open about it . . . very underground.'

'Are there many in the ballet?'

'They all are,' Ghiennadi answered.

'You know,' I started, 'Rudolf Nureyev . . .'

'Who?' They had never heard of him.

We talked about literature. Yuri was more interested in that subject. They wanted to know which Russian and Soviet – meaning modern – writers we knew in the West.

'What do you think of Yevtushenko?'

'A lot is lost in translation as it always is with poetry, but it is obvious he had talents, although in the West he was more 'known than read,' I explained. I personally did not like his 'naughty boy' act.

'I am sure,' I said, 'that when he is abroad, every time he criticizes the Soviet regime, the local Embassy is warned in advance.'

They laughed and seemed to agree. I found that Russians liked to know that some Westerners were aware that, besides the much publicized figure of Yevtushenko, there were better poets, like Akmatova, Chodasevic, Mandelstam. When we talked about ourselves, Ghiennadi explained he had three children, all boys, ranging from five to three.

Yuri, whose appetite for ladies and food was less excessive or less evident, was unmarried. Both were in their early thirties.

Tanja in the Mountains

Later we fetched Tanja, the Intourist girl who had collected me at the airport. She was wearing a tight pink and golden short-sleeved pullover, which showed off to the full her solid breasts, tightly enveloped in a white bra, which appeared through the nets of the pink and gold wool. Tanja's breasts were majestically pointed upwards. She must have had difficulty seeing her own feet when standing up. It must have been a curious experience to live with so much flesh between her face and legs.

A car arrived and Tanja chose to sit next to the driver, while the three of us sat in the back. Tanja's presence had brought to my male companions a dense sexual atmosphere which we all felt; Ghiennadi reacted to the sensuous presence with demonstrations of unrest and agitation. Tanja was tall, large, fleshy, pink and majestic. She had short yellow permed hair, a very Russian white skin and full large lips which she had painted pink. She was married to an engineer – everybody in Russia seemed to be engineers – but had no children.

'What? No children? Is he no good?' Ghiennadi immediately made heavy jokes while she smiled, half shy, half knowingly.

As she moved on her front seat, her bosom showed in profile, extravagant and attractive through its pink and golden prison. Her large arms stretched in an embrace-like gesture towards the back of the driver's seat. Ghiennadi's eyes were glued to her. He never glanced once at the landscape which he probably knew well, anyway. A tight black skirt barely covered Tanja's knees and when she sat down, it slid up showing large solid legs in her nylons. Her

133

feet strained in black stiletto-heeled sandals; a matching shiny black bag completed her gear for a mountain picnic.

Tanja's black glasses which she kept on almost the whole time suited her; she would move her lips in a very feminine way, arching them and wetting them with her pink curly tongue. They became the most prominent feature of her face.

I was officially in charge of the car, since I was paying for it, and Tanja was meant to be my guest, but there was little doubt about who was the real boss. Her attitude half irritated and half fascinated me.

Ghiennadi teased her, hinting at lovers and infidelities; the driver added a chorus of giggles to his remarks and Tanja's mouth pouted in a stately, but amused fashion.

Once out of Dushanbe, the car followed the river Darya. This was transparent with clear rushing water. All round, the sides of the mountains were steep and barren, and there were signs of frequent land-slides. Except for the trees growing around the river, the landscape was arid, although dotted with oases almost invariably hiding tiny villages. The meadows near the river were covered with wild tulips and boys sold bunches of them for a few kopeks. Ghiennadi asked the driver to stop and bought a large bunch and offered one to Tanja. She chose the best one and held it, inevitably, close to her bosom.

The wild cherry trees already had some small red cherries on them. Small torrents fell from narrow side-valleys bubbling at great speed into the Darya; over us there were snow-capped mountains with straight, rocky walls. There was no softness in that harsh landscape; it was quite unlike anything I had seen before, certainly not like the Alps. If I had seen it reproduced in a photograph, I would have guessed that the mountains belonged to Asia. This was a strong, cruel, violent landscape of great beauty.

The people on the road or in the villages were much more exotically dressed than in Dushanbe. We stopped at a small café on the way, where Ghiennadi bought some bottles of

Tadzhik white wine, a kind of salami and some brown bread. Several Tadzhik men were sitting under the shade of the trees, one of them was smoking in the Turkish fashion, inhaling tobacco through a complicated water pipe. The men were dressed in kaftans, all wore turbans, and some had large white trousers puffing out of leather boots. Near the café a woman was cooking a huge amount of large fish fresh from the torrent. She rested her huge frying-pan on some stones under which a fire was crackling. The fish, about half a metre long looked rather like carp. The woman wore a head-cap from under which her hair fell in many little plaits in the Tadzhik style. She gutted the fish in the torrent and cleaned them thoroughly in the running water. Then she rolled them in a soft pastry she had prepared on a washed stone and plunged them into boiling fat. We bought one from her though she wasn't at all keen to part with it.

The group of men watched us silently, looking solemn. They did not seem to like our intrusive presence in their landscape and resumed their conversation only as we got back into the car to leave.

We then started looking for a picnic site. The driver indicated a well-known beauty spot, a dusty corner beside the road, but Yuri and I refused it. Ghiennadi couldn't have cared less; he just wanted to get out of the car and get as near to Tanja as conventions and Tanja herself would allow.

We finally found the perfect place along the Darya, under a large shady tree. It was rather hot, about 26 degrees; Yuri put the bottles of wine in the torrent to keep them cool while the others prepared the food. I took a little walk across an unstable wooden bridge towards a green meadow where I had seen a little Tadzhik girl. As I approached three shepherds and a woman emerged from nowhere. 'Where from?' asked the older man with diffidence. He spoke broken Russian.

'Italy,' I answered.

'What you want here?' he asked, scowling.

'I just want to have a look around. Is it all right?'

'Of course.'

As I walked away, other Tadzhiks joined the elder man and I heard them repeat 'Italy'. It must have sounded to them the most remote of all places.

When I came back the Tadzhik family was united, almost barring my way to the bridge. 'Do you like it?'

'Very much,' I said, smiling and trying to caress one child who reacted to my outstretched hand as if it had been a snake. They apologized.

'Children . . .'

'Mine,' I answered, 'just the same.' It was a lie, our children favour exotic friends.

The Tadzhiks liked the idea that I had children and the elder man asked: 'Are you with *them?*' pointing at the already picnicking group at the other side of the Darya.

'Yes.'

'They, Russians?'

'From Caucasus,' I answered, trying to ingratiate my group with them as also belonging to a mountaineering national minority.

'Woman Russian,' said the old man who was no fool and was not going to be deceived by the pink Russian abundance of Tanja's body. And so he wished me good-bye.

Tanja, the driver, Yuri and Ghiennadi were eating silently; the fish was very delicate and fleshy, the wine, rather opaque in colour, had a dry muscat flavour. I washed my face in the cool water of the river, something Tanja thought odd, unfeminine, rather vulgar. She leaned against the trunk of the tree, her legs crossed: so tight was her skirt that there was a red mark along her white thighs. No one moved at all and a soft sleepiness fell on us as the result of the wine, the heat and Tanja's presence. We went on drinking while Tanja asked a few questions and Ghiennadi lay down at Tanja's side, obviously wishing that a land-slide would remove us and leave him alone with her. Yuri was silent. There was a granite boulder in the middle of the river, forming two large waves. The waves had smoothed the granite according to their own rhythm, forming two shoulders on either side, rather like a piece of Henry Moore sculpture. One day the granite would be smoothed away and covered by water.

'Let's go,' I said, reminding myself with difficulty that I was in charge, or that I ought to be. 'I would like to walk through one of the villages.'

Tanja's Intourism was aroused; it was stronger than the waves of stupor that wine and sex had settled upon her abandoned body and she looked alarmed. I walked away but only Yuri followed me. There was half a mile to cover and two wooden bridges to cross, one over the rumbling Darya and another over a smaller tributary. The village I wanted to visit was set between two narrow valleys. The houses were simple, built of wood and stone, most of them with wooden terraces. There were many trees in the village – the mountains above it were menacingly bare in contrast. A landslide had fallen on part of the village, almost totally destroying a few houses. As Yuri and I climbed, the horn began to blow impatiently; the car looked tiny beneath us. 'I came here to see things,' I said to Yuri, 'not to eat the whole time.' Yuri and I walked deeper into the village, along tiny mud roads, inner alleys, picturesque patios. There was poverty, but not misery, quite different from the villages of the 'other' Central Asia I knew.

There were so many children in each courtyard that the whole village seemed to be a kindergarten. They looked at us, laughed, and followed us along in a gay procession. Yuri tried to dismiss the swelling crowd. 'Go away. There's nothing to laugh about.'

The alley stopped at a huge wooden door. I pushed it open and we found that it led us to an inner courtyard flanked by several wooden houses and huts.

A beautiful young girl wearing a simple cotton *beshmet*, with black almond-shaped eyes and black hair just held in place by her cap, looked at us with terror. She reminded me of Mariana in Tolstoy's 'The Cossacks'. She had just the same beautifully wild features and stately dignity. Small children rushed around her, others ran indoors followed by a flurry of hens and feathers.

'How many of you live here?' Yuri asked the girl.

She looked at him with a void expression.

'How many?' repeated Yuri.

A boy aged about twelve came closer and smiled. 'Do you understand Russian?' asked Yuri again.

'No,' answered the boy.

In the meantime the beautiful girl was trying to cover her hair with a veil, and her bare arms with it too. From her behaviour and appearance she must have been an older, yet unmarried daughter.

'Don't you go to school?' Yuri asked the boy.

'Yes,' he answered. He obviously understood simple Russian. But I doubt whether the girl had followed a single word of what had been said.

As we returned, a furious Tanja, tiny in the distance, walked towards us shouting: 'We haven't got time.' She was walking with difficulty in her high heels over the stony path.

'The silly fool,' I said to Yuri. 'Time for what? I have all the time in the world.'

Getting back to Dushanbe, Ghiennadi tried to make a date with Tanja. She was playing her wet tongue on her round lips giving no answer in a cocotte rather than a coquette way.

After we left her, Yuri, Ghiennadi and myself went back to a café for more vodka and coffee.

Part Three
The Volga and the Steppes

Moscow

I had regretfully decided never to see Konstantin again. I had turned down his invitation to meet again in Moscow, half-hoping that by putting the idea out of my mind we might meet anyway.

'I knew he loved me,' wrote Tolstoy in *Happy Ever After*. 'I prized his love and, feeling that he considered me better than all the other young women in the world, I could not help wishing him to continue in his illusion. And involuntarily I deceived him. But in deceiving him, I became a better person myself.'

Happily I examined my large room at the National, the nicest of Moscow's hotels. Although I was familiar with it, I had never actually stayed there. Superior decisions had always sent me to the nightmare hotels, the Leningradskaia, the Ukraina or the Rassya. One of the National's many advantages was that one could see the Kremlin from its dining-room, and that it was adjacent to Gorki Street. It was also small enough to get to know the porters and waitresses. I liked its art nouveau lamps, its large high rooms, its pale blue stairs and white stucco flowers.

My request to stay at the National had probably been granted because of the fuss I had made over the failure of my Shushenskoye visit. I also now had a splendid black sleek *Chaica* limousine at my disposal and had been granted special passes for the Tribune in Red Square for the 22nd of April – Lenin's centenary celebrations – and for the First of May.

'I suppose you know Moscow, don't you? So there is no need for me to describe it. The streets are extremely unpleasant in November. It is even unpleasant indoors; but it's worst of all when you can't bear to stay indoors.' (Mikhail Bulgakov, *Black Snow*.)

I took a bus to visit an acquaintance who lived on the other side of Moscow. Searching in vain for the ticket collector – a lost expression on my face – I was directed to a little automatic machine in a corner.

'It is a new device,' a girl explained. 'You put in five kopeks and get your own ticket.'

'But I haven't got five kopeks.'

'We'll change them for you.' In fact some new arrivals helped me out.

'What happens if one doesn't pay? Is there any way of checking?' I asked the girl who, like all Moscovites, looked most reticent at conversing with a foreigner.

'There's no way of checking, but the other passengers would notice it. Five kopeks is not much and it is the same fare whatever distance you travel. Some months ago they discovered someone who never paid. They stuck his portrait and name on every bus. That's all they did, but he must have felt terribly ashamed. There are a few people who don't pay just for the kick of it, but that is bad.' The same goes for the underground; one buys tickets from automatic machines and the fare is the same for all distances. During the journey the bus-conductor, in this case a woman, announced on an amplifier the names of each stop.

'And where did you learn Russian?' the same girl asked me, leaning forward from her seat.

'In London.'

'In London? At the university?'

'No, at school.'

'People study Russian in London?'

'Some do.'

'That's very good.'

'Are you married?' asked another passenger. And we went through the same list of questions.

I often walked round Moscow alone or took a bus without knowing where it would lead me, but I could never come to terms with the city.

Moscow is one of the largest cities in the world with over six and a half million inhabitants. It is built over seven hills and has a unique quality: it looks neither Asiatic nor European. It gives one the impression of an enlarged country village where a megalomaniac designer has added cardboard skyscrapers and toy-like groups of churches. Its streets look temporary, old women brush them as though they were the floor of a country house. Its shops – apart from the Ielisiei or 'Gastronom One' which is a sublime gem of flowering art nouveau – are drab and seem designed to put off the customer, although God knows what queues form to grab the scarce merchandise. There are zebra-crossings, but neither pedestrians nor drivers respect them. As for traffic lights, people don't pay the slightest attention to them; luckily Moscow has plenty of underpasses, otherwise its whole population would soon be dead.

'You see,' a sophisticated Russian explained, 'Moscow is a city inhabited by peasants. That is one of its charms. No-one even knows how to use a pavement: people bump into each other, walk zig-zagging, block the way. In Leningrad, people are trained to urbanity. Here nobody is aware of living in a city.'

In Russian, Moscow has a beautiful name 'Maskva'. In 1713 Peter the Great transferred the capital to St Petersburg, but Moscow has always remained the heart of Russia, the city around which the state of Moscovy was founded and the Empire subsequently spread. Moscow, which didn't become the capital again until 10 March 1918, is today the very heart of Soviet power, the seat of a centralized government and therefore the queen of bureaucracy. People are affected by this; in Moscow there are many more social distinctions, in fact there are social classes. Moscow is also a difficult city to live in, it is difficult to find a taxi in the evening, it is difficult to get an appointment, to make a phone call, to find a telephone number, to sit at a café or to find room at a restaurant. In this way it reminds me of Rome, where life is made as difficult as possible for the citizen. But Moscow has the advantage of good public transport and no poverty. As in Rome, there are too many offices, too many tourists and one always has to wait too long in Moscow. There is one advantage: there are few cars.

Moscow also has its lovely secluded quarters of stucco

143

houses, its attractive corners, its flamboyant art-nouveau buildings, its Danskoi and Novodevichy monasteries and cemeteries, its museums and good theatres; there are many things to see. And it has the Moscovite, a tough citizen who minds his own business, not as gentle as his provincial brother whom he despises a little, as do all inhabitants of capitals.

Moscow's architecture, dating from Stalin's time, is beginning to look attractive and 'camp' in a way, but too many old buildings have been pulled down or are falling down from deliberate neglect. In their place monstrosities like the new gigantic Rassya hotel have grown up; this building illustrates *all* the mistakes architects should avoid, and it neatly blocks one of Moscow's best views.

Red Square is a perfect theatre. The immense cobblestone space has a pleasing severity and originality which is always surprising. Its name doesn't follow political changes like most of Moscow's streets and cities. 'Red' and 'beautiful' have the same root in Russian and Red Square has been *Krasnaia Ploshad* since the seventeenth century. Lenin's mausoleum is beautiful in its shiny cubist granite; it suits the severity of the scene. The Moscovites are clean and their children are taught tidiness at school. To throw cigarette ends on the pavement is considered bad form.

Larissa Vasilievna

I had some friends in Moscow. One of them rang me up one day. She was exactly my age, and had large liquid eyes and black hair. Her voice was deep, almost masculine, and she wore thick spectacles which she grasped whenever she wasn't wearing them, saying: 'I am almost blind.' She was a quite well-known lyric poet and a translator of Caucasian languages and dialects. Larissa belonged to the Writers Union. In her affectionate warm way she used to take my arm and we used to tell each other how much we liked one another.

144

She was an original woman both in what she did and in the way her mind worked. She couldn't have cared less about what she wore. 'I have no taste, I can't put two colours together without them clashing,' she said. She loved to be alone with her husband Oleg in the dacha they had bought near Moscow.

She was, as she once said, a wild Russian girl and was proud of her Slav-origins which contrasted with Oleg's Western urbanity. In the Russian schizophrenia between slavophilia and pro-Western feelings, literature has been no exception. Lara belonged to the Slav faction, but avoided the pettiness of the truly hard-line group which dismisses anything foreign. She loved old Russian architecture and customs, the language and songs, often regretting that so much had been lost. Her writing was also concerned with the revival of old Russian words, images and sayings.

She took me to have lunch at the Writers' Union in Voroscovo 25. It consisted of two buildings; the prettier of the two was isolated in a round garden which led to the golden nineteenth-century stucco residence of the family which served as a model for Tolstoy's Rostovs. Its architecture had all the coyness of the maddening Natasha. The hotel-like glass doors, watched over by a lady sitting on a chair, led into a large hall, the cloakroom was heavy with coats, boots and umbrellas. Posters, memoranda and announcements filled a notice board. Through a bar, we went into the restaurant which had been used by the former proprietor Count Olsufiyev in pre-revolutionary times as a Masonic meeting-hall.

Larissa arrived late. Most of the tables in the restaurants were full. She knew people there, although not everyone since there are twelve hundred members of the Moscow Union including translators, script-writers, prose and fiction-writers and historians. We had caviar and vodka followed by *tabaca*, a delicious Georgian dish, petit-poussin marinated in vinegar and garlic and then cooked by pressing it between red-hot stones.

We talked about literature. We both liked Bulgakov and

shared a dislike for D. H. Lawrence. I never talked to her about Solzhenitsyn. I always waited for others to approach that unapproachable subject. I asked her how one became a member of the Union.

'You submit your work to the Committee, and if you are not yet ready, they tell you what you need to do to join. But it is not easy to get in. You need to have some work already published.'

A little string-pulling of course speeds up the process. 'Being a member has advantages. Apart from the use of these premises, the library is very good, we get very cheap holidays and we can get loans, medical assistance, travel. But we have a few obligations.'

'Such as what?'

'We are expected to go on tour, thirty or forty of us, writers and poets, to give recitals in other cities. It is very interesting for us to meet the public and as you will see the theatres where we give these recitals are always full of young people.'

'Once a German poet came on tour with me and said she had never seen anything like it: she was envious of the attention and interest we Soviet poets receive from our public.'

Writers and poets are well known in the Soviet Union, in fact they become as famous as Western film stars used to be here. That is why defections of writers are so talked about.

Lara took me to one of those evenings in Leningrad; she came to collect me and we walked in the beautiful city, often asking the way.

She introduced me to the writers who were taking part in the recital. There was Sierghiei Smirnof, a tall, handsome man, very well known in the Soviet Union, who spoke good Italian and wrote poetry and prose; there was a young woman poet who disapproved of Lara being in the company of a foreigner.

The theatre really was full, mostly with young people. Some of the poetry was rhetorical and tedious, some lyrical

146

and at times there was a little satire. Archadi Arkanov recited a short story about a man who woke one morning and decided to become famous. So he walked the streets without shoes. An old woman stopped him and asked him where he had bought such beautiful feet, in Poland? In England?

He was a satirical writer with that taste for the absurd and the grotesque which is so powerful in Russian when it is not suppressed.

Lara wore her hair loose and looked very beautiful reciting her poems. When the evening came to an end, the public asked for more. It was impressive, mainly because the audience was so enthusiastic.

But at the same time the ferocious censorship sharpens the talents of such a gifted, cultured literary nation and compels them to write books which will never be published. Many writers circulate their typewritten novels among small groups of friends and readers. People talk about such books as if they were in print. 'Have you read the marvellous new novel by So-and-so?' When one asks where one could buy a copy, they look at one in amazement: 'No, no, it's not published. Yet.'

That 'yet' was added always because one was a foreigner. Others concentrate on writing children's books, which are easier to get published; some of these are really works of art.

But if the Soviet writers have political, we have economic censorship. In the West books must sell and writers are often reproached about the economic failure of their efforts. So we have to reach a compromise with the publishers. Both forms of censorship, Eastern and Western, are bad, but both exist. Although philistinism and anti-intellectual tendencies seem to be encouraged in Soviet literature today, it must be said that the bulk of the Russians genuinely resent the critical voices of some controversial writers. As far as they are concerned everybody has enough to eat and is warmly dressed and the housing problem has been solved. What do these privileged people want?

147

The Russians are hungry consumers of anything in print; books, newspapers, magazines are constantly sold out; public libraries and bookshops are crowded and if one wants to buy good new books one certainly won't find them in the shops. They are always sold out in a few weeks.

Lara showed me around the Union; there was another cafeteria-restaurant, which was 'for real conversation'.

'If you are talking to somebody here nobody will disturb you because it is understood you are here to have a private conversation.' There were libraries, reading-rooms and a boardroom. 'Do you have anything like this in London?' The answer was no. 'What do you do when you have a book you would like to have published?' I asked. 'Are there several State publishing houses?'

'There are. But the procedure is different, I imagine, from that in the West. If one hasn't yet published anything one tries to get something in print in literary magazines or weeklies. When you want to get a book published there is a special commission which judges the work. If the writers in the commission think the book is all right, they go ahead; it generally takes about a year for a book to be published because there is a long waiting list.'

I asked Larissa how much she was paid. 'Four thousand roubles for a book of poetry which has a limited edition. In the Soviet Union 10,000 or 20,000 copies is a small print number, 250,000 or 300,000 is the average number of copies printed for novels.'

Of course 4,000 roubles is much more than any Western poet ever receives, even if the book is quite successful.

'Do better-known or more successful poets receive more money?' I asked.

'No, they get the same, and this avoids a lot of envy and rivalry between writers. I think this is the best system. If my book is very successful like my last one, it doesn't mean that it is better from the literary point of view than one that doesn't sell so well. A book might be more difficult, more advanced and therefore better, in the long run. When an edition is sold out it is very unlikely to have a second printing since priority is given to new works.'

'That is a pity.'

'Yes, but at least it gives new writers a chance.'

Once we were having lunch with Oleg, who worked for *Izvestia*.

'That's Yevtushenko,' said Larissa pointing towards the pirouetting figure who moved around the table. Nobody paid much attention to him.

Larissa's House

Larissa used to take me to see the part of Moscow she loved; once she drove to a wooden house covered with falling stucco which stood in the middle of a romantic garden.

'This is my dream house,' she said.

It had a wooden portico and carved shutters. It had belonged to one of Tolstoy's cousins.

'If you wanted to,' I asked, 'could you live here?'

Larissa laughed as if I had said something witty and absurd. 'No . . . one is allotted a house. Anyway, there's probably no plumbing.'

'It could be installed.'

'A friend of mine, a painter, has painted a picture of this house,' she said. 'That's as far as I can get to possessing it. But I am writing a long poem and my main character lives there. I often come here to look at it.' We pushed open the gates and wandered about, looking through the dusty window-panes hoping to catch a glimpse of whoever lived there. Oleg had stayed outside. He was tall and thin with an absent, dreamy expression on his face and, probably, a weak constitution. Their only child was seven and was looked after by Larrisa and his grandmother.

In Novodevichy Cemetery we stopped at Bulgakov's tomb. Near Stalin's second wife's tomb a group of people were standing around, staring in silence. 'They say she committed suicide,' one of them said.

Oleg was driving his solid Volga, which he seldom used.

Moscovites like to walk and frequently use their excellent underground. An official pamphlet on the underground says proudly that more marble was used in the first fourteen stations of the underground than in all the palaces built by the Russian tsars in three hundred years. Anyway, in the winter, even the Volgas are difficult to start, let alone the Moscvitch. 'When we go out to supper in the winter, one of the guests keeps his motor on so that he can push the others and help to start them.' Some people told me that they often have to disconnect the battery and take it with them. The Volkswagen seems to cope best with Moscow's severe cold.

A Moscovite told me with horror that, although Moscow's traffic was already chaotic, there were only 600,000 cars in circulation. 'But some say that by 1973 there will be six million cars. It will be terrible. I live quite far from the centre, almost in the country, but I like it; we breathe good air, it's better for the children. And transport is good, it only takes me forty-five minutes to get to the office. With six million cars, a bus will take twice as long, apart from the fact that we shall all be breathing poison.'

We drove to a restaurant in the country, but it was full and long queues stood outside.

'There are too few restaurants in Moscow.'

'I know,' said Larissa.

'Tell me, if I wanted to open a spaghetti house – I mean, not belonging to me, but for the State – could I do it?'

Larissa roared with laughter. 'A spaghetti house in Moscow . . .'

No, the trouble was that one could not use one's initiative. That was the basic fault of the system.

One evening, after we had been at the theatre together, Oleg and Larissa asked me home for a snack. 'It's very simple,' she warned me, referring to the flat. It was off Leningradski Prospect.

As we were sitting silently in the dining-drawing-room, we all realized that we were embarrassed. We were trying to look natural, but Larissa and Oleg knew I must have been

150

curious to see their flat and I myself had suddenly become a professional at work, rather than a friend. Guessing what they felt, I avoided looking round and settled on the sofa, staring at the table.

'Would you like a drink?' asked Oleg, while Larissa prepared the food in the kitchen.

Oleg had fruit-juice and took some gin from the cupboard; there was only a little left in the bottle. 'I like gin,' he said with a concealed sigh of consternation as he emptied the last drops from the bottle. He was sacrificing a precious liquid which could only be bought at special shops with foreign currency.

As she was laying the table, Lara asked me: 'Shall I show you round the flat? Would you like to see it? I think you should; it might be interesting for you.'

I was grateful to her and that invitation relieved us all.

She first took me to her bedroom where a large double bed occupied most of the room. There was a portrait of Larissa on the wall.

'That was done by a friend of ours.'

What little furniture there was was nineteenth-century and rather heavy.

'That bed is from the house where I spent my childhood.'

Then she took me to a small gay room. 'That's our boy's room, he's away with my mother, at the *dacha* at the moment.'

Some toys, a table, a few paintings on the wall. There were two Russian landscapes painted by a rather conservative hand and the 'portrait' of Lara's favourite house. I recognized it and smiled.

'It's a simple flat. Nothing really to look at,' Larissa stressed again. There was always a note of shame in the voices of the people who showed me their flats and in the voices of those who apologized for not showing me round. Besides those two bedrooms there was a small kitchen and the room we had been sitting in; a lavatory and a bathroom. That was all.

All the rooms showed the same lack of aesthetic attention as Larissa's clothes. Yet I had found that it was possible for only a few roubles, to find attractive lithographs, but it obviously never occurred to Larissa to surround herself with pretty things. The concept of the house in Russia is that of a dwelling – a bed to sleep in and a table at which to eat. I think this is due to a deeper reason than the scarceness of rooms.

In some cities there are antique shops, selling things mostly from the art-nouveau and art-deco periods; the prices are exorbitant. Le Marché aux Puces and Portobello Road are extremely cheap by comparison although old paintings are oddly priced and sometimes one finds charming nineteenth-century water-colours or oil-paintings for as little as ten roubles, while copies of sixteenth- or seventeenth-century pictures go for three or four hundred roubles. Paintings (modern and old) are cheap in the Soviet Union, perhaps because there is little demand for them. In the past, few Russian houses had furniture, apart from the great palaces which are preserved as museums or trade-union clubs, so there is little old furniture around.

In contrast to the bareness of private flats, public places in the Soviet Union are decorated luxuriously. Tube stations, meeting halls, cinemas and theatres are gigantic and decorated with crystal chandeliers, empty refrigerators ('Don't worry,' a friend explained, 'refrigerators are a symbol of technology in our society, like the computer in America. That's why you find refrigerators in the most unexpected places.')

Now, feeling at ease with Oleg and Larissa, I looked at the high cupboard, its opaque glasses, the vase of flowers. The room really looked like a hall of a hotel decorated at the turn of the century. In fact the house itself seemed out of character with Larissa and Oleg.

In the West we treat our houses, when we can afford to, as theatrical settings in which we play the main characters.

Oleg and Larissa would have found my house very odd indeed.

The Press

I asked Oleg whether I could visit *Izvestia*'s office. With *Pravda, Izvestia* is the most widely read newspaper in the Soviet Union. While *Pravda* is the official organ of the Communist Party and is proud to have been founded by Lenin, *Izvestia* is the organ of the government and started its life on 28 February 1917 as a Menshevik paper.

Izvestia, which means 'News' is the more intellectual, rather the less dull of the two. It is slightly freer than *Pravda* since it has less party-dictat to crowd into each edition. For Moscow it is an evening paper, while *Pravda* (Truth) is a morning paper. It has a circulation of eight and a half million copies and could have more. But the shortage of paper is such that for the moment both papers are restricted to a limited printing and to a mere six pages.

When I remarked about this paper shortage, an Italian Communist official said it was a clever restriction. 'If they brought out a paper of twelve pages,' he said, 'they would have to print some news. It is a political shortage necessary in times of crisis – so it is necessary now.'

Oleg's office was bare and looked very like the Fleet Street room of an assistant editor. I went around *Izvestia*'s own library, cutting room; the printing-machine room was decorated with flowers and containing an aquarium of coloured fish. Oleg and I sat in the cafeteria and were soon joined by the former correspondent in Rome, a small man, sweet and intelligent.

Soviet journalists are not only part of an intellectual élite, but they are also politically trusted. They are something between a Foreign Office official and a political writer. Some are just dull bureaucrats, but others are highly intelligent and unlike other Soviet citizens they are allowed to travel abroad.

There is another way of spreading news in Moscow: by word of mouth. For a whole day at a time the city talks

153

about something and the rumour spreads to everyone.

This episode, which has a touch of Bulgakov, happened when I was in Moscow. The black sleek Volga of *Izvestia*'s Editor-in-Chief was found at the bottom of the Mascva river early one morning. It crashed through the stone parapet of the Daroga Milovsk Uliza Bridge, and ended up with its three occupants in the cold water beneath.

In the early hours of the morning workers were to be seen rebuilding the parapet; skin-divers plunged into the half-frozen river and a crane pulled the black car from the water. There was no doubt about it, the number plate, immediately removed, belonged to the well-known, important and powerful Editor-in-Chief of *Izvestia*. 'One less,' whispered a passer-by to his neighbour while the militiamen were trying to get the onlookers moving. 'Three less,' remarked someone else pointing at the three bodies which had been hastily removed from the car and were being hurried away under white sheets.

The whole of Moscow began to whisper: had *Izvestia*'s Editor-in-Chief died? Had he been drunk? Who were the other two? What had happened during the night? But later it emerged that the high official's private chauffeur, after taking one of his boss's daughters to a party had spent the free evening celebrating with some friends, two of whom had shared his fate in the Mascva. Using Government cars for such purposes is very much frowned on.

Izvestia and *Pravda* appear in the whole of the Soviet Union on the very same day; this means that the reader in Yakutsk can glance at his copy of *Pravda* while the same edition is being distributed in Kiev.

Both are reprinted in forty cities; to eighteen of these the matrix is sent by air. Having no commercial rivalry, all the papers are based in the same printing house which looks very much the same from Volgograd to Khabarovsk. There is no need for an editorial staff in these provincial printing houses as *Pravda* and *Izvestia* are reprinted word for word. Provincial news is to be found in the often more interesting local papers.

The history of *Pravda* is more glorious than that of *Isvestia*. The collected back-numbers of *Pravda* chronicle the internal struggles and events which have taken place in the Soviet Union since its foundation.

Pravda

When the millionaire merchant from Kazan, Tikhomirnov, died he left a huge fortune to his four sons. The third, Victor, born in 1889, left Kazan and went to see Lenin, offering him 100,000 roubles to found a legal Bolshevik daily. At that time Lenin had a weekly, *Zvezda*, which had appeared since December 1910 and a monthly, *Prosveshohenie*, a few months younger. He really needed a daily organ. *Pravda* was started in St Petersburg in 1912. The name had already been used by Trotsky when, in 1905, choosing Vienna as his residence, he had started a workers' paper for illegal distribution in Russia. Curiously enough *Pravda* had also been the title of the daily newspaper of a sort of Russian Ku-Klux-Klan, the Sacred Brotherhood, which was based in Geneva in 1882.

From exile Lenin first wanted to use *Pravda* to provoke a split in the Duma between the Mensheviks and the Bolsheviks who were at that time menacingly friendly. But *Pravda*'s editorial board started to disobey its leader by censoring and cutting his articles. Stalin was then in charge of *Pravda* and Lenin sent Sverdlov 'for the purpose of reorganizing the editorial board and correcting *Pravda*'s attitude'.

When Victor Tikhomirnov became *Pravda*'s manager, he brought with him a Kazan student called Scriabin, who used to write pompous prose under several pseudonyms. One of these was Molotov (from Molot, hammer). Molotov became the silent lackey of Stalin, the trusted presence who always took the blame and knew how to keep alive by keeping silent.

At the same time, two police agents were on *Pravda*'s

editorial staff: Chernomazov and the more famous Roman Malinovsky, trusted by Lenin, member of the Bolshevik Central Committee and the leading Bolshevik MP in the Duma.

From time to time Tsarist censorship began to prohibit the publication of *Pravda* and close it down. The newspaper would then start up again the following day with exactly the same typography, but with a slightly changed name; it became *Rabochaia Pravda, Siviernaia Pravda,* etc., both police and reader knowing perfectly well that it was the very same paper. It seems strange that Russian censorship was so much more permissive in those days than it is now.

When World War One started on 21 July 1914, the government suppressed *Pravda* in the eighth form it had taken. But its ninth life was to start again in March 1917 with the fall of Tsar Nicolas.

In 1923, during the campaign to discredit Trotsky, the board of *Pravda* decided 'to remove all present discussion from the columns of *Pravda* to a separate "discussion sheet".' This, needless to say, never saw the light.

There is an amusing anecdote in the 'Radio Armenia' series. A listener asks the 'network': 'If there were a competition between Brezhnev and Nixon to run a race round the Kremlin walls and Nixon won, how would *Pravda* publish the news?' Radio Armenia answers: 'In the competition the General Secretary of our Party honourably achieved a second place while the President of the United States arrived last but one.'

Today *Pravda* is based in a new building. The street is suitably called Pravda Street and is quite close to Bielorussia station.

I went to see Vsievolod Ovchinnilov, of the foreign editorial board. Previously he had been *Pravda*'s correspondent in China and in Japan and he had written several books. He was a sensitive man with a taste for Eastern philosophy rather than for the hectic life of a newspaperman. His editorial job, he said, was restricted by the fact that there was little room for foreign news on *Pravda*'s pages. 'The deadline for *Pravda*'s first edition is at five o'clock in the afternoon; at six the proofs are sent round the offices and at six-thirty the first edition is ready to be telexed or sent out to the far provinces. You know, we are a Party paper and we have certain responsibilities: if *Pravda* doesn't publish what a certain President says, the whole world would read some strange meaning into it. But there is only room to print 25–30 per cent of the material we receive every day.'

Pravda prints nine million copies a day, eight million of which are distributed to subscribers. When I talked to the Managing Administrator, Mr Zukasov, Secretary responsible for *Pravda*, I asked him whether he had ever had financial problems.

'Newspapers with such a large circulation as ours are always profitable. Since we depend on the Central Committee of the Communist Party, we give them part of the profit. We can in fact say that our party's budget comes from its papers' profits and from the membership fees.'

All editors of *Pravda* are nominated by the Central Committee. Its board meets every day at eleven and discusses the preliminary selection of contents for each issue; it is responsible for the political line and planning of the paper. Under the main editorial board there is an executive board of twenty deputies, five dealing with foreign news. Then there are those in charge of departments such as 'Party Life', 'Marxist-Leninist propaganda' etc. Others deal with readers' letters. 'Last year we received 400,000 letters, that is more than 1,000 a day. Selecting the most interesting keeps a whole department busy.'

There are 7,246 newspapers and over 2,000 magazines published in the Soviet Union with a total circulation of 110 million copies. Until recently the most influential literary magazine was 'Novi Mir'. It was 'Novi Mir' which published in late November 1962, after Krushchev's speech at the 22nd Congress, Solzhenitsyn's novel *One day in the*

life of Ivan Denisovich. This book startled the country with
its descriptions of Stalinist concentration camps. It has also
published works by Yuri Dombrovsky, Nekrasnov, Nina
Kosterina, etc. But recently the former editor, Alexsandr
Tvardovsky, was forced to resign when he found that his
entire board had been changed behind his back.

Journalists in the USSR have their own trade union and
the Moscow branch has good premises including a restaurant where foreign journalists are allowed one day a week.

APN is a body to which I am particularly grateful, since
without its help I wouldn't have been able to meet so many
interesting people. It is like a combination of Reuter and
USIS. APN does not try to hide the fact that it is a propaganda machine. 'If the United States Information Service
sends two correspondents to New Delhi, we send three; I
was told.

APN has correspondents all over the Soviet Union who
provide Moscow with non-political articles and photographs
from their own areas. The material is then sold to the Soviet
and foreign press. The APN people are semi-officials; they
generally belong to the Party and doors are easily opened
through them.

The Marxist-Leninist Institute

Although he is well-off, the Soviet citizen today laments the
poor service, the lack of stimulus, the queues, the five-year
plans which don't take into account the new needs of a
developing society; of a society which is becoming richer
and demands more sophisticated goods. However, all
accounts of pre-revolutionary Russia show that the *nichevo'*,
('it doesn't matter') attitude is not new. Also, the Russians
don't have a strong incentive to work, because they have
never been interested in acquiring personal wealth or possessions. Even the pioneering Cossacks gave the land they
conquered to the Crown, and they never built magnificent
houses.

'Today in the Soviet Union,' an official told me, 'food is cheaper than it ever was, taxes are very low since there are few properties. The housing problem has almost been solved: four years ago each citizen only had a right to four square metres – now he has a right to nine. And all this so few years after the terrible damage inflicted on our country by civil and foreign wars. We are building Socialism, but we have as yet no example to follow. As for the economy, we are trying out new methods, new approaches.'

'Let me tell you,' said a chance acquaintance, a factory worker, 'I work all the month and couldn't even dream of buying a dress like yours for my wife.' (The one I was wearing was very cheap.) 'We've had shortages of meat, fruit is scarce and cafés close at ten in the evening: what kind of life is this? As for spirits, recent laws have made them twice as expensive. Do you think I'd be allowed to travel abroad? Certainly not. Propaganda says we are rich, powerful and own all the raw materials in the world, but I can't travel abroad. One feels so claustrophobic here; it is a big country but, believe me, one feels shut in. If you behave yourself and never protest they might include you in one of the wretched "Sputnik" travel-groups. But they're generally reserved for trusted people, not for workers like me who are not even members of the Komsomol. Here we are lazy, we make bad products. Mechanization, they say, but you know what happens if you buy a vacuum cleaner? If something goes wrong, you can't mend it, because nobody ever thought of making spare parts. Nobody cares. Why should we? What would we gain by working any harder? We really live in a perpetual state of strike. I believe your men go on strike if they don't like something, but here it is forbidden. The only people who have to do the work are those in labour camps.'

A Moscovite journalist told me: 'Frankly we are not satisfied with the Kosygin reforms. You see, of the 50,000 enterprises existing in the USSR in the first year, 700 were selected and given managerial responsibilities and initiative in production. In the second 13,000 and in the third 17,000.

Altogether the laws affect 37 out of 50 plants. These are responsible for delivery to the consumer and for industrial planning. By increasing their production, these plants make a profit which is divided into thirteen months' wages, extra holidays, rest-homes and new machines. It is vital for us to trade with the West but this is difficult not only because of currency problems, but also for political reasons. For example, we needed tools from America for car production but the United States Government would not allow their sale because they classified them as strategic goods.' Trade between the Soviet bloc and the West before 1970 represented only three per cent of global world trade, a minute figure.

'Why,' I asked, 'is the Soviet Union so secretive about details of its mineral resources?'

'If a foreign trade group got to know that we have vast quantities of the raw material that they require – so much that we don't know what to do with it – they might lower their offer.'

A non-Soviet, but Marxist, economist told me that the basic trouble with Russia's economy was that the bureaucratic class, which ought to act as a filter between the leaders and the people, had become the leading class. In economic and sociological terms, this phenomenon cannot survive. 'The Chinese are right when they accuse Russia of being Fascist. Soviet society is static, closed. If in the present economic world situation, Russia slowed down still further its already slow production, and everyone worked five minutes less each day, the country would go bust.'

He thought that because of the economic problems the actual regime could not last in the long term unless more freedom of action and initiative was given to people in all walks of life.

The Institute of Marxism-Leninism studies and develops new theories of Scientific Communism, so I arranged to meet somebody there who could enlighten me on present economic theories. So, one sunny day, accompanied by Feodor, APN's man, I crossed Sovietskaia Square and entered the holy of holies.

A huge statue of Lenin faced us from a little garden and symbolically turned its back on the Institute. Some steps beneath it brought us to the entrance of the great and ferocious building. In the large hall, to my amazement I was confronted by a huge refrigerator. I was tempted to open it to find out if it were empty or not.

A lift took us to the second floor where we were met by a secretary and led into a large rectangular room. At the far end, a tiny desk was blessed by Lenin's portrait. Alexander Arsientivich, the vice-director of the Leninist Institute, a cigarette between the fingers of his left hand, rose to give us a rather feeble handshake with his right and returned to his seat immediately.

I sat opposite him and portraits of three extremely sad-looking people, dressed in dark clothes, their faces drawn with unhappiness. At a second glance, I recognized the faces of Comrades Brezhnev, Podgorny and Kosygin.

Before entering the large room, I had somehow expected to meet an elderly man, perhaps luxuriantly bearded, thick-spectacled, a face lined by worry. Instead Alexander Arsientivich was neat and polished, wore a well-cut suit, had carefully manicured nails and coral cufflinks. His hair was combed back to reveal a square forehead and large blue eyes. His eyes were curiously empty – like a boiled fish – free from any sparkle or expression. Although turned politely towards me, his pupils never showed the slightest flicker of attention, curiosity, anger or interest. Had they always been like that?

Perhaps even from the very earliest days of Sasha Arsientivich's life, his mother had found, to her dismay, that little Sasha's eyes did not respond to her cuddling or show any sign of recognition. Now here he was, a grown man of about fifty, with a very important job, having to face that curse of Soviet officials: a foreign journalist. Foreign journal-

161

ists always want to know everything regardless of the fact that it is dangerous for a political authority to discuss new ideas, or even think about them. Why can't they stay in their luxury hotels and read the pamphlets which are so generously distributed by the State propaganda offices?

Noticing that Alexander Arsientivich's rather worrying complexion revealed a bad liver, I told him I had come to ask him about recent economic theories. I said that as the Soviet Union was facing economic difficulties, it was obviously here that work was in progress to develop new formulae which the whole Socialist world would watch with attention.

Alexander Arsientivich looked towards me and began to speak. His voice was high-pitched and as colourless as his eyes. He didn't seem to need to pause for breath.

'I shall first tell you about this Institute which was established fifty years ago but was very different in those days.' I looked around, but as I couldn't see anything which bore witness to its novelty, I concluded that Alexander Arsientivich must have been alluding to the new refrigerator in the hall. 'First it was an organization devoted to studying the history of Communism created on the initiative of Lenin himself and it gathered information from the leading figures of the Party.' (I wondered what was the purpose of preserving archives full of papers by people one could no longer mention, such as Zinoviev, Kamenev, Trotsky.) 'Then the Institute gathered material for the history of the revolution because until 1917 it had had to remain underground, in 1921 on Lenin's initiative it became the Marx-Engels Institute and published their works after Lenin's death in 1924, it was immediately renamed the Marxist-Engels-Lenin Institute, three scientific branches were created in 1931 and in 1937 . . .'

This was very interesting, I interrupted, but I had come to hear about something more specific than the history of the Institute. I wouldn't have expected a true history of the Institute from Alexander Arsientivich anyway since the re-writing of history, the removal of documents and charac-

ters, the erasing of photographs, thoughts and actions were
more in his line.

'As neither Marx nor Engels,' Alexander Arsientivich
droned on, 'ever lived in Russia our Institute made a special
effort to collect all their writings whenever possible – the
originals or photocopies, according to Engels' wishes all his
writings and possessions had to be owned by a Social
Democratic party so they belonged to the German Social
Democrats, the Germans allowed us to refer to these works
in 1925, so for four years we had free access to the Marx-
Engels archives, what was missing from them we either
acquired or received as a present in copies or originals,
now we have here the largest collection of Marx-Engels
material, before the Second World War, our Institute published one edition of Marx and Engels' works in fourteen
volumes, we finished the second Russian edition two years
ago: it runs to twenty-nine volumes, now we are resum-
ing this work in a joint effort with the Berlin Institute in
a large International edition which will consist of 100
volumes.'

I was beginning to get annoyed: my only question had
been ignored. I looked round the room in exasperation but
my eyes only met the sad eyes of Brezhnev, Podgorny and
Kosygin, staring out from their portraits.

'The Institute popularizes the works of Marx and Engels
many of which had never been published during their life-
time, the new international edition of 100 volumes will
include comments written by leading philosophers and
scientists, we have also started an edition in English consisting of fifty volumes which will appear in 1971, the second
task of our Institute let me explain is gathered round Lenin's
works, we have produced five editions of Lenin's writings,
the first edition was in twenty volumes and the last, which
is complete, is in fifty . . .'

'Really complete?'

'We included everything that we managed to gather . . .
Lenin's letters, preparatory works and writings . . . after the
fifty volumes edition we published one special volume for

the 100th anniversary of Lenin's birth containing a further 507 documents never published before . . .'

Alexander Arsientivich, I suddenly noticed, had a nervous tic. It was not, I don't think, my presence which made him nervous, but perhaps these energetic nervous tics which made his otherwise still face palpitate were due to the repression of movement in his eyes.

'I hope that when we publish the next edition of Lenin's works in twenty to twenty-five years we shall be able to include all those 507 new documents chronologically.'

'So the Institute is just a publishing house,' I interrupted again.

Alexander Arsientivich's eyes showed neither dismay nor anger. 'Therefore our Institute is devoted to the scientific research of Marxism and Leninism apart from this the Institute works on the problems of our party. We have published a scientific biography on Lenin and secured the works of Marxism for posterity.'

Off he goes again, I thought in despair. Why had they sent me to witness the worst aspect of Soviet bureaucracy? I suddenly began to dislike Alexander Arsientivich; almost to hate him, to hate his elegant suit, his smooth head, his polished nails, his yellow face. Oblivious to my many signs of impatience, Alexander Arsientivich droned on and on.

The idea suddenly struck me that Alexander Arsientivich might be asleep. A brilliant man, he had perhaps trained himself to keep his eyelids open while reciting a speech he knew by heart. He could talk while actually asleep; or was it a record playing? Now it all began to make sense – his failure to answer my questions, his facial and vocal expressionlessness.

He went on to inform me that the Institute had a very large library and 400 scientists . . .

My attention wandered to the three portraits; I knew what I would have done to secure myself a comfortable living in Russia if I'd lived there: I would have painted portraits. I would have specialized in Lenin, since the market seemed to be inexhaustible. It was unlikely that Lenin would ever fall into disgrace, but to paint portraits of other leaders might have been risky.

Imagine finding yourself with forty unfinished portraits of Krushchev in your studio! On the other hand, if I had been stuck with eighty portraits of Comrade Stalin I would now be selling them again. Marx was not a lucrative prospect and Engels was a waste of time. Perhaps I might have revived Gorki and produced a group of 100 identical canvases depicting Maxim Gorki in conversation with Lenin. I would have had to make sure of selling them in all the theatres and spreading the rumour that literary people who did not display these portraits in their offices were looked on unfavourably. I could have settled down to paint another batch. Although I would have followed the Soviet practice of making their style identical in each painting I would have added a detail or two to my portraits of Lenin: Ilyich reading *Das Kapital*, Ilyich contemplating his first proofs of *What's to be done?*, or reading a letter from his sister Maria or looking at a photo of his brother Alexander ... this reminded me that the man facing me had the same name as Lenin's brother – and he was still talking.

'We have three Academicians in the Institute – four corresponding Members of the Academy of Sciences, thirty Doctors of Sciences and a hundred and fifty ... we have altogether three buildings in Moscow and sixteen branches in the Soviet Union ... If a post-graduate is very capable we send him to the Academy for three years to study ...'

'Alexander Arsientivich, what about the economic theories?'

'Economics is studied very generally here. We only concentrate on the future development of Communism but we develop the economic concept of scientific Communism ...'

'I beg your pardon?'

'As for pure economics – we have institutes such as the Institute of Economics and many other excellent institutes where practical problems are studied but our general economic theory is based on Lenin ...'

Yes, I thought, shaking Alexander Arsientivich's floppy

hand. He must have been asleep all through our interview. Otherwise, I was sure, our meeting would have been very exciting.

A Spokesman from the Komsomol

'How did it go?' asked APN's Misha.
'A disaster – it couldn't have been worse.'
'Perhaps you should have seen someone younger, someone from the Komsomol.'
'Who is the Marxist theoretician here?'
'Mikhail Suslov is,' Misha smiled. 'Brezhnev may be "primus inter pares" but he'll never be much more than that.'

There was a very intelligent man connected with the Komsomol, Misha told me.

He arranged a meeting.

Ghiennari Antonovich Kashoian was editor of the magazine *Roviesnik*, an organ of the Central Committee of the Komsomol. He was Chairman of the Youth Department and of the Friendship Society and a Member of the praesidium of the Youth Organization.

Roviesnik is a rather progressive magazine by Soviet standards: it includes advice on how to do one's hair, how to keep slim and fit and it carries articles from abroad with colour illustrations. The magazine was started eight years ago with a circulation of 37,000 copies, now it has risen to 640,000 and, if it weren't for the famous paper shortage, they told me, it could have been thicker and sold more copies. It is impossible to find it on sale in the newspaper kiosks, unless one knows exactly when they are coming out.

Roviesnik's offices were in one of those Moscow streets which still retain their charm. The headquarters of the magazine were gay, and a considerable effort had been made to decorate the place – unusual in the Soviet Union. Ghiennari

Antonovich's own office had a nice carpet, an aquarium and a bunch of flowers.

Ghiennari Antonovich had dark curly hair and wore dark sun-glasses – a status symbol in Russia because they are difficult to obtain. He was articulate, friendly and convincing, although much of what he said was a little dubious. But men like Ghiennari Antonovich are trained to believe what they say and to convince their audience. I think he was sincere when he spoke to me, even when he touched on delicate questions like freedom of travel, or democratic elections.

'You must first understand that the relationship between the generations in the Soviet Union is very complex,' he started, answering my first question. 'People say it doesn't exist; but of course it does. Power is in the hands of the older generation which doesn't understand young people's attraction to mini-skirts, dances, pop music and records. When it was young, the generation which now holds power had neither time nor opportunity for such things. Another problem is in the different levels of education. Although half of the young people today have had either a secondary education or been to university, this is, of course, not true of the old. So the young are better educated. But there is no conflict between youth and power in the Soviet Union because the revolutionary spirit of this country is directed towards youth. Besides, the young have great political power; one-third of the deputies in the Soviets are young. After the Party and the Trade Unions, the Komsomol is the largest organization in the Soviet Union; it has twenty-seven million members. For example, we wanted to build the palace for the young Pioneers in modern style but it wasn't easy to push the project through. However, we succeeded. Through conflicts, we settle problems. I am very often asked to talk in the West about the Virgin Lands, whether we compelled people to work there. Well, in 1953 I was secretary of the Komsomol in Tiflis and we had so many volunteers that it was impossible to send them all. People aged twenty-seven, twenty-eight can now be managers of huge projects.

'To answer your question: do they influence the Party? Not by formal means. I am sorry to say that in the West the energy of young people is sapped by things of secondary importance; Western youth is organized as a consumer and not as a creator; the young are regarded as a consumer class to be cultivated by industry: records, clothes, make-up. That's why they demonstrate in the streets asking to participate. Here they do participate: in Moscow the young have more luxuries than in Bratsk and perhaps we could do more to supply the young generation with records, clubs and clothes. But if youth does not develop a taste for fashionable things, it will find better things to enjoy: like literature and good music. I must be frank, I know we don't satisfy young people and have some problems with them, but we give economic precedence to such things as culture clubs; some thirty million young men participate in youth circles of folk-songs, drama, national dance ensembles, Dixieland jazz. Money here is distributed according to the needs of groups. In the West if a pop group succeeds, the record industry produces millions of copies of one record, but those who would prefer another kind of music are not provided for since it's not profitable. But we cant' do that.'

I then asked Ghiennari Antonovich why the régime was so prudish and why was 'sex' more or less banned in print.

'What are sex books? Explanation of methods of sexual intercourse. Frankly, I can do without that. But it's wrong to say that we don't allow sex books. Take Shokolov's *Quiet Flows the Don*, one of the most popular books in this country. A young man falls in love with his neighbour's wife. She becomes his mistress. His parents compel him to marry another woman. He returns to his old mistress who, during the war is unfaithful to him with an officer, so the young man beats her up and leaves her for his wife. But after many years he goes back to his mistress. What is this, if not a sex story? But we are against open naturalistic scenes and sexual permissiveness, sadism, homosexuality. Also all that show of violence and masculinity on Western television and films cultivates inferiority complexes, I am sure. Freedom to travel abroad? Well, you know, our currency is not convertible, so we generally organize travel groups called "Sputnik". Currency is the property of the State and, of course, there are many more people who would like to go than it is possible to send. But we are sending more and more. Travelling to Socialist countries is no problem at all. This is a collective state and we insist that every Soviet man abroad represents our country: so we don't allow people to travel who might behave indecently or get drunk. I think this is normal. And when we send a young man abroad we always check up on his references. I think this is correct. '

I told Ghiennari Antonovich that I had heard complaints about difficulties to obtain permission to travel.

'I have heard that too. My driver was always complaining until one day I told him to try. He went to his trade union and then to the Sputnik organization and next day he returned with a ticket for Yugoslavia. The trade unions pay for half of such trips and since each trade union is allotted a certain number of journeys from Sputnik, success depends on the number of requests. People here are very spoiled, they are accustomed to having everything paid by the State. For a cure you get seventy-five per cent.'

I told Kashoian that some young Soviet people seemed to want 'to go back to Lenin'. How did he interpret that?

'You must have spoken to young people who don't know that it was much worse twenty-five years ago than it is now. And they can't have meant it from a material point of view. In Lenin's time class exploitation still existed; there was more than one party in parliament, there were more class differentiations. Under Lenin, the leadership was not elected, but now under the new constitution anybody can vote and anybody can be elected. At that time national republics were formed into federations: now they have autonomous self-government. Democracy has increased since Lenin. People make a mistake when they say that today

169

is not a continuation of yesterday; the way from proletarian revolution to Communism is only one: collectivism. People who regret Lenin's times are naive. Lenin was a beginning, but now people are closer to Communism than they ever were. People today study ideology, we don't want to build a state of fools who cannot criticize, who just utter banalities. Communism is close . . .'

'How close?'

'Closer by fifty years. We have not got a utopian Marxist Communist society, of course not. But we have taught people to fight for it; and that was Lenin's concern, Marx said "a nation of fighters . . ." '

But he had also said: 'A nation which oppresses another nation cannot itself be free'. And Lenin had said almost the same: 'Can a nation be free if it oppresses other nations? It cannot. The interests of the freedom of the Great Russian population demand a struggle against such oppression . . .'

I would have felt happier if Ghiennari Antonovich had not mentioned democratic elections. Concerning the 'Return to Lenin', he had either misunderstood me or wanted to misunderstand. But at least he had talked, energetically and articulately.

Moscow's Lenin State Public Library

Moscow's central library was founded in 1862 as the Rumyantsev and renamed after one of its many users. It is a gigantic affair: with the Leningrad Library, the British Museum and the Library of Congress, it is one of the four biggest in the world – and certainly one of the most recent. It is located in a huge cement building just off Marx Prospect, in Prospect Kalinin; it would take months to familiarize oneself with it and to be able to find one's way around its labyrinths.

It certainly gives one a good idea of how lively culture is in the Soviet Union; the reading and working rooms are so crowded that often people have to wait to find a seat. I was taken around by Mark Mitrofonovich Klieviensky, the Library's deputy head, a big man of around seventy, devoted to his job. 'I have been a librarian for forty years,' he said.

Under international law the library receives a copy of every publication from abroad and from inside the Soviet Union. In pre-revolutionary times, seventy-two years ago, it received two copies of *The Development of Capitalism in Russia*, written by Vladimir Ilin, another of Lenin's pseudonyms, during his Siberian exile. The censors, who knew well that Ilin was Lenin, didn't forbid the publication as they hadn't forbidden the first volume of Karl Marx's *Das Kapital* in 1872. But after that, all Lenin's books were published illegally.

The library is divided into departments dedicated to science, fiction, history, typography etc; it has twenty-two reading-rooms and around eleven thousand visitors a day. Its cataloguing department (I visited both Russian and foreign sections) is not worked by computer and is very impressive.

'We have the biggest collection of catalogues,' Mark Mitrofonovich said, taking me through a huge room divided by tall bookcases. 'Even the BBC admits this. And this is the British Museum Library catalogue: 263 volumes in all.' Two thousand six hundred people work in the Lenin Library. 'In order to use the library, people have to ask for a special pass; over 200,000 such tickets have been issued and the users can come in whenever they want.'

There are three 'universal' reading rooms for the ordinary reader, and 200 specialized ones divided according to different subjects. For example, the social science reading room is a large hall with 550 benches and tables where the ticket holder can work from nine in the morning until ten at night, Sundays included.

The system of public libraries in the Soviet Union is very impressive. Every small city I visited had its own; something taken for granted in Britain, but still astonishing to me as an Italian. In Khabarovsk's public library I came across two beautiful leather-bound copies of Byron's *Don Juan*. How these precious volumes had arrived in Eastern Siberia started me off on romantic speculation.

Leaving Moscow

'I am sure they do,' I said to Misha, 'but where?'

'You'd be surprised, people in love always find a way and a place.'

Houses are crowded, hotels restricted to travellers from other cities, the countryside can be cold or covered with snow and it is unlikely that a young man or woman would possess a car anyway. Where do people make love?

'Well,' said a friend as we walked in the Kremlin, 'if you take one of the boats that tour the river, you'll see great crowds at departure time which disappear then until arrival time. The point is that the boats have cabins.'

A girl giggled: 'Then there's the night train, Moscow-Leningrad. It leaves at twelve and arrives at eight in the morning. You spend the day in Leningrad and come back the same way.'

Women in Russia are very much a liberated sex; emancipation must have come violently and it started from the tougher and more important angle: work.

Women work in factories and have all kinds of jobs; but there are almost five hundred forbidden as excessively heavy. Just as in the West, it is difficult to find women in top political bureaucratical or journalistic positions, but in the Soviet Union wages are the same for women as for men. Today three out of four Soviet doctors and teachers are women; they get pensioned at fifty-five. In divorce cases, wives get half the property, and pregnant women are given 112 days paid leave and if they wish to return to their former jobs, they can within one year.

Apart from the difficulties of being a Soviet housewife –

172

the queueing and lack of delivery service – the Russian woman is much less of a second-class citizen than women in the West.

Thinking about that I went round the corner to the post office to send an inland telegram and filled in a form: 'Shall be Rostov for one week stop if possible reach me there.' I had changed my mind about Kostia.

The post is very temperamental in the Soviet Union; a parcel sent by surface mail from Novosibirsk to London may take just a week, and sent by air from Moscow it may take a month. Anything coming from Moscow takes much longer. Not all that is sent from abroad gets to the Soviet Union: postal communications and parcels are under tight control.

Internal communications are equally strange. Stamps are cheap but so large that they often take most of the space for the address. The large stamps featuring Lenin, cosmonauts, sporting youth, often need an additional dab of glue which slows the clerks down still further and prolongs the patient waiting of the long queue.

'The smaller and the more repetitive the stamps, the more civilized the country.' I agreed with my Soviet friend and we gave a high prize for civility to Switzerland and Great Britain, while Jordan, Yemen, Argentina and the Soviet Union seemed to come at the bottom with continuous series of new and gigantic stamps.

To send a parcel within the Soviet Union or outside one has to have it carefully checked by the postal assistant. Then the parcels are wrapped and tied up, glued and stamped – all of which can take up to twenty minutes while the rest of the queue has to wait.

In 1701 the Russian merchant Ivan Pososhkov wrote that foreigners

' . . . have cut a hole leading from our land into their own, and through this hole they observe all our political and commercial relations. This hole is the post. The harm it does to the realm is incalculable. Everything that goes on in our land is known to the whole world. The foreigners become rich by it, and Russians become as poor as beggars. The foreigners always know which of our goods are cheap and which are dear; which are plentiful and which are scarce. Thereupon they bargain, and . . . in this way trade is made unequal. It is very bad that foreigners should know everything that happens here.'

22 April

Red Square had been closed all morning. Preparation had started some days earlier; the cobblestones of the square had been marked with mysterious coloured signs, the amplifiers on the terraces of Lenin's mausoleum had been tested by young men counting – and the numbers echoed against the bannered façade of GUM, the largest of the government stores, against the dark-red History Museum, and the Spasskaya tower. The flags of the fifteen republics flapped in the crisp Moscow wind. No-one knew what was going to happen on the 22nd, for Lenin's birth centenary – no-one knew whether the government would participate or not.

Feodor, the APN man who looked after my main and many demands, came to collect me with the ticket bearing my name: it was necessary to show it, together with documents, at the various army blocks barring the way to Red Square. We had to make a large detour in order to reach it from the river side. The demonstration for Lenin's anniversary was quite modest by comparison with that of the 1st of May. Hundreds of little Oktyabrists (children from seven to nine) placed themselves in orderly rows flanked by Pioneers (children from nine to fourteen) and finally by Komsomols (fourteen to twenty-six)* – after that the doors

* The Komsomol, Young Communist League, was founded by Lenin in October 1918 and is a powerful organization of twenty-seven million members.

of the Communist Party proper are open but members of Komsomol can remain so until the age of twenty-eight.

The air was ringing with the din of recorded marches, sung by tenors praising tractors, Lenin, youth, the Komsomol. The colours of the different uniforms formed attractive patterns on the huge square, little arms waved with pre-ordained movements, flagging red scarves in the wind; it looked like a flight of red birds departing towards the Kremlin. It was beautiful and yet it was strongly reminiscent of those film sequences of Nazi youth: the gymnastics, the children, the uniforms, the discipline, the quasi-goose step of the soldiers. I felt a strange shiver going down my back.

The ceremony proceeded very simply: Komsomols, Pioneers and Oktyabrists exchanged rosettes: the latter were thus promoted Pioneers who, in turn, became Komsomols.

The members of the Politburo arrived on the famous balcony over the mausoleum at the end of the ceremony: Kosygin looked like a tired grandfather. I liked his face: his manners and his tone of voice were reassuring and honest. The children clapped; but banners, music and gymnastics did not succeed in turning my thoughts to the person who, born a hundred years before in the town of Simbirsk, had set himself to change the world.

'I have a great request to make to you. Do not allow your mourning for Ilych to take the form of external reverence for his person. Do not raise memorials to him, palaces named after him, solemn festivals in commemoration of him etc.; to all this he attached so little importance in his life; all this was so burdensome to him. Remember how much poverty and neglect there still is in our country. If you wish to honour the name of Vladimir Ilych, build crêches, kindergartens, houses, schools, libraries, medical centres, hospitals, homes for the disabled etc., and most of all, let us put his respects into practice.'
(Krupskaya's letter of thanks for messages of condolences published in *Pravda*, 30 January 1924.)

'We insist
Don't stereotype Lenin.
Don't print his portrait on placards, sticky back
plates, mugs and cigarette cases.
Don't bronze over Lenin.'

(Mayakovsky in 1923.)

Subsequently I learned that delegations of foreign Communist parties sent to attend this ceremony were kept out of
sight in very elegant houses on Leninsky hill. Champagne,
chandeliers, caviar, chauffeur-driven black Chaika cars were
at their disposal but only for officially-authorized trips. In
fact, they wanted to walk, to have a look around by themselves. The North Vietnam and Cambodian delegations got
very impatient and met up at the Cambodian embassy for a
relaxed dinner – escaping some official meal. But the Italian
delegation did not include the leader, Enrico Berlinguer;
after his open criticism of Russia's invasion in Czechoslovakia, he likes to keep his distance.

That night I went to the 'Queen of Spades 'at the Bolshoi.
Then I set out to have dinner at the house of some friends.
The night was damp and drizzly, and I was shivering inside
my hood. Suddenly I looked up towards the sky. I was
startled: was I seeing things? An immense, illuminated head
of Lenin was floating in the sky over Moscow. Perhaps it
was a ghost, perhaps it was Lenin angered by the poor
treatment he received during his celebrations. To my equal
amazement, a taxi stopped for me.

I gave him the address. 'Oh, it's too far,' he said.

'All right, I'll pay double.'

'OK, jump in.'

I sat next to him to stress my gratitude and my willing-
ness to chat.

'Aren't you afraid of walking in Moscow by night?' he
asked.

'No, frankly Moscow doesn't scare me at all, unlike other
cities.'

'You are Polish, I imagine. You have been at the Bolshoi,

lucky you. Not so easy for us Moscovites, you know, we have to book months in advance if we are to get a seat . . . When I was a student I used to go often . . . when the old lady sings about her past beauty, do you remember? alone in her bedroom . . . the Queen of Spades, that's a lovely song, really lovely . . . and when Lisa sings of her sadness . . . oh, what a masterpiece . . . Have you read Pushkin's short story of the Queen of Spades? Oh, good – it is quite different from the opera, isn't it? Pushkin is our great poet, you know. Look, you really shouldn't walk alone at night, in Moscow. There are a lot of drunks about, you know. The portrait in the sky? Oh, it's hung from a balloon, you can't see it because only the face is lit by some powerful lights from the ground. It was first invented by . . . by Stalin. It's very impressive, isn't it? He used it a lot. In the morning, it's all taken down. Look at him, shining in the sky, like an apparition, like . . . like . . .'

God.

Lenin Pilgrimage

'The Volga is the mother of Russia, the Amur its father.' So they say, though this would mean that Russia's father would be embarrassingly recent. In the nineteenth century the Amur used to belong to China.

The Volga is an enormous, slowflowing river punctuated by villages and cities, interrupted by dams producing power for the inexhaustible needs of big industrial Russia. The vital artery starts in the heart of Russia, midway between Leningrad and Moscow, winding its way to Gorki and Kazan, then on through the Tartar country, passing Togliatti, the new car city, Ulyanovsk, Kuybyshev, Volgograd down to Astrakhan into the Caspian Sea.

The right-hand side 'European' bank of the Volga has the curious feature of being high, while the left, which is flat, is invaded by the river with the thaw, drowning the thin white birch trees.

Villages on the 'Asian' bank are, for this reason, set inland and when the overflowing Volga reaches them, the villagers build a wooden path over which people walk to the river embankments. The boats leave from these and take them to the other side; it is always on the 'European' bank that cities, factories and harbours are built. It is the Volga rather than the Urals which divides West from East, the Volga which made Russian history, where the Nazis were stopped, where the great Cossack rebellions of the seventeenth and eighteenth centuries gathered momentum with Stenka Razin and Emelyan Pugachov; and it was the Volga which nursed Lenin.

Lenin's father came from Astrakhan, and his mother from the province of Kazan, both on the Volga. Lenin himself was born in Simbirsk, today Ulyanovsk, and lived there until he went to study in Kazan and Saratov, spending his police-surveillanced holidays in Kukushkino (in the province of Kazan). Near Samara he worked as a lawyer. Before reaching St Petersburg, Lenin's earlier life had been nursed by the great river.

'HERE LIE THE ASHES OF ILYA NICOLAIEVICH ULYANOV 1831 – 12 January 1886 MAY GOD REST YOUR SOUL IN PEACE' is written on Lenin's father's tomb, the only stone which has been spared by Soviet bulldozers in what was once Simbirsk's cemetery and is now a recreation garden in Ulyanovsk.

The brownish stone was sculpted in the shape of a book resting over a stone cloth; the symbol of Ilya Nicolaievich's work to which he dedicated so much effort. He had attained the rank of Councillor of State, which gave him an hereditary title. He had come to Simbirsk, the forgotten, feudal little town, as school inspector for the whole province.

They had first settled in a group of three houses situated just on the borders of the elegant district but near the old prison, now destroyed. The Ulyanovs mixed little: they were odd – intellectuals; they were not the kind of people to be welcomed into the 'Club de la Noblesse' which Baedeker describes at length.

In Chuvash language the old name of the city, *Simbirsk*, means 'green mountain': this hill, called the 'Vieniets', used to be covered by grass but is now being cemented and decorated with a prim, municipal-style garden. At the foot of it is the Volga, at its shoulder the river Sviiaga. It was there that the Lenins lived and in one of the three tiny houses, Maria Alexandrovna had her third child, Vladimir. It is a tiny wooden house constructed with graceful white-washed boards, and it has a pointed roof. The house containing the 'living quarters' was next door, rather like at Sissing-hurst; the Ulyanovs had to move from one to the other under umbrellas, wearing galoshes. There, an arch divided the drawing-room from the dining-space. Out of those windows there was a beautiful view of the Volga; the table-cloth in the dining-room was made of white lace. Ilya Nicolaievich's study was tiny, warmed by a black majolica stove. The bedrooms, too, were small, decorated simply but with taste. Near the children's quarters was their nanny's room – Varvara Grigorievna Sarbatova, who spent all her life with the Ulyanovs. The kitchen was large and white with a typically Russian stove, small windows and samovar.

When the Ulyanovs lived there, the city was the residence of a Greek bishop, it had forty-four thousand inhabitants and twenty-eight churches of which one was Catholic and one Lutheran (*'une jolie église luthérienne'*) where Maria Alexandrovna went from time to time. A mosque and two convents also enriched the massive presence of religion there. The low city around the hill was made in timber and cut across by roads of mud.

The little house where Lenin was born is now enveloped under the gigantic arches of Lenin's memorial building, a square block of Karelian marble, partly decorated from the outside with a huge mosaic: it looks like a jumbo air terminal, with a touch of Loreto or Lourdes. Facing it, the new Hilton-like hotel, with a thousand rooms, twenty-two floors high, several restaurants, most of them impenetrable.

'Do you like it?' asked Misha who had mysteriously accompanied me to Ulyanovsk.

179

'I think it's horrid,' I answered.

The new town of Ulyanovsk has been built to impress visitors with the miraculous change from pre-revolutionary Russia to Soviet times: modern houses, industries, monuments, a glittering airport although most of what is new is in a state of upheaval and mostly doesn't function. Since Misha was an official, I kept tormenting him: it was awful! a waste of money! Think of what 'he' would have said! But Misha answered that the masses loved it; the gigantic, the mastodontic: quantity rather than quality appealed to the masses as the Vatican had found out several centuries earlier. But at least the fountains in St Peter's function.

Once Misha and I met an old man walking down the hill towards the banks of the river. The old man wore the flat cap and the high collar of the old-fashioned Volga man. He had a beautiful Alsatian with him. Few Russians have pets, since the custom disappeared during the famine when pets were eaten. Anyway, keeping pets was considered 'bourgeois'. The old man was handsome, and thin, but seemed lonely. 'How old is he?' shouted Misha pointing to the dog.

The old man turned slowly: 'Old, like me. A writer gave him to me. We were together in Sverdlovsk during the war. I had another Alsatian in those days. When he came to Ulyanovsk he asked me where my beautiful dog was, and I told him that I had had to give it up to the government. At that time we had to. Then he gave me this one.'

One day I took a solitary walk in the old residential Simbirsk, on the hill over the Volga, on from Novoi Vieniets. I felt as if I was playing truant, but nobody came and told me to go and inspect the new skyscrapers instead. The houses in the old, intact quarter were laced by intricate woodwork, the wind had swept the sky clear, somebody was playing an old record of a sonata by Chopin, the sunset was glowing.

People were at home, a clatter of dishes in the silence of the evening suggested that they were settling down to dinner; the lights were being switched on, a few couples were whispering near the gates of their gardens, two young people were kissing. The peace of family life, of the night settling over the Volga, was the same as it always had been – the same peace that the Ulyanovs had felt evening after evening. What would have happened, I thought, if Lenin had had a son? Would he have been a 'dauphin' or would he have been intimidated like his hypothetical mother (Stalin menaced Krupskaya to appoint another 'official' widow).

The breeze shook the tops of the birch trees and as the sun disappeared, the water in the pools and in the streets began to form a trembling crust of ice. I soon turned back home.

When, after Vladimir's birth, the family had grown larger, the Ulyanovs moved several times until in 1878, Ilya Nicolaievich bought a timber house in the birch-lined Moscovskaya street, number fifty-eight, where they lived for nine years. This was no longer smart Simbirsk, but it was on the border between the peasants' *izbas* and the upper-class Vieniets.

The drawing-room was on the first floor and it opened into an enchanting glass veranda filled with green plants; there was no stove and it must have been cold in the winter; that's why the family preferred to spend its evenings in the dining-room. There are no paintings or photographs on the wall. Maria Alexandrovna used to play the piano and sing songs and teach the children. A nice table, a mirror flanked by two cane chairs, is set between the two windows which look over Moskovskaya street.

In Ilya Nikolaievich's study there's an elegantly-carved desk with a neat brass desk *nécessaire*, a bell, two candelabra. His books, still left there, are mainly academic: on geography, teaching, history, poetry, physics. He used to say that his children were divided into pairs and that 'the second pair, Vladimir and Olga, are perhaps brighter; they will go even further than Sasha and Maria'.

The brownish wallpaper had black-flowered garlands which gave the room a certain severity.

The dining-room overlooked another glass veranda on its left side which filled the room with light and gave an impression of space; there was a wall clock, chessmen laid out on chess-boards, a sewing-machine near the window. A silver samovar was on the veranda sill, an oil lamp in white opaline hung from above. The wallpaper, over which hung two large maps of Europe and Asia, had an almost art-nouveau motif of mauve flowers on a brown background.

Vladimir's and his brother Sasha's rooms were on the other side of the house, separated from the younger children and from Anna. Sasha had pinned up a map of European Russia. Vladimir, in keeping with his name, which can be translated as the Lord of the World or as the Lord of Peace, had put a map of the world on his wall. His room was tiny, carved out of the back of the staircase; his small bed near a white stove, he must have felt warm in the bitter, windy Simbirsk nights.

The headmistress of the gymnasium where Lenin studied, received me kindly and showed me the hundreds of letters she receives every week as headmistress of the school where Vladimir Ilyich had been a pupil. Built in 1786, the institute is still used as a school and children run about chatting and laughing, just as the Ulyanov children must have done. The only difference is that the school is now co-educational.

The class where Vladimir firꜱt studied is large, with three vast, double-glazed windows overlooking the wide square and the Vieniets. The white majolica stove is near the black-board, and the floor is wooden parquet.

A pupil from the school had been chosen by the headmistress to take me and Zoia, a friend of Misha's, around. The little girl had thick spectacles, two badges, white sandals, black school overall and large plaits: a creature out of St Trinian's. 'He was nine and a half,' the girl said in a religious tone; 'he was the youngest of the class and the best. He never made mistakes.'

Documents concerning the famous pupil were kept in

one room. I stopped in front of the letter Fyodor Kerensky, the father of the last Prime Minister before Lenin, had written to recommend his bright pupil Vladimir for entrance in Kazan's university. It wasn't easy for him to be accepted there since he was the brother of that Alexander who had been condemned to death for attempting to assassinate the Tsar.

'Very gifted, always neat and industrious, Ulyanov was first in all subjects and, upon completing his studies, received a gold medal as the most deserving pupil in ability, progress and conduct . . . Ulyanov's mother intends to be with him throughout his university career.'

'Don't tell her who wrote that,' somebody whispered to Zoia.

'Nonsense,' she said, 'she can read, anyway.'

I liked Zoia, she was an intelligent girl.

Once on the Volga, I came to terms with Ulyanovsk. Misha, Zoia, her husband Ievgheni, with a bottle of brandy, and myself all took a speed-boat and, closing my eyes to the monstrous new buildings, I opened them again when we reached the undulating wooded landscape. 'I was born under the same sky. I breathed the same air. I heard the same peasant songs and played in the same school playground. I saw the same limitless horizons from the same high banks of the Volga . . .' (Alexander Kerensky.)

The captain of the boat was a handsome young man who knew his own country very well. 'But,' he said, 'there is no place like this. Look at the Volga, it is fourteen kilometres wide and over thirty metres deep here, it is like the sea but more beautiful. We get sturgeons and caviar, and breathe the best air in the world. What more could anyone want?' Captain Boris, as he was called, had allowed me to smoke in the cabin. 'Just because you are our guest, otherwise it's strictly forbidden. It's not good for you; we don't like our women to smoke. Really, look, don't you think it's the best place in the world? Here the summer is summer and the winter really winter, all frozen and beautiful. And just look at our spring. Isn't it magnificent?'

183

It was a lovely sight, the birch trees just turning bright green against the dark of the fir trees, the round hills plunging into the vast Volga.

'I am the captain so I'll take you a little further. We shall be a bit late, and I might get into trouble, but I can say I did it for our foreign guest.'

It was from this city that Lenin left with what remained of his family to study law at the university of Kazan.

His choice was obviously influenced by political considerations as social sciences were taught in the faculty of law. 'The time now is such,' he had once told his cousin Nikolai Veretennikov, 'that it is necessary to study science, law and political economy. Perhaps at some other time I might have chosen other sciences.'

Kazan is the capital of the middle Volga. Today it is the capital of the Autonomous Republic of the Tartars which is part of the Russian Federation, seventy per cent of Kazan inhabitants being Tartars. It has mosques and monasteries, churches and an old Kremlin.

Although advertised in pamphlets and posters, Kazan is not an easy city to reach. All I was allowed, after a great deal of pressure, was a single day there with another APN man – nice Feodor – and a taut, silent Tartar student who emphasized I should not take panoramic photographs of the Volga, although I could not see a single suspect item on the skyline.

With almost a million inhabitants, it is an industrial city. It has a large harbour on the Volga which is immense around Kazan, at one point twenty kilometres wide; they call it 'the Volga ocean'.

But Kazan looks like a provincial centre. Somehow it reminded me of a north Italian town, with its long boulevards, stucco-painted houses in golden ochre and bright white, a touch of Este, a southern torpor. Yet southern it is not; winters there are frozen, they say, and beautiful, the white and ochre city glittering with icicles.

The main hotel was the usual mixture of grandiosity and discomfort, capriciously wide, gilded corridors and hole-like

184

offices. Nothing seemed to be on sale in the shops of Kazan, and the restaurants were lamentable. But Kazan was very charming. I didn't see the mosques, and only managed to glimpse some baroque churches. My curiosity met with intolerant fury from my Tartar watch-dog and soon I had to give up such decadent pleasures.

Until Ivan the Terrible* took over the Kazan *khanate* in 1552, that city was one of the main seats of Mongol domination. The other *khanates* were in the Crimea, Astrakhan and in the city of Sibir, all three along the southern and eastern Russian frontiers. Four years after the conquest of Kazan, the Russians took the *khanate* of Astrakhan and became masters of the Volga.

What had two hundred and fifty years of Tartar domination contributed to Russian culture? Pushkin said that the Mongols were 'Arabs without Aristotle or algebra'; that is to say, they contributed nothing. Christianity took the Tartar domination as a sign of punishment for the sins of humanity, and this contributed to the withdrawal of men to monasteries and hermitages, into deeper and deeper asceticism, and it led to an acceptance of calamity which was to mark the Russian character for ever.

Kazan is dominated by a splendid Kremlin founded by Khan Ulu-Makhmet in the fifteen century and surrounded by a palisade. But the stone walls which still remain were built by Ivan IV, Ivan the Awesome.

'In passing, I took Kazan,
Brought Tsar Simeon under my power,
Stripped him of his imperial purple
Conveyed it to stone-walled Moscow
Christened it in Moscow.
I then dressed myself in the purple
Whereupon I became the Tsar Terrible.'

The Kremlin, or fortified citadel, is enclosed by these whitewashed walls and guarded by three squat towers. It makes a beautiful ensemble – with straight roads leading

* A mistranslation of a word which really means 'awesome' and not 'bad'.

to the main group. This is made up of the former residence of the Archbishop of Kazan, the castle, former residence of the governor of Kazan, and the beautiful seven-storey Sovioumbek tower, the only remaining piece of Tartar architecture. The tower looks as if it had been built by a boy playing on a beach with sand, superimposing square blocks of sand, decreasing in size towards the top.

Kazan is Russian history: it is of strategic importance, dominating the Volga and communications with the Caspian Sea. The Virgin of Kazan, excavated from the grounds of the Bogoroditsky convent became the emblem of Christian Russia on the banner of Alexander Nevsky and was brought to St Petersburg, where a whole cathedral was built for it.

Lenin's father had studied at Kazan University, as indeed did his brilliant seventeen-year-old son Vladimir. It must have been a relief to breathe a different air from that of the suffocatingly provincial Simbirsk. Yet the Ulyanovs could not escape the label of notoriety: 'Wouldn't that be the brother of the other Ulyanov? Didn't he come from Simbirsk, too?' an official marked on the margin of a paper concerning Vladimir.

Maria Alexandrovna found a tiny wooden house in Komlei uliza, off the Siberian highway, and there the Ulyanovs lived in the summer and autumn of 1887 until, on 5 December, Vladimir was arrested during the night and banned from the university and from Kazan. The previous day there had been a student demonstration at the university and Vladimir had taken part in it. The little wooden house in Komlei uliza, today a public library, retains the aroma of wood polished with meticulous care by Maria Alexandrovna. Somehow there is more atmosphere in the house where the Ulyanovs lived for such a short time, but which is not a museum, than in all the others I had seen.

On the basement floor the large window lit doll-sized rooms, doors were still covered in black soft leather and the unpolished timber stairs leading to the upper floor were small and steep. Those rooms upstairs were even smaller and some of the tiny windows overlooked an internal court-yard and fountain.

The librarian, a young girl, took me around gladly, but there wasn't much ground to cover. The Ulyanovs must have been very cramped in Komlei uliza. There was an attic at the top, its ceiling following the pointed line of the roof.

Every day, until December, Vladimir used to walk to the university; it was a long way to the central square where the 1804 solid white colonnaded building in classical style was located. Today it is still alive with students, with their high cheekbones, small noses, handsome young Slav-Tartar faces. Along the wide staircase, a small, simple plaque reads: 'Here, in the Law faculty, Vladimir Ilyich Ulyanov-Lenin studied in the year 1887.'

The room where Lenin studied still contains elegant brass gas lamps with dark green shades hanging like rigid geometric mobiles from the high ceiling, the white wallpaper had a fine gilded motif, the large stove is finished in brass. It reflects the atmosphere of Tsarist universities, elegant, selective and intimidating. Students were made to feel that they were lucky to be there at all.

After the ban from Kazan, the Ulyanovs left the wooden box and joined Anna who was living under house arrest in Maria Alexandrovna's paternal house at Kukushkino, a lovely simple house surrounded by birch trees, with a river close by where the young ones swam. Vladimir was a good and energetic swimmer. There was a pergola near the house. Vladimir used to read in the open: he had read a great deal in this period, he later was to say, and fled the house to the garden whenever visitors arrived. The Ulyanovs were a close family, preferring each other's company to most. Somebody new had joined them, Anna's fiancé Mark Timofeyevich Elisarov, who was to become Lenin's brother-in-law. Maria Alexandrovna never gave up trying to persuade the authorities to accept an application for Vladimir's continuation of his studies. This failed, but she obtained permission for him to go back and live in Kazan.

This time they rented another house. It was outside Kazan, on the eastern Tartar peasant side and in front there was a wooded garden, and at the back a steep ravine – at the bottom of which the poor peasants lived, and still do live, in wretched wooden boxes. On the first floor, there was a large terrace-veranda in carved wood – a perfect shelter for summer reading. At the back of the house there was another smaller entrance which Vladimir used, climbing down from it to the ravine to escape police surveillance. This is an important house. It was there that Vladimir read Marx's *Kapital* for the first time. 'When I came down for a chat, he would be sitting on the kitchen stove, strewn with back numbers of newspapers, and, gesticulating violently, he would tell me with burning enthusiasm about the principles of Marxist theory and the new horizons it was opening for him,' wrote Anna Ilychna Ulyanovna in her *Memoirs*.

Vladimir was discovering at the time scientific methods of revolution to replace the 'terrorist' methods applied by the anti-régime groups, of the Narodniks, which had wasted so many lives, including his own brother's.

After a brief period living near the Volga, Vladimir Ilyich went to St Petersburg with his sister Olga, where he was allowed to take his final examinations and where he graduated brilliantly. But the talented, good-looking and hard-working Olga came down with typhoid fever and died. She was only nineteen.

Nothing is left of the original Finland Station, the destination of that famous train which in April 1917 carried the yeast of the revolution across Germany. It was wiped out by German bombs. There is only a huge and famous statue of Lenin, erected in 1926, standing high on the square facing the new building. But there is still the steam engine that belonged to the train which Lenin took when he went into hiding to escape the provisional government in what was then Finnish Razliv and is now Soviet Razliv. The landscape there is marvellous, with lakes and rivers reflecting high dark woods. In the interior of a long, thin peninsula where the trees are high and dense, Lenin lived in a hut placed in a sunny glade. The hut, when I visited it, was surrounded by a meadow covered with wild lilies-of-the-valley. His office was in the open air: two trees had been cut down and the trunks served as a chair and as a table. In Razliv Lenin wrote one book, several articles and conducted the activities at the Smolny, the headquarters of the Soviet.

In the Smolny Institute for Young Ladies of Noble Birth, built in 1805 near the Smolny Sabor (by Rastrelli) is one of the most beautiful ensembles of beautiful Leningrad. When Lenin arrived, the headquarters of the Soviets was in ferment; on 10 October, presiding over the Central Committee of the Bolshevik party at 32 Naberezhnaya karpovsky, Lenin decided to rise against the Kerensky government.

'The blue and gold cupola of Smolny Convent announces from afar the headquarters of the insurrection' (Trotsky's *History of the Russian Revolution*). It is situated on the edge of the city where the tramline ends and the Neva describes a sharp turn southwards, and it separates the centre of the capital from the suburbs. That long grey three-storey building, an educative barracks for the daughters of the nobility, is now the stronghold of the Soviets. Its long, echoing corridors seem to have been designed to illustrate the laws of perspective. Over the doors of many of the rooms along the corridors little enamelled tablets are still preserved: 'Teacher's room'. 'Third Grade'. 'Fourth Grade'. 'Grand Supervisor'. But alongside the old tablets, or covering them, sheets of paper have been tacked up in casual fashion, bearing the mysterious hieroglyphics of the revolution: Tz K P-S-R, S-D Mensheviki, S-S Bolsheviki, Left S-R, Anarchist-Communists, Despatching Room of the Tz-I-K etc., etc. The observant John Reed noticed a placard on the walls: 'Comrades, for the sake of your own health, observe cleanliness.' Alas, nobody observes cleanliness – not even nature. In October, Petrograd is deluged with rain. The streets, long unswept, are dirty. There are enormous puddles in the court of Smolny. The mud is carried inside by the soldiers' boots. But nobody looks down; everyone looks forward.

The memorial plaque on the Smolny reads: 'Here, in Smolny, were the headquarters of the armed uprising of workers, soldiers and sailors in the days of the great October revolution of 1917. Vladimir Ulyanov Lenin himself directed the armed uprising from Smolny.'

Lenin died at Gorki, the former residence of the ex-Governor of Moscow. His body was carried forty-five kilometres along the snow-covered road to Moscow, under the white birch trees glittering with icicles.

The villa near Gorki where he had spent his last days was secluded and remote. He and Krupskaya first lived in the right-hand wing of the villa; typically, Lenin wanted to avoid the grand main residence.

On Lenin's bedside table was a book by Plenkhanov and Heine's works. The room was small, from his bed he could see through the double-glazed window to the birches in the garden below. In this room, as usual, he wrote and worked. On his desk lay his pen and many of those famous little pieces of paper on which he noted down ideas, communications and orders. The décor of the room had a Swiss touch: the small sofa and chairs were covered in blue-and-white striped cotton. In Krupskaya's room (they never shared a room, like Lenin's parents) petit-point decorations hung from the wall and there were many books: Tolstoy, Shakespeare and the History of German Social Democracy.

Next were the rooms of Lenin's sisters: what would he have done without those women, his patient, dedicated and skilful secretaries?

When the doctor ordered Vladimir Ilyich to move to a less damp room, the family settled in the main house which opens into a colonnaded portico in the garden. It was there that Lenin died.

While he was still able to walk and could go downstairs, Lenin used to receive delegations in a large study on the ground floor: he still read an immense amount, mainly political works, but I also noticed a book by Goethe.

There he would receive the visits of Maxim Gorki, a man for whom he felt a deep affection in both pre- and post-revolutionary days, a friendship dictated neither by political struggle nor by blood ties (as was often the case with Lenin). Vladimir Ilyich had even gone to rest at Gorki's villa in Capri: Capri! a decadent place void of revolutionaries or Marxists; Lenin must have liked his friend a great deal to allow himself to waste his time in rest, playing chess in the blue Gulf of Naples.

Gorki, and also Krupskaya and Anna Ilyichna, wrote about Lenin and left details and observations which would have never reached us otherwise. It is a pity that while they were writing, Stalin was breathing censoriously down their necks, but their accounts are still fascinating. Lenin surrounded himself with literary people; a contrast to Stalin whose own writing was very poor.

In the last of Lenin's residences one can feel the sorrow of his enforced rests; his wheel-chair had been motorized, yet it was still a wheel-chair. The banisters of the stairs had been reinforced so he could lean on them safely: the man who had trained his body to be strong in prison cells and exile must have been reduced to exasperation by his enforced inactivity.

And yet, one can imagine that he must have had moments of peace on the veranda of that house, drinking tea from the samovar which is still on the dining-table, sitting on the straw chair with Gorki and Krupskaya and his sisters, looking at the long avenues stretching from the house down to the woods. That house at Gorki was enchanting, with large rooms surrounded by trees, and flowery or white lace curtains.

When he could no longer go downstairs, Lenin worked in a large room which was also Krupskaya's bedroom, connected to the dining-room from one side and to Lenin's own bedroom on the other. The large window over a terrace had rich, soft pink curtains. On a *directoire* desk there was a pot of glue, books, pieces of paper for notes and messages.

Lenin died in a room lit by four double-glazed windows, brushed inside by white lace curtains and outside by the branches of the trees. A screen discreetly sheltered Lenin's bed; next to it there was a brass bell, Jack London's *Love and Life,* the last book he read, Gorki's *My University* and three bottles of medicine. The room was glittering white in contrast with the dark wooden parquet, which gave it a hospital atmosphere. On a table, there was Lenin's stick, which he needed when he left his bed. The room opened into Krupskaya's bedroom and into the room in which he was to lie in state. At Gorki I looked at the masks of Lenin's hand and face: they were marked by the lines of a man of iron.

I went down to the large hall in the Mausoleum in that Square where Lenin's body lies under glass. Soldiers stood all around it, the dim light of the flame barely showing the shiny inlaid marble walls, with the strong lighting focused on the metal and glass coffin, on the short body dressed in a black suit. Walking round those walls and looking down at the coffin, I felt almost ashamed to turn my eyes towards the body I had come to inspect, as if such curiosity was demeaning both to the observed and to the observer. Glimpsing 'it', I stared with more determination at the faces around me, all turned towards that small body. What did they feel? If only I could have asked them, there and then. Yet the silence was total, except for one unfortunate creature who, walking too fast, tripped noisily and was silenced, still more noisily, by the militiamen.

But I found the Mausoleum fascinating, severe and austere, a work of architectural genius, combining the materialism of the cubist age with the spiritual atmosphere of the Nile tombs. I felt like queueing all over again and going back in.

When I reached the open air, the crowd followed the path behind the Mausoleum where Stalin's tomb had just received the fresh homage of a bunch of flowers. Beside it, there was also a plastic rose, undatable. The Mausoleum was really a phenomenon of reverence and devotion which I had also felt. But Lenin's presence I had found elsewhere, in public libraries, schools, but always far, far from Moscow.

Volgograd

I was walking along the banks of the Volga looking at what was listed as Volgograd's 'curiosities': the Square of the Dead, the Avenue of Heroes, the Square of Fallen Fighters: Volgograd's topography sounded like the 'In Memoriam' column of *The Times*.

A city of 800,000 inhabitants, Volgograd has been rebuilt to three times its original size since its almost total destruction in the famous battle of Stalingrad. Since the ground is sandy and marked by ravines, and the houses are not built higher than six-to-seven floors, so the skyline is low.

Until 1925 its name was Tsaritsyn, it then became Stalingrad but after Khrushchev's 'secret speech', the city voted to become Volgograd. It was a good idea to rename the city after the river. Of course, even the Volga could be renamed. But though Soviet leaders have named mountains, cities, factories after themselves, they never thought to rename rivers. Could we be sailing on Brezhnev river? Or could the Volga have the honour of being named after Suslov? Suslovia, Suslovrieka, Suslovna: the name already sounded familiar. 'The floods of the Suslovia . . . the beautiful woods overlooking the windy Suslovia . . .'

Volgograd is an industrial centre stretching for seventy kilometres along the European bank of the Volga. The factories are all close to the river, their transport artery. Volgograd produces tractors, and also the special steel with which the Sputniks were made, fifty-five per cent of Soviet mustard (its flowers blooming in the steppes) and ninety-nine per cent of the world reserve of caviar, which swims between Astrakhan and Volgograd.

The area of which Volgograd is the capital is as large as Holland, Denmark and Belgium put together, it is a steppe area containing only five per cent of woodland and is inhabited by the Saigak, the antelope of the steppes, an animal with a long nose and legs. It can survive for days without water and can run at over eighty kilometres an hour.

Not even the most optimistic eye could classify Volgograd as a beautiful city, but the strength and the pride of the city is catching and indeed Volgograd was one of the cities I liked most in the Soviet Union.

While I walked, a steppe-wind pushed me about; I had been told about those winds which come in turn from the south, breathing sand and hot air, and from the Arctic finding no obstacles in mountains or trees, changing the climate from one day to the next. In 1968 the ground froze two-and-a-half metres deep, killing over seventy thousand trees. If that wind were to blow for the rest of the week, I would be stuck in Volgograd and would never reach Rostov.

As I walked slowly along the embankment, I suddenly thought that I recognized the couple next to the gigantic white-chalk monument. The sight of the tall, pink man and the fragile woman flanked by an unmistakably Intourist guide was familiar.

As I approached, the big Australian and his tiny wife stopped listening obediently to the guide. 'Hi!' he said. 'Fancy meeting you here . . . How've you been?'

That encounter surely meant that Kostia would have been waiting for me at Rostov's airport.

'Well, so long, I guess we'll meet around the place.'

The Australians had tracked me down.

Valentin Liednuv was APN's man in Volgograd; since he was going to report on a meeting of the Volgograd Writers Union, he took me along. The Union was located in the 'Press House', the building where all newspapers, *Pravda*, *Izvestia* and local papers, are printed. The smell of typographical ink mixed with the smell of fried onions as we climbed the steep cement stairs; the atmosphere of the building was that of a run-down bed-and-breakfast Cromwell Road hotel rather than of a 'Communication house'.

We sneaked into a crowded room where twenty-five writers sat on wooden school benches discussing and listening to a speaker. Valentin interrupted and introduced me to the President of the Union, who seemed to have received a great deal of medals. 'I have with me a foreign writer, Citizen Mostran-Vove, who lives in Italy but comes from England and is writing a book about Lenin.'

I bowed my head and we all smiled at each other in a Japanese fashion, after which the debate was resumed.

There were various proposals and speeches, some of which were of a length and verbosity worthy of Italian parliamentarians. There was trouble in Volgograd: the most famous and talented poets were leaving the city; what was the Union to do? One speaker who had been already talking for an hour, emphatically waving his hands in the air and speaking as if he were declaiming a poem by Blok or Lermontov, gave no sign of ever coming to an end. 'We like to talk here,' said Valentin, rather hoping the message would reach the ear of the orator. It did not and so I left, bowing and begging to be forgiven.

With me came Svietlana, a girl of twenty-eight whose ambition was to become a writer and journalist.

'Give me some advice,' she said.

But how did journalism work in the Soviet Union? I asked her. Surely differently, if people had to write articles forty-eight pages long, as one journalist told me.

'It is very difficult for a woman to work in this branch,' she added.

She was married, Svietlana, to the proverbial engineer and had the proverbial one child looked after by the proverbial mother-in-law. Her hair was yellow as scrambled eggs and lined at the roots with a severe black halo.

'You know,' she said confidentially, 'this is not my natural colour.'

Nature had also not been left to itself as far as Svietlana's eyebrows were concerned: these had been severely plucked, leaving her with a thin Rosalind Russell arch and a constant expression of wonder.

She wasn't quite satisfied by the results, but what could she do?

I set to work to improve Svietlana's looks, giving her a detailed demonstration. She was sweet, full of good will, naiveté and warmth. She also had a flattering attitude towards me. She had been waiting for the arrival of someone like me. She wanted to learn everything at all costs and we had long chats, meals, and went to the theatre together. She came from the south near Rostov, and she had come to study at Volgograd University where she had met her future husband.

Svietlana had shocked her parents by her modernity, smoking cigarettes, dyeing her hair, wearing short skirts. She had her own clothes made by a woman who sewed privately for ten roubles a dress and twenty for a coat (in Moscow one couldn't find anything so cheap). Or she would go to what they call an *atelier* where prices were higher, but the dresses prettier. She was in fact neatly and smartly dressed.

As usual in the Soviet Union, Svietlana thought that few cities in the world could rival Volgograd in modernity, power and beauty. She wasn't politically-minded although when we once discussed Trotsky, she was shocked by my fascination for the disgraced leader. But she said: 'Portraits of Trotsky were shown everywhere when my parents were young after the revolution; he was very popular then. But he wasn't a good man. They discovered that he wanted to give St Petersburg to the Germans because that was the most revolutionary city in Russia. After the revolution Trotsky regretted it and wanted to crush it.'

The hotel I was staying in was marvellous, with large halls, stucco decorations, immense marble stairs, huge rooms, crystal chandeliers, a large dining-room whose guests consisted of a delegation of Bulgarian army officers, the Australian couple, Svietlana and myself. It surprised me that the war had spared this Ritz-like hotel. 'Oh, no. It was built in 1958,'

196

Svietlana explained to my astonishment. A city full of surprises!

Another pleasant surprise was in the hotel restaurant, the Volga's fish, the *Stierliad*, the *sudak*, the sturgeon were fresh, well cooked and quickly served, the vodka iced, the waitresses sweet and the caviar, oh the caviar, was large, fresh, plentiful, and served with parsley butter and black bread. What wouldn't a Moscovite have done for such caviar? Startled by my voracity, the Australian couple remarked on the poor quality and monotony of Soviet cooking. I suggested they try the caviar.

'But I don't like caviar,' said the Australian wife.

The Left Bank

I was hoping to cross the Volga by boat and visit the other side. The many landing stages along the Volga beckoned tourists invitingly. There were busy crowds on the landing stages carrying parcels, bursting bags, baskets, oddities, pieces of wood, vegetables. One of those landing places served the boat which crossed the river to a small village facing Volgograd. When I said I was heading there, Svietlana looked a bit doubtful, although I stressed that I was going on my own and she should not worry. But then she decided to join me.

The wooden landing stage was poetic, painted in white, displaying red flags; the charm of communications, travel, the importance of the Volga spelled out in visual terms.

The usual two militiamen stopped us and asked Svietlana why I wanted to cross the Volga. She explained that I was a writer. 'We'll take the same boat back to Volgograd; it will give us twenty minutes on the other bank,' she said to me. What was there to hide? The view of the factories? It couldn't be that: tractors and steel are not such mysterious products. But a knowledge of the Soviet mind told me that on the other side of the Volga I would have found a poor village in great contrast with the cement city of Volgograd, a village where roads were turned into rivers of mud by the flooding Volga, leading to small timber houses, where the peasants would carry their poor possessions and would remind me of the Volga *muzhik* of bygone days.

Svietlana and I settled down on the deck of the boat, since the wind had at last dropped, though the Volga looked grey. We passed the island of Tsaritzin.

The boat was filled with old people, the men wearing the peaked Volga hat, their wrinkled, suntanned faces sheltered from the violent light; the women had covered their heads with the traditional scarves and carried bags filled with bits and pieces. The young people, on the other hand, looked modern in their clothes and behaviour.

We all sat close together. 'Have a cigarette.' I offered one to Svietlana.

'Not here, it's not done for women to smoke in public.'

'But you generally smoke.'

'Yes, but not in public, people would talk; this is a provincial city.'

I lit mine. 'You can do it, you *should* do it,' she added.

After a few minutes we started to chat with the group around us. Where? What? How? Why?

The women from time to time digressed among themselves. 'What do you think of her coat?' 'It is an evening coat, it shouldn't be worn like that.' 'But if she has a good coat, she ought to wear it in the morning as well as in the evening.' 'But the shoes are too much of a contrast, I wouldn't wear them. They are too masculine.' 'You are right, they don't go well with her coat.'

'What sort of house have you got?' a young girl asked.

'Who's looking after your children when you are away? Your mother?'

'She lives in Italy.'

'Your mother-in-law?'

'No, I work and with most of what I earn I pay somebody to look after my family.'

'Some rich people do the same here.'

'Sorry,' Svietlana whispered, 'you're getting so much attention because few foreigners come to Volgograd.'

'We have few English visitors,' one woman said.

I felt ashamed to come from Italy, the former ally of Nazi Germany in a city like Volgograd. In the same way I almost dared not show my face in Yugoslavia.

'But we have delegations of German visitors.'

'Really?' I asked 'And what do you feel about them now?'

'Phew, you know Germans protest here, saying that in telling the history of the battle of Stalingrad, the Russians are one-sided and don't mention the heroism of the German army as well.'

'Why do you wear those shoes?' insisted another woman.

The boat was almost touching the other bank and sailors hooked it to the small wooden raft. We all descended and walked down a sandy peninsula with small boats moored alongside. Birch trees were reflected in the flooding Volga and flowers covered the meadows. Half a kilometre away stood the wooden village reached by a sandy path, most of which had been covered with wooden planks to save it from the rising, thawing river. The water formed capricious shapes, islands, tiny bays shaded by thin tall trees growing out of the water. On the opposite side, Volgograd stretched in all its seventy kilometres, factories and high monuments, Mother Russia in cement towering high over the Mamai hill.

People walked towards the village carrying baskets on their heads.

Since Svietlana and I had to return to please the militiamen who were waiting our return on the other bank, I made a point of coming back the following day.

In order to avoid Svietlana's overwhelming company, I pretended to have an earlier appointment at ten and sneaked away from the hotel one hour sooner. This time I knew my way about the different landing stages and found no militia. A quantity of peasants disembarked from a boat arriving from the village – to sell flowers and vegetables at the market. One man was carrying a table over his head, children were playing on the sunny deck, staring at me with their limpid blue Volga eyes.

As we arrived on the other side, the procession rolled on again and women carrying bread-filled baskets on their heads, walked towards the village.

The slow procession gave one a timeless sensation of peasants walking patiently to and fro, a constant human wave in slow and continuous motion – as bulky as the Volga, hiding a strength under their loaded heads, a strength of endurance and patience.

Bigger boats passed on the river on their way to Saratov.

'Hey, *dievushka*,' an old woman loaded with parcels shouted towards me, 'is that what they wear in your country?'

'Yes, *babushka*,' I answered. 'Do you like it?'

'And do you like it here? This is no place for foreigners, you know.'

'It's a beautiful spot,' I said.

'But poor. Now I'm going home to rest,' she said and waved at me, freeing one hand from her parcels.

I walked on to the village, but I wasn't welcomed there. Yet the village had its beauty and in contrast to Volgograd, which was a symbol of achievement, it represented the past. Volgograd with its monuments and factories, the wooden village with its tiny rooms and huge stoves.

'Hey, *dievushka*.' I turned.

Dievushka means 'young girl' but everybody of female sex is called *dievushka* until she reaches sixty, the age of the *babushka*. The waitress, the postal employee, Svietlana, they are addressed as *dievushkas*. 'Since the word "Mrs" has been abolished,' Svietlana once explained, 'we now need new words for addressing people. The Soviet Academy is studying the problem.'

'Will they invent new words?'

'They might.'

A man in a peaked cap shouted: 'You are not supposed to be here surely?'

'Don't you start,' I answered angrily.

'No, no, I think it is silly to forbid tourists to come and see what they like, but I know they are forbidden.'

Alexei ('Call me Alioshka') was crossing the river back to Volgograd, so we went together.

'Alexei is Alioshka,' he told me, 'always. Nicolas is Kolia or Nikita, like Khrushchev. Sierghiei is Sierioshka or Seriosa, Grigori Grisha, Lara Larissa Larinka Lala, Mikhail Misha, Alexander Sasha, Nadia Nadieshda and so on. We never use proper names here.'

'I like that.'

He explained that family names were comparatively recent since before the liberation of the serfs, the bulk of the population only had first names and patronymics.

'But the aristocracy and the bourgeoisie had surnames. Those in "ov" like mine, Alexandrov, is simply the genitive plural. My father is called Sierghiei, so my full name is Alexei Sierghievich Alexandrov.'

'So I shall call you Alexei Sierghievich.'

'No, you can call me Alioshka. If I were an older man, a professor or a big boss, you would use the patronymic, but I am not so old, am I?'

He had been married and divorced. 'Volgograd has the highest number of divorces in the Soviet Union. I don't know why, but if one doesn't get along, what's the good of living together?' Had it been easy to get a divorce? Yes, it always is if both partners agree, although it had been made slightly more difficult recently.

'You are the first foreigner I've ever talked to in my life and you arrive in Volgograd, have a look and go back to your country. Our country is big, yet one feels claustrophobic; I have my passport, I have money, I would like to see the world. Why can't I?'

'You know perhaps one day it will be possible . . .'

'One day, one day . . . but you travel now. What is it like in the West? Is it different? What is better there? Is it true that it is so corrupt, that young people are so lost? I am curious to know, please, tell me.'

We were walking slowly. 'I am a shop-assistant, and I don't do badly, but I am simple and yet you talk to me and you are a Westerner. So I see that Westerners are not all like we are told they are.' We drank *kvass*. 'Everybody looks at your coat because everybody would like one like it. Our clothes look bad; if they could, people would like to have a coat like yours and then buy a better one still. Shoes are not expensive, though. Good ones cost thirty to thirty-five roubles. The trouble,' Alioshka said, 'is politics. We spend too much money on foreign countries, like Vietnam, while we don't have money at home. Look, we had civil wars, we had to rebuild everything, now we need money to spend on ourselves. You saw it with the militia, we are not free here. They also build too many monuments and too few houses and places for us to go and have a cup of tea or a glass of beer. I would like to go to England and see more British tourists come here. Thirty of you, a hundred of you, so we would get to know each other. You know why we didn't get to the moon first? Because we haven't got the money.'

'Look, Alioshka,' I said, 'be careful when you talk like this.'

'That's the Institute for Party Workers,' said Alioshka pointing at a huge building. 'When they graduate, they work for the Communist Party. It is an institute that just teaches the art of conversation. Perhaps I shouldn't speak like this,' he warned himself.

We went to the market where many people were crowded in front of the wooden stalls. I bought some pretty cotton scarves printed in Slav motifs, more attractive than the ones in the *Berioshka* foreign currency shops. Then we went on to the flower market. 'My British guest,' Alioshka would say, 'wants red and yellow tulips. Yellow is for goodbye, you shouldn't get that colour, red is for love and white is for beginning.'

We went to the embankment. 'Do many women smoke in England?'

'Rather a lot.' I looked at my cigarette. 'Do you mind?'

'We are very conventional here. I don't mind at all. I like the way you do what you like.' His blue liquid eyes looked sad under his large cap. 'What Russian products do

foreigners like best? I have heard they like Russian sweets.'
Somebody must have been spreading that odd rumour.
'What do you like best in Russia?'

'The people,' I said.

We went to the Droujba fountain. 'Let's have a photo
taken in colour, so that we'll remember our meeting,' he
said.

We walked towards the photographer who stood next
to a large camera.

'Comrade photographer, I have a British friend with me.
She has come all the way to Volgograd, so you must take a
beautiful photo so I can send her a copy. When will it be
ready?'

'Comrade, what is your name?' the photographer asked
me. 'Good, then, I would like to see you standing like that,
putting the flowers next to your face, and smiling, a big
smile . . . in the background we'll get the monument . . .'

'And the Volga . . . ?'

'In that case, you'll have to move further, there.'

'Shall I keep my cap on?' Alioshka said.

The photographer and I came to the conclusion that no,
Alioshka should take his cap off. 'She is a British writer,'
Alioshka explained proudly.

'Do you know our Lermontov and our Pushkin?' asked
the photographer who began to recite Lermontov.

We finally posed, very stiff, and smiled, the Volga in
the background.

'I shall send you a copy,' said Alioshka.

'And send me your address, so that I can answer.'

'I promise I shall.'

I never received either, though I am sure Alioshka sent
both photo and address.

Stalingrad

Stalingrad was the gateway to the oilfields of Baku, to Asia,
to the inexhaustible labour forces and mines Hitler dreamed
of.

The story of the battle of Stalingrad is well known; for two hundred days the city fought, every house, every wall becoming a front. Children who were sent to safety by boats to the other side of the Volga on those *pieraprava* died in sight of their helpless parents when the boats were hit by bombs. Eighty-five per cent of the city was destroyed. Of the débris, one building is preserved, the Mill. This gives an idea of what the city must have been like: every brick has been burned, hit by bullets.

As it stands today, Stalingrad-Volgograd is a monument to the Russian will to survive – of its optimism. The modern city is large, pulsing with life; it looks as if the Germans hadn't been able to touch it. Volgograd affects one emotionally and gives one an understanding of the Russian character: it is not a city of laments, it doesn't provoke the pangs Dachau or villages like Marzabotto do. In fact, it is gay and proud.

There is a cemetery on the hill within the city where ten thousand Russian soldiers killed in battle with the Germans are buried. It contains a complex of monuments, dominated by a gigantic Mother Russia brandishing a sword and calling her sons to her defence. On the sides of the hill are many tombs. There's a kind of Pantheon whose roof is open to the sky: a huge fist holds an eternal flame, a chorus sings Schumann in perpetuity, and sentries stand to attention.

Descending past realistic statues describing the history of the battle, is a huge flight of stairs flanked by walls bearing inscriptions left by the dying. It is a popular monument which just misses being ugly. It tells a heroic story, rather like a Greek epic recounted by the more prosaic Romans. It has not the lightness and beauty of the 'Victory of Samothrace', but my heart went out to it. I thought of those colossal battles which could have changed history, like the Greek victory over the Persians. Had Stalingrad been lost, Hitler might have been victorious.

Stalingrad fought for the West as well.

The Sturgeons

After paying a visit to the Volgograd Planetarium, I decided to dedicate my day to the queen of the Volga: the sturgeon.

The wind had started blowing again and the high walls of the gigantic dam outside Volgograd were deserted except for a good-looking young woman with short hair blowing in the wind, dressed in a white PVC jacket, red skirt and matching shoes.

'Are you interested in the dam?' she asked.

'I have come to see the sturgeons. Do you know where I should go? Do you know anything about it?'

She looked at me with a surprised expression I couldn't quite understand. 'Come this way.' She took me to the southern side of the dam. 'There, you see, are two "cages" which are opened in turn and filled with sturgeon which are going north to spawn. Every three hours one of the "cages" is moved along the width of the dam and then a net lifts the fish up to another "cage" to the level of the higher side of the Volga. The cage is then opened and the sturgeons can progress on their journey.'

The dam was so high, one got vertigo. 'Does the sturgeon die after spawning?' I asked.

'No, but it is so exhausted from its journey, since it doesn't eat on its way north but just uses its fat reserves, that on its return it is very weakened. It tends to roll on the bottom of the river and often gets wounded by stones.'

She was pretty and looked like a heroine from 'The Avengers'.

'Why do you know so much about it?' I asked.

'Me? I am the engineer in charge.'

I looked at her again in amazement: she certainly looked efficient.

'They start producing the caviar when they are fifteen years old, and they are fertile every three or four years.'

'How long can a sturgeon live?'

'Sixty or sixty-five years; some sturgeons don't catch the current and don't get into any of the gates of the "cages". So they spend the winter at the bottom of the river in a layer of fat which they form round themselves to protect their bodies from the cold; in the spring they resume their journey to spawn, but it is too late; the caviar is no longer fertile.'

'Do they all migrate at the same time?'

'No, there are autumn, summer and spring sturgeon, but the migration always follows the warm season. Now it is rather cold, so you won't see many animals.'

She showed me the way into the concrete dam – we descended steep iron steps towards a deep square chamber. At the bottom there was the water of the Volga.

'You wait, the net is coming up with the sturgeon.' And she left me saying: 'I must go, I am on duty upstairs.'

I stood in the deep chamber over a strip of metal hung half-way across the emptiness. There were two other people opposite me: a man and an elderly woman with a camera. She shouted: 'It's coming up. There'll be other kinds of fish as well.'

A big cable lifted the net and as the sturgeon came into view, strong reflectors lit the bottom of the square chamber; the lady took a photograph.

There they were, the colossal inhabitants of the Volga. Belugas, Sevrugas, their pre-historic muzzles, their big bodies struggling in the air. Soon the water coming from the upper side of the Volga submerged the animals and they disappeared from sight.

'Did you enjoy it?' said the woman. 'At times we get many more. I have photographed up to 450 at a time.'

'Do you work here?' I asked. I had thought she was an eager tourist like myself.

'I am the fish biologist here and I take a full record of how many sturgeons pass each season, each year.' She told me that a sturgeon of thirty-five kilos gives seven of caviar – that a female carries a fifth of her weight in caviar.

'We have a nursery near here and we spawn the caviar artificially. About one third of the sturgeon in the Volga today comes from there.'

Easter in Rostov

Nobody at all was there to meet me at Rostov Airport, least of all Kostia. But later I was handed a telegram.

Before I opened it, I made a mental bet with myself that the text would have started *K soshalienniu,* the Soviet word par excellence, the 'unfortunately' with which everything is forgiven, the *nichevo* of modern times. Little consolation, I won my bet: 'Unfortunately unable come Rostov please let me know exactly when you will be in Moscow again Kostia.'

To hell with him, I thought. I decided to wipe Kostia from my memory, and, in a bad mood, I joined Piotr Alieksievich Iashenko, APN's correspondent in Rostov. But Piotr Alieksievich was too nice and gentle a person for my temper to last and, helped by a sunny day and the sight of the busy river Don, my mood improved.

Rostov-on-the-Don is a southern city where vines grow, but winters can still be harsh, although not in the full Russian sense. It is the centre of the Don Cossack country. The origin of the word Cossack is Turkish; it means 'free man, independent man'. It doesn't indicate a race, but a group of people who from the sixteenth to the seventeenth centuries, unable to pay debts, living in conditions very close to slavery, fled the state of Moscow and formed autonomous entities at the border of the country. So they colonized the land lately taken from the Tartars or expelled them and became lawless frontiermen, living on horseback. They were the masters of the steppes. Bands of Cossacks swollen by criminals, run-away slaves, Tartars, romantic noblemen (like Oleghin in Tolstoy's *The Cossacks*) lived by brigandage. There was also a strong democratic element among the Cossacks and it was around these anarchic nuclei that rebellions sprang up. The main groups of Cossacks lived in southern and south-eastern Russia, particularly along the Don, in the Caucasus and in the Lithuanian-controlled Ukraine. To the west there were the Zaporogian Cossacks – whose headquarters were on an island on the Dnieper 'below the rapids' *za porogi*.

The Tsars began to use the Cossacks without subduing them and they often became auxiliaries in the Tsar's army as in the conquest of Siberia and later, in the White army.

It was Russian Easter. The large cathedral surmounted by numerous domes became the centre of the city. Crowds swarmed around its walls and formed a long queue waiting to get to the inner courtyard. It was finally swallowed up in the darkness of the interior. There were old women wearing black shawls over their heads and carrying baskets full of coloured eggs and cakes covered with candles. The dark air was sticky with sweet incense and oily sweat.

The icons were positively ugly, though their strong colours were softened by the dimness of the light. The crowds pushed inside and formed separate circles leaving empty spaces in the middle. Coloured eggs, cakes and ears of wheat were laid on the floor and a line of dignitaries in rich golden robes, their long hair and beards flowing over the glittering embroideries, came to bless the offerings. An egg from each group of blessed items was placed in a large basket and taken into the church.

Piotr Alieksievich and I walked away under the large boulevards shadowed by huge trees. He was around forty-five and had a daughter of fourteen who studied English at school.

'I thought we might go out together, tonight, with my daughter so she can practise her English a little. Perhaps we could go to the circus? We have one of the most beautiful circus halls in the Soviet Union here in Rostov, and there is a new performance by a Latvian group.'

A circus . . . there it was again; that would have meant inevitable references to the circus at Irkutsk, and would have reminded me of Kostia, whom I had decided that very day to forget. But Piotr Alieksievich was too sweet for me to improvise some obvious excuse. He had a tired, sad smile which opened on a line of brown teeth, some capped with gold. 'So you write books,' he said as we sat at a café. 'Lucky you; I have been writing articles and articles, but I could never write a book. Whenever I try to start one, I think of Pushkin. What can I do? He has said everything already.'

A father figure, but a man who needed help for some reason I couldn't guess.

'Tell me,' he asked, 'do you feel you can write about us? About Russia? Such an impossible task. Tell me, what kind of questions do people here ask you?'

'They ask about the differences between "you" and "us". Sometimes I find people here who talk the same language as I do, more so than at home, but sometimes I don't understand them at all. People are more accepting – not critical enough.'

'That's not the answer.'

Piotr Alieksievich's daughter wore her hair in stiff brown plaits, had an enchanting smile and greeted me in English. She was shy in speaking it, doubly so because her father was constantly urging her to say something in English.

She had made a little doll and gave it to me for my children.

Why do Russians like the circus so much? It is their national entertainment and they are certainly very good at it; their disciplined training and courage is shown in the acrobats, and their heavy sense of humour is well suited to the art of their clowns.

The Russians love dwarfs, midgets and freaks just as Renaissance noblemen used to. And the animals in a circus automatically become freaks as well; clothed leopards, elephants trained to perform human acts, bears who play instruments. The circus hall in Rostov was indeed beautiful, it looked more like an opera house, a delicate Fenice. It was full, the stairs, cafés and the corridors smelt of onions, blocked lavatories and animals.

'I thought you might like to go to the steppes,' said Piotr Alieksievich. 'Would you be interested in a horse farm?'

We decided to start the next morning at eight. Piotr Alieksievich, who in the meantime had become Pyetya, said he could not take his daughter with him because she was going to school, but the Intourist amazon Lelia was coming with us. I had already met her and had disliked her deeply.

The Steppes

Towards the Courgan steppes the road was flanked by an immense flatness, the sky falling on the steppes bluer and larger than I'd ever seen.

The wind waved the wheat in the fields in rippling irridescent ochres and the curving grass shimmered. The running wind whisked up a new gigantic green wave in a race towards the infinite horizon of the steppe.

At times, lines of trees broke the flatness; these were the sentries of the harvest, the agronomist's protection against the violence of the steppe winds. Immense areas in the Don steppes have been barricaded in this way to shield the ploughed fields.

We passed through little stone villages grouped around the main road, police blocks and steppes, steppes and steppes.

After two hours' driving we finally turned off the main road and arrived at the Kirov State Farm – former Trudiskoy. A simple square faced the main building which housed offices and an entertainment centre.

Pyotya looked about and then led the way to the director's office. We crossed a large hall, climbed steep stairs and found ourselves in a deserted office, where several telephones and bronze statues of horses occupied the table while on the walls a portrait of Lenin and paintings of more horses looked down in triumph.

A large Ukrainian burst into the office wearing a light

grey suit and a mini-tie under a heavy, shiny face. He had cunning blue eyes. Yuri Gheorghievich was accompanied by Vladimir Alexandrovich, his commisar for culture, Larissa the specialist in economics and Misha, whose line of work I forget but who seemed to me the jolliest of the lot.

'Sit down,' Yuri Gheorghievich commanded us. We all obeyed. 'This is the Kirov State Farm which specializes in breeding horses. I am the Chairman; we sell horses all over the world: to England, West Germany, the Democratic Republic of Germany, Italy, Holland and our own country, of course. In the Mexican Olympics we had five from here.'

'Are they Don Cossack horses?'

'I must disappoint you there. We breed a cross. The Don Cossack horse has stamina, can suffer hardship, requires little attention, eats little and can be overworked. It is the ideal war horse. The English horse is brave too. Ours is a mixture of the two. We started in 1930 when the State Farm first emerged. We have over 25,000 hectares of land, 23,000 of which are arable. We have a specialized staff of forty-four. Three thousand people including women and children live in the farm, and we have four secondary schools in the area. Everything is produced within the farm except new tools and machinery which have to be bought from outside. It is the director – myself . . .' he pointed at his chest, as if I hadn't understood who was the boss around there, 'who decides. Our State Farm is a multiple enterprise. Although the main effort lies in the breeding of horses, we sell 17,000 tons of grain to the State, 1,200 of flour, 4,000 tons of castor oil.' (Yuri Gheorghievich enumerated the statistics he knew by heart like reciting a prayer.) '1,000 tons of fruit – apples, pears, plums, cherries, grapes, apricots, nuts, even strawberries. We have a special plan for selling carp, and a special lobster which we breed in our local lakes. We also have a small plan for selling honey. We produce milk, meat, half a million eggs.'

'How much does a horse sell for?' I asked shyly, aware that I was interrupting a powerful flow.

'Difficult to say, it depends on its quality: from 5,000 to

211

15,000 roubles. But the main purpose of this farm is not to sell so much as to breed. Ours is mainly a jumping horse for steeple-chasing.'

State Farms are owned by the State (unlike the *Kholkoz* which is owned by a community) and operate on a self-supporting basis. They sell their products to the State and receive money which covers all their production expenses, wages, etc. Yuri Gheorghievich was the new type of manager, the overall boss, the new 'Kosygin law' man.

We went back downstairs. In the large arched hall a group of peasants had gathered, wearing their Sunday best. There was a holiday air about the place: after all, it was Easter. A handsome young boy was playing the harmonica. He had slanted blue eyes under short blonde hair: his short nose turned upwards. The scene was so gay that I climbed into Yuri Gheorghievich's black Volga car with regret.

'We have 190 mares,' he explained while driving, 'and twelve stallions, altogether 520 animals, including foals. Annually we produce seventy-two foals; we take them from the mother when they are six months old and start training them. When they are one and a half, they are broken in: a horse is ready when it is three years old. The specialist decides if it is worth keeping for running, jumping or breeding. It is ready to start when it is four years old. Now we are going to see the stables.'

We drove over the large plain along tracks flanked by high grass, over fields where mares and foals were grazing, watched by a guardian on horseback. The novelty of the scenery made me happy: had I met Kostia in Rostov, I wouldn't have been there.

'What is fiction?' Kostia had asked me once. 'And what is true in writing? Once you transform an episode by describing it, it has already lost its entity and becomes a point of view, even if you did not mean it to be so.'

In his Durrellian viewpoint, Kostia had touched a sore point. Why was I thinking about Kostia, anyway, instead of enjoying the fields of apple-trees in bloom? Hectares of white, translucent petals filtered through by pearly light, what beauty, what a ballet of flowers in the wind. The field stretched away forever, white against the sky, like a flight of thousands of seagulls along the blue sky of the steppes.

Whenever we stopped at a new stable, a table had been prepared, chairs all round it and bottles of mineral water, fruit juice and glasses. We all took a seat and the director signalled that we were ready to be shown the best horses. These were brought into the hall where we were sitting by a man dressed in full fox-hunting style, pink coat, white waistcoat and breeches. I found this detail extraordinary, that costume on the steppes, on a Soviet Farm . . .

The horses were beautiful, every name and detail marked on a piece of paper which we were handed. 'The initial of each horse's name has to be the same as that of its mother,' Yuri Gheorghievich explained. 'It is a tradition.'

Larissa, the economist, lived in a stone house between the central hall of the State Farm and one of those steppe lakes full of sweet-water lobsters. It was a simple house with a veranda, two bedrooms, one living-room and a kitchen. She had a son of eight who went to a local school.

I was tired and the heat of the day had made us all silent. Larissa gave me a clean towel and took me to the wash-room. The lavatory was nearby.

'It is a simple house,' she said in that apologetic tone which so often accompanies Russian hospitality, 'but very comfortable.' She showed me around the simply furnished room. I felt at ease there and we washed and chatted and combed our hair like women do together, exchanged comments on housework and the education of children.

The tiny hotel of the State Farm was enchanting. Yuri Gheorghievich had arranged a memorable meal there. It opened with hors d'oeuvre, Russian style – salty sturgeon and salmon, caviar, pickled tomatoes, gherkins, plenty of butter from the farm, black bread, all accompanied by iced vodka served in a huge carafe.

'Let's have a toast,' said Misha Vasilievich. At the third toast, Pyetya warned me in a fatherly way to drink with moderation; Lelia and Larissa didn't drink vodka.

'You must drink it all in a gulp, you must see the bottom of your glass after each toast,' protested Misha Vasilievich at my slower pace.

A consommé, with tiny strips of egg-noodle, arrived with bottles of local wine.

'This is a soup for emperors,' said Yuri Gheorghievich. An old woman came in carrying food; she had also done the cooking.

'We are eating like Khrushchev...' somebody said.

'Tss, tss.' The others at the table reminded us that we shouldn't go too far. The presence of a foreigner was still a barrier to total *détente*.

Champagne arrived with an immense quantity of chicken cut in pieces and fried fish from the local lakes. 'We have a tradition. We all have to propose a toast in turn, saying no more than ten words about some happy moment in our lives.'

'To my marriage,' said Misha Vasilievich standing up. Everybody clapped such a sweet and grateful toast.

'To these steppes and to your hospitality and warmth.' I raised my glass and we all drank until the bottoms of our glasses were over our noses.

Part Four
Russia

A Performance: The Demonstration

Imagine that one day the director Stanislavsky had received from the Moscow Art Theatre an order to *stage* something that, by its very title should have been spontaneous: a demonstration.

Only Stanislavsky, with his knowledge of how to make actors perform naturally, would have been equal to the task. Let's say he chooses a choreographer, a playwright and a mad designer. They all sit down and discuss the plans for the performance. These are their recommendations and directions:

(1) Take as a stage a vast space called 'Red Square', an oblong, cobblestoned expanse. The setting is perfect: on both sides it slopes down so that actors can appear and disappear without disturbing the scene.

(2) But the perfection of the stage is flawed: there is no room for the public. Therefore, the director is advised to put the most important section of the public, twenty to thirty people, to watch the spectacle from the top of a tomb or mausoleum and build two stands for a small selected audience. Most of the public for whom the performance is intended, the Moscovites, will either have to participate or they will watch it on their television sets.

(3) Although the performance is to be directed, designed and timed, the play will be called *Demonstration*.

(4) Clear the centre of Moscow from traffic for four hours. Block all entrances to Red Square to any living soul not carrying special invitation cards and documents. Gather the actors into the area four hours before the beginning.

(5) Decorate the square, pull down all previous banners and put new ones up (never mind the cost). Hand draperies of twenty by forty metres at least.

(6) Fill all the roads of Moscow with crowds. Place buffets with sandwiches and drinks in strategic positions. At night,

lay on lighting and glitter (inspired by the carnival of Nice or Viareggio).

From the sky drop pieces of paper printed with: 'Long live the 1st of May', 'Long live the Internationale'. Release large numbers of white doves and pigeons into the sky. Also: colourful balloons. Aeroplanes carrying banners. Ideally, there should be a heavy downfall of rain, in keeping with tradition.

Other directions for the staging of the play:

The actors will not be listed: there will be over a million of them. They will consist of groups of children in various uniforms, bus-loads of Komsomols, thousands of stocky girls in colourful costume, gymnasts of all denominations, militia, Red Army, people in factory overalls; plump, smiling beauties in national costume with ears of corn and wheat.

On the stage, various objects will be needed:

Branches of paper-blossoms, one thousand motor-cyclists, two and a half thousand lorries, one thousand vehicles of different kinds carrying banners which read: 'He lived, he lives, he will live'. 'Long live the Internationale and the Communist party.' 'Marx, Lenin.' Gigantic portraits of several people (some of whom will also take part in the play as spectators watching it from the terrace of the Mausoleum) will be carried over the square.

The play must develop in an orderly fashion.

Although the director must bear in mind it is meant to be a spontaneous demonstration, he will be responsible for any disorder which may occur during the performance.

Upstage, on both flanks of the Mausoleum the public should be colourful. Perhaps as many negroes in national costumes as possible, Arabs, Czechs, Poles, Hungarians, Russians. Any Chinese-looking spectator would be a good idea, if you can find any willing to take part.

Hot coffee, orange juice, ice-creams will be sold around the stands, but try to prevent the appearance of a football match. The play will start at ten o'clock in the morning and last four hours.

First Elaboration:

The play-demonstration will open as the Kremlin clock strikes ten. A huge crowd in civilian clothes will invade the stage from Revolution Square. Amplifiers on the Kremlin walls will play the Internationale.

Over the top of the squat red porphyry building, a group of people in dark coats wearing felt hats will appear. The actors in the square will clap them, and they wave back as though blessing the crowd, and clap back in the Russian tradition. One of the men in dark coats, preferably played by the retired baritone Brezhnev Leonid, speaks on several microphones. The actor is required to improvise, but never to say anything original on the usual subjects of victory of the proletariat, Leninism, Komsomol, youth. He should have a Ukrainian accent. We recommend Brezhnev for the part, since he had a special talent for platitudes and has already had much practice at giving these kinds of speeches.

The actors will cheer the speech, and leave the Red Square. More actors will fill the stage. All will make spectacular patterns choreographed by the limited but mathematical fantasy of our Chief Choreographer.

Scattered over the stands and on the stage, several actors will wear huge numbers of medals on their capacious chests. These can be cut out of gold paper, as long as the effect is glittering, and the gold catches the television lights. The Kirov *corps de ballet* could participate if they have not all defected to Monte Carlo. After this long scene, thousands of actors dressed in contemporary and ordinary suits will march past the square carrying banners.

The director thinks that the impresarios of the *Demonstration* should be warned that it will cost a great deal to produce.

The Theatre

The theatre in the Soviet Union is a popular entertainment which retains some of the holy and magic elements that the Greek theatre must have had. A performance is a real treat and people flock to the theatre, prepared to see anything. The choice is somewhat limited to contemporary plays about Lenin, electricity, and an excessive amount of Gorki and Chekov. Before a good performance there are always queues in front of the theatre, hoping to buy tickets at the last moment, a hope which is always disappointed.

Although plenty of talent exists in Russia, there is not enough freedom for it to develop to the full. The Russian stage is strictly a vehicle for a message, but, unfortunately, in the Soviet Union there is only one message.

The most famous theatre in the Soviet Union is, of course, the Moscow Art Theatre, known as the Mkhat. Its insignia is a seagull since it was through that company that Chekov was established. It is a rather small, elegant theatre, with a fascinating museum.

Today the theatre for which Konstantin Stanislavsky and Vladimir Nemirovich-Danchenko developed their theories of modern realistic theatre appears not only to us, but to the Soviet intelligentsia, old-fashioned and tired.

It was at the Mkhat that Stalin went to see Bulgakov's *White Army*, after the author had written to him several times complaining that his play had been banned from the repertoire. The company hastily revived the dusty costumes and sets and performed the forbidden play in private for the *Generalissimo*. After some cuts, it was allowed to appear again. But recently the Mkhat has lost all its popularity among the Moscow intelligentsia and could not even perform to full houses. The criticism is not only that the performances are too old-fashioned but that too many old actors were still taking the leading parts.

In September 1970 it was announced that Oleg Yefremov, the actor and director who formed the Sovrimmienik, a new excellent Moscow theatre in 1957, had been made chief director of the Mkhat. Mr Yefremov was reluctant to leave the Sovrimmienik.

In Moscow there are thirty-one theatres, and all but the Bolshoi, the Mali and the Moscow Art Theatre were founded after the October Revolution.

The best company in the Soviet Union today is the Na Taganka, in Moscow. It sprung up in the sixties – a bit of Andrei Vosniesiensky's theatre – as an experimental group working under the direction of Yuri Andrievich Lyubimov, a short, intelligent-looking man. The group works in rooms which were hastily transformed into a theatre and it has kept the flavour of a pioneering, experimental group. The actors walk about in the foyer of the theatre until a few minutes before the beginning of the play. Yuri Andrievich circulates, stops at the bar for a fruit juice, looks at his audience, chats with people. I spent some time talking with him in his office, facing a wood-cut of Pasternak beside a red carnation which must have been renewed every day, judging from its eternal freshness. 'You can see for yourself what we do. I don't like talking about my ideas, I prefer others to judge them. We stress group-acting, we use plenty of singing, lighting effects, projections, politics and controversy.'

The Na Taganka is really a theatre of poetry. It seemed to me that its best productions were based on poems rather than plays, and it deals in concepts and images.

Molière's *Tartuffe* was staged in a symbolic way, every character kept behind a screen in the shape of an enormous card and the play was conducted indeed as a game of cards. *Pugachov*, by Eisenin, is a long lyric. *Antiworld* by Vosniesiensky, a series of poems. The best production I saw there was *Listen – Mayakovsky*. It is based on Mayakovsky's poems and words and brought out how he is misinterpreted, 'the victim of his own ideas', as a Soviet friend calls him. The character of Mayakovsky was played by five actors always on the stage together, wearing the large felt hats of the twenties; he is constantly accused, criticized, misinterpreted by an 'audience' of actors who fill the stage. Then they mount the poet on a pedestal, and the petty bourgeois make him adopt the position of the famous statue of him in the Moscow square which bears his name.

Lyubimov, an ex-actor, obviously rejected the influence of Stanislavsky in his conception of the theatre. There are all those visual enrichments, films, projections, songs with which Brecht rejuvenated the existing theatrical situation. In the by now famous *Ten Days Which Shook the World*, which in fact retains only the marvellous title of John Reed's book, the play starts even before one enters the building. One is admitted not by a ticket collector, but a moustached Bolshevik or a sailor, who collects the tickets onto the point of his bayonet. In the hall, where the audience assembles, groups of sailors and of 1917 workers come and sing revolutionary songs, pushing their way rudely through the crowd and staring round at the people with the threatening look of men who can bear it no longer and are about to change the world. The play itself takes place in the small theatre. The stage is narrow, but the company seems to have stretched and changed it just by an intelligent use of lighting, shapes, reflectors and voice. The repertory and the public here are always unusual, but they too are sometimes reminded that they have gone too far when a play is taken off after one or two performances.

In Moscow I was told that the very best company in the Soviet Union was in Leningrad, the Akademichesky Dramatichesky, at the Gorki Theatre. In Leningrad itself, the intellectual seemed to prefer the theatre company for children. One play I saw called *Nothing-Nothing* was about a little girl who had red plaits and was annoyed by the fact.

After considerable difficulty in obtaining a ticket for the Gorki Theatre, I took a bus to Na Fontaku and walked by the broad Leningrad canal before entering the theatre. The interior was very beautiful, elegantly painted in white and blue, a stage better suited for the performance of *Cosi fan tutte* than for straight theatre.

There I saw a new play by a L. Rachmanoff, *A Welcomed Old Age,* about an elderly couple of 1905 and the difference of opinion with the new revolutionary generation; I also saw an arrangement of Shakespeare's *Henry VI,* performed in Brechtian style. Both evenings were of a high professional level, though rather academic; the company didn't have the compactness and sparkle that Na Taganka has. The audience was composed more of elderly couples and ladies dressed up for the occasion than of young people. Although very large, the Gorki Theatre is always full up and one needs to book considerably in advance.

A Sudden Visit

Why is there something so special about Russian trains? Or is it the magic of those people, those crowds, talking that beautiful language which sounds like one long piece of classic literature, that makes them so very appealing? Or is it the countryside which passes by the window-panes monotonous and spacious, bathed in lakes and rivers reflecting ample skies?

I knew I had contracted that special disease: Russophilia. Already I could visualize myself in London looking for Russian books, for the company of Soviet people, listening to Russian music with a partial ear.

What is it that makes that nation, or rather that continent, so fascinating? Perhaps the melancholy and loneliness of the vast plains, the scepticism, the untouchable contrasts.

I trust them, I thought, looking at the inscrutable faces of my travelling companions – nothing evil will ever come from them. I'd rather have them as a ruling power presiding over world affairs than any other kind of people; it's hard to remember that there could be a Stalin amongst them still. But Stalin was a product of Tsarism, a Jesuit, the son of a starving family, and he was not a Russian anyway. Contemporary Russia would give birth to generations separated by millennia from Stalin's world – generations which were more aware but still retained the Russian depth, passions, tremendous physical endurance, patience and courage. The nineteenth-century French historian Leroi-Beaulieu observed that the Russians' 'capacity for suffering is unknown to the nations of the West . . . they would march across the steppes of the south until totally exhausted, when they would die by the roadside by the hundred thousands, not a cry of revolt, almost without a moan or murmur . . . and yet the Russian people are naturally the least pugnacious, the least warlike in the world.'

What a complex nation, I thought, as my eyes rested on Kostia, who was sitting opposite me in the train. His eyes were lowered under his heavy lashes and seemed to focus on somewhere in the middle of the floor of the compartment.

'You are sad,' I said aloud, interrupting the silence which enveloped the travellers. They all looked at us in confusion and curiosity. Kostia lifted his eyelashes and shifted his eyes from my face to the passing landscape.

'I am sorry, yes, I am sad.'

But then his mood would be altered by outbursts of joy as we wandered around Suzdal, walking from monastery to church, from kremlins to wooden buildings, looking at the undulating landscape shaded by a brilliant watery light, reflected in the river, stopping to buy some food and picnicking near the wooden bridge where a lonely fisherman was wading among the reeds.

'You were angry, weren't you?' Kostia suddenly asked.

'About your telegram? Of course I was.'

'I knew that you would be, but I really couldn't come. I tried, but I couldn't leave my work.'

'It was silly of me . . . I am sorry, I should have thought of your work. It's only that I thought . . .'

'Thought what?'

'Well...'

'That if I really wanted to see you, I could have managed it. Isn't that what you thought? Well, in a way you were right. But now I have found you.'

'How did you manage it?' I asked.

'It took a lot of time and telephone calls and I had to conceal the fact that it was you that I wanted to trace. But a Siberian boy always succeeds if he wants to.'

Suzdal was beautiful, it was really breath-taking and one couldn't get accustomed to the continuous changes in landscape, dotted by thousands of onion-shaped cupolas painted in blue and gold.

'You must have thought that that telegram was oddly phrased.'

Since he had pointed it out, I nodded: 'Yes, really, and to start with it was *K soshalienniu,* that's what I couldn't forgive.'

'It had to have an official tone, I thought it would be read by others before you.'

'Yes, of course.'

'Forgive the *K soshalienniu.*'

'Forgiven.'

But after the joy of running about and looking at so much beauty, Kostia fell again into a state of deep misery. Next day he had to go back to Siberia and I was to fly to Leningrad.

He stopped talking altogether as we passed among the pale monasteries, the trees, the cupolas painted with golden stars which the sunset had transformed into shining meteorites. His eyes were cast down and his face was gloomy.

'Are you angry, Konstantin? Are you angry with me?'

He just wouldn't talk. He looked slightly different outside Siberia, without his sable hat and heavy coat. He wore an almost black suit and showed his total contempt for clothes by wearing a tie which was so small it might as well not have existed, a little black knot almost strangling him.

He was wearing 'city' shoes to which he was not accustomed and he seemed out of place mentally and physically outside Siberia.

'I can't enjoy anything any more,' he said. 'The only thing I can think about is that we will never see each other again. I wore moustaches once,' he added suddenly.

'You? Moustaches?' I burst out laughing, trying to visualize that already serious face with a thick, black drooping moustache, or one that was brushed upwards or with Yagoda-style black patches under his nose. 'How ridiculous ... I wouldn't have even looked at you if you'd been wearing them.'

'I shaved them off quite recently, just like that. I looked at myself in the mirror and realized how funny I looked.'

We talked about names. 'Why do your children have many names instead of only one? Is it a custom?'

It was more often so in Italy, I answered, than in England. One called a child after someone one wanted to honour or remember. 'My daughter's third name is Aglaya, after Dostoievsky's character in *The Idiot*. I wanted it to be her first name, but then my husband pointed out that the English word "ugly" sounded like Aglaya and children might have made fun of her at school.'

'And her second name?'

'It's Gemma, after my grandmother who died at Auschwitz.'

Somehow the thought that I was half-Jewish disturbed Kostia.

'And why are you Konstantin?'

'I don't know and I can't ask. My parents are dead.'

'Did they die a long time ago?'

'My father did.' He didn't want to talk about it.

'And your wife?'

'She was terribly ill. We spent three months going from doctor to doctor, but there was nothing we could do about it. She had cancer, and she suffered horribly.'

'You must have had a difficult life.'

'No, I am all right. You don't pity me, do you?' The suspicion that any feelings I had towards him might have originated in pity seemed to horrify him. His face became hard. 'You don't like me because you pity me, do you?' he repeated.

And yet, Konstantin was pitying himself then, not for his past, but for his immediate future. He was clearly torment-ing himself and I never saw him smile until we parted.

'I only smile to make you happy, but I shall come to Leningrad.'

'When?' I asked.

'I don't know, when I'll be able to. I'll just come, so expect me.'

Valery

I had forgotten the spectacular beauty of Leningrad. The city was enveloped in a clear Arctic light, perfectly still through a cold sweeping wind; the trees had just started to cover their branches with tender green, the evenings were beginning to melt into dawns in those white, shadowless nights which transform Leningrad into a ghost city, a vision from John Martin's romantic brush, reflecting itself a hundred times in the still whiteness of its river and canals and over the Gulf of Finland.

I used to wander about the city, on foot or taking river boats, feeling there was no end to the painful sense of beauty this city could give me, looking at façades which seemed to be made from precious stones, the amber of the Mikhailovsky Palace, the turquoise of the Winter Palace, the pale malachite of the Smolny, the pure gold of the Admiralty tower.

I paid a visit to Maria Feodorovna Edovina, the vice-director of the Hermitage and to Martha and Irina, whom I hadn't seen for nine years. I went to meet Yuri Kuznetzov, the head of APN Leningrad Bureau, a gay person full of life, enthusiasm and energy. He had decorated the office personally. It was on the embankment of the Neva, facing the battleship *Aurora*. He had furnished the large rooms with modern Finnish and Russian furniture, the first contemporary décor I ever saw in the Soviet Union. It was very neat and attractive. Yuri had also made two chandeliers himself out of an enormous *directoire* crystal candelabra which he had found in bits and pieces. The effect was splendid and he was rightly proud of them He once took me to have dinner at a restaurant on the Finnish border, where we ate venison with cranberry sauce and met several friends. There was an attractive girl who looked like Marina Vlady and the solemn manager of the restaurant who complained he was seeing too little of his wife, and that his work kept him on duty most of the time.

One day I rang up Gheorg Mikhailovich Krasoursky whose name had been given to me by a Moscow acquaintance. He had told me I would enjoy the company of Mikhailovich, an elderly man of great culture with a passionate knowledge of Leningrad. He lived with his old mother and taught French at the university, although he was really an architect.

But Gheorg Mikhailovich could not meet me for a few days: he was very busy with the examinations of his pupils, and we made an appointment for the following week.

Instead I met Valery, a former student of his, a diffident young man whose body seemed knotted like a thin young tree which has grown too quickly and whose head of foliage was out of proportion, towering over the thin trunk it had built for itself in the course of a few springs. Valery could not quite control his light contempt towards my curiosity, my wish to find out all about everything at once. We spoke in French; his was flawless and he used it with absolute grammatical precision and a few antiquated phrases.

Valery never dropped the *vous* or called me anything else but *Madame* and later, after I had asked him to call me by my first name, that '*Madame*' assumed a contrived sarcastic tone.

Valery became a favourite companion. While walking along the grim Griboedova canal, Dostoievsky's quarters, and stopping in the courtyard where Pushkin had lived, I gradually became more involved in Valery's personality and began to lose interest in the secretive canals and little roads through which Valery, a knowledgeable guide, was chaperoning me. He had a sarcastic, mocking vitality hidden behind a cloak of provocative stillness and inscrutability. It took me some time to decide whether his ironical *Et vouse, Madame, qu'est-ce que vousen pensez de tout ça?* was an infuriating way of making fun of me or whether he was trying to provoke a critical answer: it was, in fact, a mixture of both.

We visited the former palace of the Yousupov, now the cultural centre for the teachers' trade union. It boasted an entrance hall in the grand manner, an exquisite marble staircase rising from two squat white sphinxes which, under a crystal candelabra, divided into two branches which gracefully reached the *piano mobile*. The rooms were small in comparison with the Tsar's residences; Russian nobles were kept in their places, no such building as Buckingham Palace was allowed to rival the palaces. At the union I talked to the person in charge of the English Club, where teachers used to gather to speak English and to stage plays by Bernard Shaw. Valery and I exchanged glances, we could well imagine what the plays must have been like.

On a freezing evening, Valery took me to the former residence of the Strogonovs on the Moika canal; in the courtyard enclosed by the spectacular house built by Rastrelli, a group of young people were singing with a guitar under the trees.

The Old Capital

Leningrad always seems familiar to me because it contains so many famous things; from the Nevsky Prospect described in so many books, to the Finland Station. There were the houses of Gogol, and Kirov and Pushkin. There was the model for Raskolnikov's house (Dostoievsky always situated his characters in 'real' houses). In the double cathedral of St Nicolas of the Seas, Tchaikovsky had his own special icon, and Catherine the Great used to make appearances there as the Head of the Church and Autocrat (it wasn't until the first revolution that a Patriarch was appointed). And the familiarity of the place includes the name of the hotel Astoria, a name which resounds with American capitalism.

The architects who built the jewel-city had the un-Russian names of Rastrelli, Rossi, Cameron, Quarenghi, but the shapes they devised could never have been conceived in any other part of the world.

St Petersburg was the city of the Tsars and for the Tsars, built oblivious of cost. Almost every Autocrat made a new palace for himself or herself and the aristocracy lived in graceful residences provided with private theatres and enough luxury to be able to entertain the Tsars. Only in a city of that kind, built for the very rich instead of the working class, could architects have such freedom. Here they did not need to paint *trompe l'oeil*, they went ahead with the real thing; St Isaac's columns are *made* of malachite and lapis-lazuli ... and Rossi was able to plan not only the main theatre, but the streets leading to it, including its ballet school and conservatory.

In the trade boom early in the twentieth century, Nevsky Prospect changed its appearance, and extraordinary art nouveau shops sprang up. Here, as in Moscow, there is an Ielisiei Gastronom, a beauty of crystal cascading from the super-decorated walls; the former Singer shop is now an immense book shop.

Much of Soviet history was made in Leningrad: there is the battleship *Aurora,* permanently anchored at Petrograd-skya Naberezhnaya and no less than seven Lenin Memorial Museums. In Leningrad there are still some 'original' Bolsheviks whose number seems suspiciously to swell rather than decrease, and who describe events of revolutionary days in trembling voices.

During the war most of the population of Leningrad died in the nine-hundred-days' Nazi siege of the heroic city. 'Now it's all different. The old population died and the city has been invaded by peasants. Although the Moscovite is a little rough-mannered, he's more accustomed to urban life than the new population of Leningrad. This is also a very provincial city, very *petit bourgeois,* if we can use that expression. . . .'

Apart from some high buildings and the unnecessary demolition of some old palaces, modern architecture has so far respected the old city.

I went to see Mr Travnikov, of the Atelier 12 of the Leningrad architects. He looked like the proprietor of an inn. I don't know why his image seemed so noticeably out of keeping with his profession, but somehow I could only see him as an innkeeper recommending good dishes while the horses were changed outside a country inn in pre-revolutionary days.

The vast group of studios where the architects worked was on the northern bank of the Neva, near the house where Gorki had lived.

Valery and I climbed to the fourth floor of a decaying cement building where Travnikov received us in a tiny office swamped with papers.

'Yes, the old city has been respected,' he said, 'and no house has been built higher than nine floors so as to preserve Leningrad's skyline. Whenever it was necessary to build a house in the old district along the canal, special care was taken to match the style of the new house with the surrounding architecture. We are preserving, building and restoring,' he said. 'Restoration, which includes repainting the grand façades of so many buildings, is very expensive. It costs a great deal to protect the whole city against the weather we have here which corrodes stone so fast.

'Now we are working on a totally new district to be built on 350 hectares on the Vassily island, where the ground is particularly difficult because it is sandy, right on the Finland Gulf. Until recently it would have been impossible to build there, since the ground is constantly inundated by the sea. But technology has now made it possible.'

The district, Mr Travnikov explained, was to house 140,000 people who now lived in Leningrad: it was to be totally self-contained, provided with schools and shops.

'The project was all elaborated here at the Atelier 12 where one hundred architects work, but there were only ten principal architects involved in the project. The district will be ready between 1980–5.'

Mr Travnikov took us round to see the vast model of the project for the Vassily island district. I noticed high elevations. 'Yes, this will be a hotel twelve or fourteen floors high and over there we'll build the House of Youth with sixteen floors.'

This contradicted his previous statement that they never build higher than nine floors. And there was to be a great monument twenty metres high to the defence of Leningrad, and Mother Russia, and two obelisks and a restaurant built in the shape of a gigantic globe. Again we looked at the details of the project in a separate section of the studio. It looked like an old-fashioned version of a World Fair. Oh well, I thought, descending the stairs, it will be one of the many capitals ruined by bad taste. In the meantime we still have ten years left to see it.

'Yes, it was disappointing,' I confessed to Valery, who hadn't expressed any opinion, 'and that monument will be visible from everywhere.'

'With any luck it won't be built. Nineteen-eighty is still far away,' he answered.

The Cemeteries

Once Valery and I went to visit cemeteries. In Leningrad there are many old ones where stone and grass melt into one another and paths lead to corners of chaos and upheaval.

232

It's as though the Last Judgment had already shaken the tombstones with a violence worthy of Signorelli's frescoes.

Glinka, Tchaikovsky and Dostoievsky are buried in one of the three cemeteries attached to the Alexandr Nevsky monastery. Towards the Neva, we visited the Nikalskoye, the largest of the three, through a mossy, battered gate along a romantic lake under thick trees. The only other people in the place were a young pair murmuring to each other.

We stopped by a gallant tomb: lying on a simulated wooden coffin, resting his stone elbow on two stone cushions, a mocking ussar laughed, with all the decorations and embroideries of his uniform carefully sculpted in stone.

'Give me your hand, Comrade, and follow
me here; we tasted happiness
let us taste the flavour of the earth, now.'

No date, no name. The hand of the ussar which had fallen off, must have once been pointing towards the rhymed inscription.

'He's marvellous,' I said.

'Yes, isn't he. I love this kind of Russian poetry; it is just so bad.' Valery adored 'kitsch', especially those postcards with roses and couples, old-fashioned, sending each other messages under a hand-painted full moon.

Plants were growing out of some tombs; in some cases Orthodox double crosses had fallen over onto other graves. 'There's a special day, I think it is May 25th, the day of the Trinity . . . when people come to the cemeteries with their families and sit on the tombs of their parents. They drink and eat and spend the day here.'

'It is a nice way to look at death; it sounds like an old custom.'

'It's a tradition. Many people come with children and they play around.'

'It sounds gay.'

'It is very beautiful to look at.'

We went on to the Volkovo cemetery, an immense place containing thousands of tombs of known and unknown people; part of Lenin's family was there and so was Turgenev, whose body had been sent from Paris at the author's will.

The Volkovo is divided into sections: writers, scientists. . .

'Now we are walking over the ballerinas,' Valery's sharp-edged voice announced.

'Yes, it does seem grotesque to be walking over ballerinas.' That those celestial bodies trained to defy gravity should have been brought low by death, seemed particularly unjust.

'To die is not new under the sun

neither is living new any more.'

So wrote Sergei Eisenin, the poet and husband of Isadora Duncan, in the very last verses he composed before killing himself.

'Did you know he had died at the hotel Angleterre, next door to you?'

'No, I didn't know. Do you like Eisenin?'

'He's meant to be decadent.'

I was left with that. Valery had read so much, he never stopped amazing me with his literary knowledge and good taste. He didn't show off, but it was obvious from his conversation.

'I fear you are a Romantic,' Valery announced.

'I am not,' I answered speedily, coming to my own defence.

'No need to be so touchy, *Madame*, everybody is a romantic.'

'And you?'

'I am a simple-minded fellow.'

'You? Simple?'

'To be simple-minded makes life much easier.'

We went to the modern Piscarovskoya cemetery where the victims of the siege had been buried: six hundred thousand of them, a huge space swept by wind and covered with flat stones.

In a pavilion where documents and photographs had

been gathered, there was a notebook in which a little girl had written in a shaky, childish hand: 'My mother died today.' In the next pages, followed by dates, the child noted the death of her brother, her uncles, her grandmother, her father. In the last page she had written: 'I have been left alone. They have all died.'

Winter

In December Leningrad had become glittering and icy, the sun rose at eleven, the Neva and the canals were frozen, the tourists had left, the cafés were full. Some of these were so pretty, the tables made of white marble, the décor art nouveau. People go to have a glass of white wine or champagne or a coffee and chat. Once I was sitting at a high stool on a cocktail bar in Nevsky Prospect waiting for somebody. Cocktails are very new things. Chatting with the barman, I told him how to make a whisky-sour. 'It sounds very complicated,' he said, 'and we don't always have lemons. But you know, I mix anything together that is handy and everybody seems to enjoy the concoctions I produce.'

In houses, friends prepare large quantities of hot soup, with mushroom and sausages, fish and onions, which one consumes with vodka and revives, forgetting the cold outside.

Valery's grandmother would prepare a boiling *borsch* or a soup of meat and potatoes.

'Tell him to eat,' she would say to me. 'He never does. If he goes on like this, he will die. And if he dies during the winter, it is a bore; the transport is difficult and anyway he is so tall that the coffin would have to be specially made.' Of course she adored him and it was just her way of expressing her love. Once, Valery took me to an extraordinary place. He had just warned me that we were going to a reading of Byron's *Don Juan*. He took me to a large room full of barrels, with a huge table in the centre, surrounded by chairs, half of which were occupied. A plump lady was lecturing at the top of the table, with a vast number of bottles in front of her. We sat down. In front of us was a wooden tray with a plate of nuts and pieces of chocolate. So I realized – and Valery enjoyed my amazed surprise – that Byron it was not, but a scholarly lecture on Soviet wines. After each bottle had been described, another lady would pour a glass for each of us, people would drink it and ask questions.

By the time we got to the Georgian and Armenian wines, my capacity for storing such variety and quantity had come to an end. Some of the people present had come to acquire a genuine knowledge on the subject, the other half to get drunk. At the end of the lecture we went into another room, a kind of night-club, the décor of which was surprisingly sophisticated, like a smart Parisian 'cave'. There was pop music, no dancing, further drinking, plenty of people.

In the evenings, Valery would sometimes take me to see his friends.

'We shall walk, it is quite near; so-and-so might be at home.' It always turned out that 'quite near' meant long walks through the frozen nights but almost always the friends were at home, as if expecting our visit. We would chat, drink tea, or vodka, and eat.

After some time, Valery would say good-bye and, going downstairs, would tell me:

'Now we are going to see another friend, a very nice girl who lives very near.' And off again, we would walk through the immense still squares, along the green façades, sheltering one's face from the gusts of frozen wind coming from the Neva. One night Valery and I even quarrelled in the gardens of Isskustv Square, sitting on a bench covered with ice. I had to give in, or I would have died of cold: it was minus 15. Next day Valery didn't seem to remember anything about our clash except for the colour of my face

– mauve – and when I reminded him of the excessive sarcasm he had used on the previous evening, he remarked: 'I hate an evening companion who has a good memory on the following day.'

Valery never really forgave me for the terrible inconvenience I caused him by not being Russian.

Dom Culturni

'I was a worker,' said Nikolai Vasilievich Tchmuchin. 'And I received my higher education while working during the day in a factory.'

The portly man with white hair and explosive energy was the head of the main house of culture in Leningrad, named after Kirov. These houses of culture are typical landmarks of Soviet society. They are places where the public can go and spend its spare time in hobbies or educating itself – learning foreign languages, playing instruments, singing, plant-growing, skiing, skating, and it is all free. They naturally become meeting-places and people are encouraged to organize plays, concerts, ballets, which are then performed in the Dom Culturni theatre and concert hall.

The one in Leningrad was particularly large and active, thanks to the dazzling personality of Nikolai Vasilievich; there was a library, a dance-hall and a restaurant.

'Before this I worked at the Gorki theatre; the work there was much quieter than here. But I didn't really like working with actresses. You never know if they are speaking the truth or not. I don't like that world, and that's why I prefer this work; it is so much more lively, and I am nearer to the people. We have many activities here and besides, there are lectures every day and lessons in English, French and German: 2,500 people attend. Sometimes we get real companies to perform at our theatre; from abroad we had the

American ballet company of Robert Jeffry and Porgy and Bess and the Japanese ballet.'

The Soviets feel that houses are for eating and sleeping while social life should be carried out in the community, in public buildings made for that purpose. This one was a pleasant sort of building demonstrating once again the Soviet feeling for communal life.

'We must speak quietly in here,' said Nikolai Vesilievich leading us into the public library where several people were reading. Walking quickly among the shelves, Nikolai Vasilievich suddenly shouted in the direction of the librarian: 'Svietlana? How many volumes are there here? Twenty-five thousand? You see, twenty-five thousand volumes,' he said turning to us.

Happily but nervously, Nikolai Vasilievich walked quickly away. We then reached the large theatre where an amateur group was rehearsing a kind of musical before going to Riga in an exchange performance.

'Not ready yet?' he shouted as he entered the hall, and every face turned towards him. He seated us in two stalls seats and climbed on the stage. He immediately took over the direction, acting and lighting.

'Now, Valodya,' he shouted towards someone, 'we must start immediately. Silence.'

The first scene began: a group of girls dressed in modest but sequined attire, performed a little dance accompanied by a scratchy song emanating from large amplifiers.

'Warm applause.' Nikolai Vasilievich ordered the small audience as the first scene had reached its end.

This was followed by singers, and guitar players and more dancing. 'Change the scene quickly, hurry up. More warm applause.'

A singer had started his own composition on the city of Leningrad, when Nikolai Vasilievich interrupted him. 'You come on the stage as if you were about to gather mushrooms!' And to a group of girls: 'You mustn't sing with those gloomy faces. Smile.'

At the end of the performance, Nikolai Vasilievich welcomed us once more to his office and gave us drinks.

'Did you like it?' And, thank God, without waiting for an answer, he added: 'Good, wasn't it?'

Valery and I exchanged electric glances.

'Who was the director?' I asked, to distract myself from an imminent fit of giggles.

'For such an important performance,' Nikolai Vasilievich explained, 'we engaged a professional director, not an amateur, you could see that, couldn't you?'

I burst out laughing, but tried to hide it by picking up an imaginary pencil under the table. Valery was struggling with his own giggles under handkerchiefs and scarves.

'Well, you are in a good mood,' said Nikolai Vasilievich, not at all disturbed by such an outburst.

He was a really lovely man, full of spirit and enthusiasm which had lasted all his fifty years, and would probably be with him for the rest of his life, lucky man.

A Last Encounter

I had had no news of Kostia until the telephone in my room rang and his voice sounded so far and faint that I thought that he was ringing from Irkutsk. 'I am packing,' I said, gazing out at St Isaac's façade which was splendidly framed in my window. 'The place is in total upheaval, but come up.'

He had arrived just in time to see me off. I was suddenly scared by the possibility that our last meeting might turn out to be ridiculous, as last meetings sometimes do. I almost felt like escaping there and then by taxi to the airport.

Kostia knocked and without waiting for my feeble answer, opened the door, his pale face hidden by a bunch of garden roses. He couldn't bring himself to put them into my arms, but clumsily thrust them across the table. And while I busied myself putting the flowers in water, to cover my embarrassment, Kostia sat tongue-tied, his hands over his knees gazing at the suitcases.

'Have a drink,' I said, tormented with embarrassment as I stretched towards a half-empty bottle of vodka which Kostia glanced at censoriously. I should have remembered: he did not drink. I could have done with a drink myself, but I gave up the idea.

I couldn't concentrate on Kostia who was allowing himself to be carried away by a particularly black Russian gloom: I had to finish packing. 'Heavens! Where have I put all those customs declarations?'

'You must write to me.'

'I will. Do you know, when I came in, I forgot to declare a necklace I was wearing. Do you think I should explain?'

'When do you think you'll be able to come back?'

'I am terrified of policemen, they always make me feel guilty of something. And where did I put those bank exchange receipts?'

Kostia had not moved from his chair and looked miserable.

I suddenly realized that I was in a certain haste to leave. I was seized by my customary panic of missing the plane and I masochistically began to imagine all the terrible things that could happen: what if I lost my passport at the last moment, dropped my wallet, or couldn't find a taxi? What if I was arrested by the police? I sat down, considering these possible disasters.

'I am very sad,' moaned Kostia, breaking the chain of those disagreeably realistic images.

'I can see that. But I must pack.' And I got up again.

There he was, that Siberian boy I had so often thought about, and I behaved as if my sister had been in the room. 'What's the matter?' I asked stupidly, sitting down again, this time beside him.

'I am unhappy.'

'But you knew I would be leaving. You shouldn't have come just to see me off ... I mean ... it is very nice of you, but ... you know, when one is packing, one is in a private mood, one talks aloud ... one needs to be alone. ...' That wasn't the loving voice of consolation. I was getting everything wrong, so I decided I'd better get on with my packing.

'I will never marry again.'

Where the hell had I put the keys of my house? 'Oh yes, you will.'

And where was the visa? Christ! The most important paper of the lot, those grey pages listing in Cyrillic letters the cities one was allowed to visit, with a photograph of myself looking like Groucho Marx. ... These bureaucratic countries ... one is tormented by pieces of paper which must not be lost. ...

'I don't want to see anybody for months. I need to be alone and to think. Why don't you want to stay? Wouldn't you like to live in the Soviet Union?'

My visa was expiring that very day. And, anyway, where was it?

The suitcase was turned upside down. Kostia watched me in a silent stupor.

And when that vital piece of paper had been rescued from the greedy embrace of some woollen socks, I began to realize that I was performing a rite. I started packing again, putting away letters and images, books and notes, Feodor and Misha, Larissa and Alioshka, Yuri Grigorievich and Kostia. ... In a moment of practical absent-mindedness, I seized the bunch of roses Kostia had brought and packed them as well.

In London, for a short time, they revived.

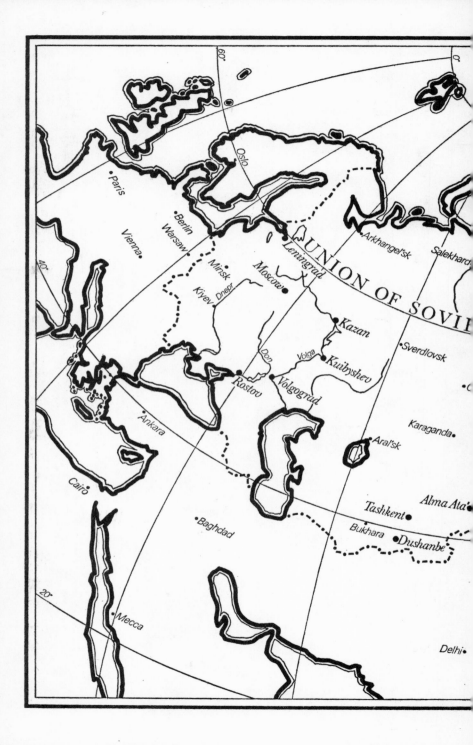